Exploring the core content of socio-economic rights: South African and international perspectives

Exploring the core content of socio-economic rights: South African and international perspectives

EDITORS
Danie Brand
and
Sage Russell

PROTEA BOOK HOUSE
PRETORIA
2002

Exploring the core content of socio-economic rights: South African and international perspectives
Danie Brand and Sage Russell (editors)

First edition, 2002
Protea Book House
PO Box 35110, Menlo Park, 0102
protea@intekom.co.za

Typography and design by Hennie Vermaak
Cover design by Tienie du Plessis
Reproduction by PrePress Images, Pretoria
Printed and bound by ABC Press, Cape Town

ISBN 1-919825-87-8

© 2002, Danie Brand and Sage Russell
© All rights reserved.
No part of this book may be reproduced in any form, without prior permission in writing from the publisher.

CONTENTS

List of contributors	vii
Acknowledgements	x
Introduction – Minimum state obligations: International dimensions .... *Sage Russel*	11
The essential components of the human right to adequate housing – a South African perspective .... *Pierre de Vos*	23
Core obligations related to the right to health and their relevance for South Africa .... *Audrey R Chapman*	35
South Africa's commitment to health rights in the spotlight: Do we meet the international standard? .... *Karrisha Pillay*	61
The right to adequate food: Violations related to its minimum core content .... *Rolf Künneman*	71
The minimum core content of the right to food in context: A response to Rolf Künneman .... *Danie Brand*	99
Social security as a human right .... *Lucie Lamarche*	109
The right to social security: A response from a South African perspective .... *Sandra Liebenberg*	147
In search of the core content of the right to education .... *Fons Coomans*	159
Of floors and ceilings – minimum core obligations and children .... *Geraldine van Bueren*	183

Children's rights: A response from a South African
perspective 201
    Frans Viljoen

The right to work: South Africa's core minimum obligations 207
    Richard L Siegel

The right to work: A response to Richard Siegel 237
    Kenneth Creamer

The minimum core content of trade union rights in the
South African context 245
    Colin Fenwick

Index 266

LIST OF CONTRIBUTORS

DANIE BRAND, Senior Lecturer in Law, Researcher
Department of Public law and Centre for Human Rights
University of Pretoria
Pretoria
South Africa

AUDREY R CHAPMAN, Director
Science and Human Rights Program
American Association for the Advancement of Science
Washington, DC
USA

FONS COOMANS, Senior Researcher
Centre for Human Rights
Maastricht University
Maastricht
The Netherlands

KENNETH CREAMER, Public policy analyst
Johannesburg
South Africa

PIERRE DE VOS, Professor of Law
University of Western Cape
Belville
South Africa

COLIN FENWICK, Professor of Law
Centre for Employment and Labour Relations Law
University of Melbourne
Melbourne
Australia

ROLF KÜNNEMAN, Secretary General
FIAN International
Heidelberg
Germany

LUCIE LAMARCHE, Professor of Law
Faculty of Law
Université du Québec à Montréal
Montréal
Canada

SANDRA LIEBENBERG, Professor of Law
Community Law Centre
University of Western Cape
Belville
South Africa

KARRISHA PILLAY, Advocate of the High Court of South Africa,
Member of the Cape Bar
Cape Town
South Africa

SAGE RUSSEL, Senior Program Associate
Science and Human Rights Program
American Association for the Advancement of Science
Washington, DC
USA

RICHARD L SIEGEL, Professor of Political Science and Faculty Associate
Grant Sawyer Center for Justice Studies
University of Nevada-Reno
Reno
Nevada
USA

GERALDINE VAN BUEREN, Professor of Law
University of London
Queen Mary and Westfield College
Director
Programme on the International Rights of the Child
London
England
UK

FRANS VILJOEN, Professor of Law
Department of Legal History, Legal Philosophy and Comparative Law
University of Pretoria
Pretoria
South Africa

ACKNOWLEDGEMENTS

This book is the product of a conference that took place in Pretoria, South Africa, in August 2000, entitled *Exploring the minimum core content of socio-economic rights*. The conference was presented jointly by the Socio-economic Rights Project of the Centre for Human Rights, University of Pretoria and the Science and Human Rights Program of the American Association for the Advancement of Science.

The international perspectives in this volume originated as a series of papers written under the auspices of the AAAS/HURIDOCS (Human Rights Information and Documentation Systems, International, a Geneva-based NGO) Economic, Social and Cultural Rights Violations Project. Contributions from the international authors represented in this publication, along with chapters on the rights enumerated in the International Covenant on Economic, Social and Cultural Rights that do not also appear in the 1996 South African Constitution, are scheduled to be published in a related book resulting from the AAAS/HURIDOCS Economic, Social and Cultural Rights Project, Intersentia Uitgevers NV in early 2002. For ordering information contact:

Intersentia Uitgevers NV
Churchilllaan 108
B-2900, Schoten (Antwerpen), Belgium
Tel: 32/3/680.15.56   Fax: 32/3/680.15.58
Website: http://www.intersentia.be

Our thanks to the presenters at the conference for readily making their papers available to us and agreeing to have them published.

We were able to collect all but one of the papers and two of the responses presented at the conference.

We received invaluable assistance from a number of people, whom we thank heartily. Gina Bekker and Lawrence Mashava from the Centre for Human Rights organised the conference; John Adolph, Nina Brune, Karina van Dalen and Henry Badenhorst, research assistants at the University of Pretoria, checked footnotes and generally tracked things down; and Nico Stassen of Protea Publishers unhesitatingly supported the project and carefully managed the publishing process.

Finally, we are grateful to the Ford Foundation Southern African Office, which provided the funding for this book and for the conference on which it is based, and the European Union Foundation for Human Rights, who assisted with funding for the conference.

D.B.
S.R.
October, 2001

MINIMUM STATE OBLIGATIONS: INTERNATIONAL DIMENSIONS

Sage Russell

INTRODUCTION

Some of the truisms about economic, social and cultural rights that have been stated fairly reflexively over the years are no longer as true as they once were. The last ten to fifteen years have witnessed a significant advance at the international level in the theoretical and conceptual development of these rights. Economic, social and cultural rights are no longer as neglected as they once were relative to civil and political rights.

There now exists wider agreement on the core elements of these rights, development of international standards, and guides to monitoring and evaluation. Recently, the United Nations Committee on Economic, Social and Cultural Rights (the Committee) has been holding days of general discussion and adopting general comments on the individual rights in the International Covenant on Economic, Social and Cultural Rights (ICESCR).[1] Prior to

---

1   International Covenant on Economic, Social, and Cultural Rights, *opened for signature* 16 Dec 1966, *entered into force* 3 Jan 1976, 993 UNTS 3.

1999, the only rights-specific general comments addressed the area of housing.[2] We now have general comments on the rights to food and health and two general comments on education.[3] The UN Commission on Human Rights and the Sub-Commission on the Promotion and Protection of Human Rights have appointed special rapporteurs to investigate and report on the implementation and violation of a number of human rights around the world, including education and housing.[4] The influential 1986 Limburg Principles on the Implementation of Economic, Social and Cultural Rights[5] and the 1997 Maastricht Guidelines on Violations of Economic, Social and Cultural Rights[6] have achieved wide currency internationally and de facto official status within the Committee on Economic, Social and Cultural Rights, as demonstrated by their incorporation into the recent general comments.

The Limburg Principles and Maastricht Guidelines were developed by international experts in economic, social and cultural rights at two meetings held approximately ten years apart at the University of Limburg (now Maastricht University) in the Netherlands. The Limburg Principles provide guidance on interpreting the ICESCR, especially Articles 1-5. They define a human rights violation in terms of states' obligations: "A failure by a State party to comply with an obligation contained in the ICESCR is, under international law, a violation of the ICESCR.[7] The Maastricht Guidelines build on the Limburg framework by clarifying the nature and scope of violations of economic, social and cultural rights, along with appropriate responses and remedies.

A framework is developing for thinking about these rights that includes identifying the core elements, setting standards, and identifying minimum state obligations. There is also renewed

---

2 *General Comment 4: The Right to Adequate Housing* (1991) CESCR reprinted in *Compilation of General Comments and General Recommendations Adopted by Human Rights Treaty Bodies* (1994) UN Doc HRI\GEN\1\Rev1 at 53; *General Comment 7: The Right to Adequate Housing* (1997) CESCR UN Doc E/C.12/1997/4.
3 *General Comment 11: Plans of Action for Primary Education* (1999) CESCR UN Doc E/C.12/1999/4; *General Comment 12: The Right to Adequate Food* (1999) CESCR UN Doc E/C.12/1999/5. *General Comment 13: The Right to Education* (1999) CESCR UN Doc E/C.12/1999/10. *General Comment 14: The Right to the Highest Attainable Standard of Health* (2000) CESCR UN Doc E/C.12/2000/4.
4 To obtain reports submitted by the Special Rapporteurs, visit http://www.unhchr.ch/html/menu2/7/b/tm.htm.
5 "The Limburg Principles on the Implementation of the International Covenant on Economic, Social, and Cultural Rights" (1987) 9 *Hum Rts Q* 122.
6 Van Boven, Flinterman, and Westendorp (eds) *The Maastricht Guidelines on Violations of Economic, Social, and Cultural Rights* (1989) Netherlands Institute for Human Rights.
7 "The Limburg Principles on the Implementation of the International Covenant on Economic, Social and Cultural Rights" (1987) 9 *Hum Rts Q* 122, para 70.

attention and activity in the area of developing indicators and benchmarks, which is facilitating monitoring and evaluating the implementation of these rights.

Complementary efforts on the part of nongovernmental organisations (NGOs) and other civil society actors are reinforcing these trends. The AAAS/HURIDOCS[8] Economic, Social and Cultural Rights Violations Project is one such effort, but there are others. The project commissioned the series of papers that forms part of the structure of this Conference. We asked international experts to write papers on the individual rights that are listed in the ICESCR, using a four-part framework. First, they sketched out the legal basis of the right in international law. Second, they described the scope of the right. Next, we asked them to identify the minimum state obligations. And finally, based on the preceding analysis, they described some common violations of the right.

Another important sign of progress with respect to ESC rights is in the area of their justiciability. It has been said for a long time that economic, social and cultural rights, unlike civil and political rights, are too vague to be justiciable or consist of elements that cannot be tested in court. On closer scrutiny, this generalisation begins to break down too. In its General Comment No. 3, on the nature of States parties obligations,[9] the Committee identified several aspects of economic, social and cultural rights that have already been incorporated into many domestic legal systems and that are therefore justiciable. On the general level these include nondiscrimination and equal treatment under the law. More specifically, the Committee stated that in many legal systems the following provisions of the ICESCR will be justiciable: equal pay for equal work; trade union rights; child labour laws; a number of educational rights; and academic, scientific and artistic freedom.

South Africa has gone further than most countries by incorporating many of the economic, social and cultural rights listed in the ICESCR into its Constitution,[10] along with several that are not

---

8 HURIDOCS (Human Rights Information and Documentation Systems, International) is a Geneva-based NGO focusing on documentation of human rights violations.
9 *General Comment 3: The Nature of States Parties Obligations* (1990) CESCR reprinted in *Compilation of General Comments* (1994) UN Doc HRI\GEN\1\Rev1 at 45.
10 Constitution of the Republic of South Africa, 1996. This is often referred to as South Africa's "final" or "permanent" constitution, to distinguish it from the "interim" constitution of 1993, that regulated the drafting of the 1996 constitution and regulated government while the 1996 constitution was being drafted. Economic and social rights are entrenched in section 23 (labour rights), section 25 (the right to have access to land), section 26 (the right to have access to housing), section 27 (the rights to have access to health care services, sufficient food and water, and social security and assistance), section 28(1)(c) (children's right to basic nutrition, shelter, basic health care services and social

explicitly stated in the ICESCR, such as access to water and to a clean and healthy environment. By definition, then, these rights are justiciable in South Africa, as has been demonstrated in recent Constitutional Court cases, most notably the *Grootboom* case.[11]

There are compelling reasons to share ideas and information between the international and the South African levels. Since South Africa is ahead of other countries in this regard, and economic and social rights are relatively new in South Africa as well, international law is an important source of interpretation for these rights. Indeed, the Constitution recognises the importance of international law as a valuable source of guidance in interpreting the economic and social rights it contains.[12] The work done in South Africa is equally important internationally. Although considerable progress has been made recently in understanding economic, social and cultural rights, most of it has been theoretical, and we have not seen an equivalent improvement in the way people around the world are living their lives. Since economic and social rights are more than abstract concepts here, progress in South Africa in interpreting, monitoring, institutionalising, educating, litigating, promoting and otherwise realising these rights will move the equivalent processes forward internationally as well.

Minimum state obligations, the theme of this conference, is one of the more difficult and controversial concepts in economic, social and cultural human rights, bridging the gap as it does between fundamental entitlements and scarce resources. There are a number of complexities associated with this concept, starting with the very basic one of terminology. It is variously referred to as minimum core content, core content, essential elements, core obligations, minimum state obligations and other variations on these themes. These terms are related, but not synonymous. They can be divided into two main groups, centering around the notions of content and obligations respectively. There seems to be

---

services), section 29 (the right to basic education and, under certain circumstances, further education) and section 35(2)(e) (detained persons' right to the provision, at state expense, of adequate accommodation, nutrition, reading material and medical treatment).

11 *Government of RSA and others v Grootboom and others* 2001 (1) SA 46 (CC). The Court considered the concept of minimum core obligations at some length in its judgment in *Grootboom*. As the judgment was delivered well after the conference on which this book is based took place, the authors of the papers contained in this book where not expected to incorporate the judgment in their work. Some found time to do so, but most did not. Their contributions should be understood in this light.

12 Constitution of the Republic of South Africa, 1996, section 39(1) and section 233.

an emerging consensus toward adopting the minimum state obligations approach. That is the phrase we use in our project, because it manages to avoid or at least reduce some of the problems with the minimum core content designation.

Minimum core content is often defined as the nature or essence of a right. That is, it is the essential element or elements without which a right loses its substantive significance as a human right and in the absence of which a State party should be considered to be in violation of its international obligations. It has also been described as a "floor" below which conditions should not be permitted to fall. The problem for many human rights activists is the risk that the "floor" will become a "ceiling." The concern is that the identification of minimum core content will reveal to States parties how little they are required to do to be in compliance with their obligations, and that they will do that minimum and nothing more. However, if states actually did live up to their minimum obligations, that would in many cases represent progress. It is probably also temperamentally difficult for people who work for human rights to apply the term "minimum" to something they passionately believe is an entitlement of all human beings everywhere.

Referring instead to minimum state obligations is at least a partial way out of this dilemma. Although the semantic shift is slight, the focus changes to a new question: when a state ratifies the ICESCR, what things must it do immediately to realise the right? Rather than ranking the various components of a human right in some sort of hierarchy and assigning relative worth, the question becomes one of timing. All the components of the right are important, and the ultimate goal is full implementation. To get there, what must the state do first? Clearly the two concepts are closely related. What the state should tackle first are those elements of the right that are considered the most essential or fundamental.

The minimum state obligation formulation is the one the Committee on Economic, Social and Cultural Rights favours, and it is the one that appears in paragraph 10 of General Comment No. 3, which is the most authoritative rendering of the concept:

> The Committee is of the view that a minimum core obligation to ensure the satisfaction of, at the very least, the minimum essential levels of each of the rights is incumbent upon every State party. Thus, for example, a State party in which any significant number of individuals is deprived of basic foodstuffs, of essential primary health care, of basic shelter and housing,

or of the most basic forms of education is, *prima facie*, failing to discharge its obligations under the Covenant. If the Covenant were to be read in such a way as not to establish such a minimum core obligation, it would be largely deprived of its *raison d'être*. By the same token, it must be noted that any assessment as to whether a State has discharged its minimum core obligation must also take account of resource constraints applying within the country concerned. Article 2(1) [of the Covenant] obligates each State party to take the necessary steps "to the maximum of its available resources." In order for a State party to be able to attribute its failure to meet at least its minimum core obligations to a lack of available resources it must demonstrate that every effort has been made to use all resources that are at its disposition in an effort to satisfy, as a matter of priority, those minimum obligations.[13]

Paragraph 11 goes on to say that "the Committee wishes to emphasise, however, that even where the available resources are demonstrably inadequate, the obligation remains for a State party to strive to ensure the widest possible enjoyment of the relevant rights under the prevailing circumstances."

It is important to emphasise that the purpose of the minimum state obligations approach is not to give states an escape hatch for avoiding their responsibilities under the ICESCR. It is in fact the opposite: a way to take into account the fact that many economic, social and cultural rights require resources that are simply not available in poor countries. This approach states that even in highly straitened circumstances, a state has irreducible obligations that it is assumed to be able to meet, and it shifts the burden of proof to the state if the state claims that it cannot meet even these most minimal obligations.

One potential weakness in this approach is that its basic assumption – that minimum state obligations are by definition affordable – may be untenable. The obligation to make primary education free and universally available is commonly considered to be part of the minimum state obligation of the right to education. It is also not a particularly controversial one since governments are widely accepted to be in the education business. But primary education is not cost-free, especially if quality standards are attached – if students are expected to learn something.

---

13 *General Comment 3: The Nature of States Parties Obligations* (1990) CESCR, reprinted in *Compilation of General Comments*, (1994) UN Doc HRI\GEN\1\Rev1 45 at para 10.

The somewhat abstract and theory-bound international system has not grappled fully with the potential contradiction in the minimum state obligations approach. States are assumed to have access to the resources needed to meet their minimum state obligations, but in fact they may not. How does one resolve this dilemma? The literature and theory of economic, social and cultural rights have developed several approaches to deal with the problem, although they do not resolve it.

The ICESCR and the general comments do not anticipate that necessary resources will all come from the state. The resources are those that are available within the society as a whole, from the private sector as well as the public. It is the state's responsibility to mobilise these resources, not to provide them all directly from its own coffers. Further, the ICESCR underlines the international obligations of states – the obligation of wealthier countries to make resources available to poorer countries. Many resource problems center around the misallocation of resources: to expensive tertiary-level health care, rather than primary or preventative health care; to university education rather than primary education; to expensive weapons systems rather than food; to the privileges of the governing elite rather than to low-cost housing. A reordering of priorities will alleviate some of the resource burden in any country. In addition, a country faced with severe resource constraints can begin to meet its minimum obligations by developing a plan for the accomplishment of the goal over time – that is, for its progressive realisation. Article 14 of the ICESCR requires exactly that in the area of compulsory, free primary education.[14]

Still, we live in the real world. There are already more than six billion people in the world and the numbers continue to grow. There are gross and grotesque disparities in resource allocation, both within and between countries, and states that can afford to be generous frequently do not live up to their international obligations. It is often said that in a time of increasing globalisation, large corporations may have more power than the governments of the countries within which they are located or incorporated. This can further frustrate the state's ability to mobilise private sector resources. As the Maastricht Guidelines state, "The impact of these disparities [in wealth] on the lives of people – especially the

---

[14] Article 14 expressly requires States parties that have not managed to secure free compulsory primary education for its people to: "within two years, ...work out and adopt a detailed plan of action for the progressive realisation, within a reasonable number of years, to be fixed in the plan, of the principle of compulsory education, free of charge for all".

poor – is dramatic and renders the enjoyment of economic, social and cultural rights illusory for a significant portion of humanity."[15]

Against this general background, as well as the particular circumstances and history of South Africa, what is taking place in South Africa to make the promises of economic and social rights real, rather than illusory, and what is being learned in the process, are extremely important. This is true not just within South Africa's borders, but in the rest of the world as well.

Since scarce resources are one of the key questions in economic and social rights, if not the key question, it is worthwhile to say more about the relationship between resources and minimum state obligations. The Maastricht Guidelines refine the concept of state obligations, by dividing them into three types:

> The obligation to respect requires States to refrain from interfering with the enjoyment of economic, social and cultural rights. Thus, the right to housing is violated if the State engages in arbitrary forced evictions. The obligation to protect requires States to prevent violations of such rights by third parties. Thus, the failure to ensure that private employers comply with basic labour standards may amount to a violation of the right to work or the right to just and favourable conditions of work. The obligation to fulfil requires States to take appropriate legislative, administrative, budgetary, judicial and other measures toward the full realisation of such rights. Thus, the failure of States to provide essential primary health care to those in need may amount to a violation.[16]

The obligation to fulfil has been further subdivided by some commentators into obligations to facilitate, promote, and provide, and there may be other formulations as well. There are differences among these terms, but it is not necessary to make those distinctions for the purposes of this analysis.

It is frequently stated that the respect-bound obligations are cost-free because they require the state *not* to take action, *not* to be a rights violator itself. It seems rather straightforward and obvious that a state that is charged with realising economic, social and

---

15 Van Boven, Flinterman, and Westendorp (eds) *The Maastricht Guidelines on Violations of Economic, Social, and Cultural Rights* (1998) Netherlands Institute of Human Rights para 1.
16 Van Boven, Flinterman, and Westendorp (eds) *The Maastricht Guidelines on Violations of Economic, Social, and Cultural Rights* (1998) Netherlands Insitute of Human Rights para 6.

cultural rights for its people has no business getting in its own way by violating them. Since the obligation to respect is both fundamental and presumably cost-free, it is a short step to assign the respect-bound obligations to the category of minimum state obligations.

The protect-bound obligations are a little harder. The obligation to protect is sometimes said to be cost-free because it is also a negative obligation – *not* allowing third parties to violate rights. One of the principal ways that states meet their protect-bound obligations is by creating and implementing the necessary policy, legislative, regulatory, judicial, inspection and enforcement frameworks. Creating and operating these systems requires considerable human, financial and other resources. They are not cost-free. But legislation, regulation and enforcement are also widely understood to form part of the basic responsibilities of government. A government is expected to use its resources in these areas. Therefore, one can claim that the protect-bound obligations form part of states' minimum obligations, despite the cost. Although creating the legislative, administrative, judicial and enforcement frameworks to prevent or redress violations by third parties may be seen to be part of minimum state obligations, given the limitations of state power with respect to corporate power, implementing them effectively is likely to be considerably more difficult and expensive. This raises the distinction between obligations of conduct and obligations of result, discussed below.

The obligation to fulfil is harder still and this is where some of the difficult resource questions come in. Part of the obligation to fulfil, like the obligation to protect, consists of setting up "the appropriate legislative, administrative, judicial and other measures". These are among the fundamental processes of government. It therefore seems reasonable to assert that they form part of states' minimum obligation under the ICESCR, in spite of the cost. Unlike the obligations to respect and protect, which are often viewed as negative obligations, the obligation to fulfil is seen as a positive obligation, requiring the state to make sure that the essence of the right – its minimum core if you will – is provided to its people. People can pay the cost themselves – either directly or through taxes – the state can require private sector actors to pay the costs, and, if and when necessary, the state can implement the right directly.

As stated earlier, non-discrimination is subject to immediate implementation and is a fundamental tenet of all human rights. When we add that to the respect and protect-bound obligations and the dimension of the obligation to fulfil that engages the basic processes of governing, it is apparent that there is a great deal that can be considered part of a state party's minimum obligations under the ICESCR. Minimum state obligations is actually not a minimalist concept.

Another refinement to the concept of minimum state obligations is the distinction between obligations of conduct and obligations of result. According to the Maastricht Guidelines:

> The obligation of conduct requires action reasonably calculated to realise the enjoyment of a particular right. In the case of the right to health, for example, the obligation of conduct could involve the adoption and implementation of a plan of action to reduce maternal mortality. The obligation of result requires States to achieve specific targets to satisfy a detailed substantive standard. With respect to the right to health, for example, the obligation of conduct requires the reduction of maternal mortality to levels agreed at the 1994 Cairo International Conference on Population and Development and the 1995 Beijing Fourth World Conference on Women.[17]

Obligations of result lead straight to questions of effectiveness and realisation of the right. It is no longer a question of whether children are going to school, but of whether they are learning to read and write when they are there. Obligations of result introduce some difficult issues of measurement and monitoring, and they are likely to be more expensive than obligations of conduct. According to the Maastricht Guidelines, "[t]he obligations to respect, protect and fulfil each contain elements of obligation of conduct and obligation of result."[18]

This book reproduces the papers presented at a conference held in Pretoria on 30-31 August 2000 that focused on the minimum core content of economic and social rights. The Conference was structured as a series of paired presentations on the economic and social rights that appear in both the ICESCR and the South African Constitution, albeit not always in the same form.

The authors of the papers take a variety of approaches to the notion of minimum state obligations (or minimum core content). Differences in the approaches among the papers are conditioned

---

17   Van Boven, Flinterman, and Westendorp (eds) *The Maastricht Guidelines on Violations of Economic, Social, and Cultural Rights* (1998) Netherlands Insitute of Human Rights para 7.
18   *Ibid* at para 7.

by the views of their authors as well as by the nature of the rights themselves and whether the right is discussed from the international or South African perspective. Education or housing, for example, may be viewed as programmatic in nature, while realisation of trade union rights depends on having the appropriate legal and administrative framework in place and enforced.

The interplay among these factors – the varying opinions of the authors, as conditioned by the rights themselves – provides a multidimensional approach to minimum core obligations, enabling the reader to grasp its meaning in a more complete and rounded way than would otherwise be possible.

THE ESSENTIAL COMPONENTS OF THE HUMAN RIGHT TO ADEQUATE HOUSING – A SOUTH AFRICAN PERSPECTIVE

Pierre de Vos

1 INTRODUCTION

From a South African perspective[1] the paper by Miloon Kothari on the essential component of the human right to adequate housing confronts us with a fascinating but complex problem regarding the justiciability of social and economic rights generally and the right to adequate housing in particular. On the one hand, the concept of "adequacy" (elaborated upon at some length in the paper under discussion) and the insistence on a holistic approach to housing rights provides us with an important but – in the context of a developing country like South Africa – a very ambitious benchmark for measuring the state's compliance with its negative and positive duties engendered by the right to housing. On the

---

1 Or, to be more honest, I should say from my personal perspective as a South African legal academic with more than a passing interest in social and economic rights.

other hand, it becomes clear that it will be difficult if not impossible for courts or other adjudicating bodies to intervene effectively to ensure that all aspects of this right to *adequate* housing are realised by the state within a reasonably short period. Put differently, while a growing body of work is assisting in slowly coaxing courts and other tribunals into acceptance of the justiciability of social and economic rights in general and the right to housing in particular, judges will, at this point in history, surely bolt from the blocks if asked to provide individual relief for petitioners claiming a right to be provided with adequate housing in the sense that it is set out in General Comment 4.

Kothari's paper acknowledges this extremely difficult problem of constitutional adjudication and provides us with the very helpful list of "inherently justiciable"[2] aspects of the right to housing with reference to the final report of the UN Special Rapporteur on housing.[3] To my mind this list of "inherently justiciable" elements of the right to housing is a very sound starting point for any discussion about the "core content" or "essential components" of the right of access to adequate housing. There are three main aspects to this list that might be of specific importance for the advancement of the justiciability of the right of access to housing in the South African setting.

First, the list reflects the obvious reality that the major stumbling block in the judicial enforcement of the right to adequate housing is the lack of adequate resources available to the state and other relevant actors. Hence it recognises that this right places a set of duties on the state to respect and protect the right to adequate housing; duties that, on the face of it, do not place a heavy burden on the state to spend vast and indeterminable sums of money. Although some of these obligations must obviously entail budgetary allocations and may have economic consequences, these costs are either incidental or they are costs that a government can plan and budget for in a particular year. For

---

2   These are: (a) Protection against arbitrary, unreasonable, punitive or unlawful forced evictions and/or demolitions; (b) Security of tenure; (c) Non-discrimination and equality of access in housing; (d) Housing affordability and accessibility; (e) Tenants' rights; (f) The right to equality and equal protection and benefit of the law; (g) Equality of access to land, basic civic services, building materials and amenities; (h) Equitable access to credit, subsidies and financing on reasonable terms for disadvantaged groups; (i) The right to special measures to ensure adequate housing for households with special needs or lacking necessary resources; (j) The right to the provision of appropriate emergency housing to the poorest section of society; (k) The right to participation within all aspects of the housing sphere; (l) The right to a clean environment and safe, secure and habitable housing.
3   E/CN.4/Sub.2/1995/12.

example, the duty on the state to ensure protection against arbitrary, unreasonable, punitive and unlawful forced evictions, may have economic consequences and may place certain budgetary obligations on the system in relation to the enforcement of such provisions, but will not lead to a sudden and unplanned increase in the amount of money that the state will have to spend.

Second, the right to equality and non-discrimination runs like a golden thread through the elements judged to be "inherently justiciable". The argument here, as I understand it, is that very often access to adequate housing is denied to individuals *not* because of resource constraints but because of discrimination or because the victims find themselves in circumstances where they are so vulnerable and disempowered that they are incapable of accessing existing legal, political and social remedies that might very well allow them to gain access to some form of housing. This line of thinking moves us closer to a practical understanding of rights as being interdependent and indivisible; the understanding, also, that there is no *conceptual* difference between civil and political rights and economic and social rights. This also implies that the different rights operate in support of each other, since the realisation of one right might be dependent on the realisation of another. Starving people may find it difficult to exercise their freedom of speech while a restriction on freedom of speech may make it difficult for individuals to enforce their right of access to housing.[4] In the case of the right of access to adequate housing in the South African context this means that an evaluation of the state's obligations regarding housing must not only have regard to the right to housing (s 26) and the right of children to basic shelter (s 28(1)(c)), but also – very importantly – to the right to equality (s 9) and the right to human dignity (s 10).

Third – and this is not unrelated to the second aspect – the list acknowledges that there is a duty on the state to take *special measures* to ensure that the most vulnerable people in a society are

---

4   See De Vos "Pious wishes or directly enforceable human rights?: Social and economic rights in South Africa's 1996 Constitution" (1997) 13 SAJHR 67, 70-71. The approach of indivisibility is one adopted by the South African Constitution makers and is reflected in the documentation of the Technical Committee of experts to the constitutional committee (Theme Committee 4 of the Constitutional Assembly), most notably in an undated memorandum "Supplementary Memorandum on Bill of Rights and Party Submissions" drawn up by the Technical Committee after publication of the first working draft of the Constitution in October 1995. In the course of objecting to a request by the Theme Committee to group social and economic rights together in a separate section of the Bill of Rights, the technical experts argue that grouping these rights together will devalue them and will make them seem "like some special species of rights".

not left without any protection against the elements. What is required is to view the right of access to housing from a specific contextual perspective. In South Africa, this means that the particular history of our country and the material consequences of that history, the transformative nature of our constitution in general and the equality provision in particular, and the importance of the value of human dignity entrenched in the Constitution must be taken into account when looking at the scope and content of the right of access to housing. Put differently, the right of access to housing must be approached with an appreciation that the state has a special duty to take steps to protect those individuals and groups most disadvantaged and marginalized by our apartheid history. A failure to take such special steps may thus, in the context of the right of access to housing, result in a Constitutional infringement of either that right and or the right to equality.[5]

These issues are important, not only because they provide us with very specific markers about the scope and content of the obligations engendered by the right of access to housing, but also, I would argue, because they might assist us in persuading rather reluctant courts to engage more fully with social and economic rights in general and the right of access to housing in particular. I would argue that the identification of "inherently justiciable" aspects of the right of access to housing might be an important way of convincing courts to begin to enforce this right in an effective way. There should, of course, be an appreciation of the interrelated and mutually enforcing nature of the concept of inherently justiciable aspects to the right on the one hand and the idea of a set of minimum core obligations on the other. In the South African context especially, the very specific understanding of the

---

5   This is supported by the international law opinion. See *General Comment 4: The Right to Adequate Housing* (1991) CESCR UN Doc E/1992/23, para 7, where the CESCR acknowledged that the right to housing stems from a right to dignity and stated:

"In the first place, the right to housing is integrally linked to other human rights and to the fundamental principles upon which the Covenant is premised. This 'the inherent dignity of the human person' from which the rights in the Covenant are said to derive requires that the term 'housing' be interpreted so as to take account of a variety of other considerations, most importantly that the right to housing should be ensured to all persons irrespective of income or access to economic resources.

"The Constitutional Court has accepted the view that the rights in the Bill of Rights will often be interrelated and interdependent. In *National Coalition for Gay and Lesbian Equality v Minister of Justice* 1998 (12) BCLR 1517 (CC) at 1537 par 31 Ackermann J stated that:

"In Bernstein v Bester, it was said that rights should not be construed absolutely or individualistically in ways which denied that all individuals are members of a broader community and are defined in significant ways by that membership."

nature and scope of the right to equality might often assist to show that many of the "minimum core obligations" regarding the right of access to housing are indeed inherently justiciable.

2 SUBSTANTIVE EQUALITY, THE RIGHT OF ACCESS TO HOUSING AND JUSTICIABILITY

Karl Klare has argued that South Africa's 1996 Constitution can be understood to establish the project of transformative constitutionalism. This project rejects the fiction that our community was founded at a magical moment that froze its meaning for ever, and embraces the Constitution as a transformative document, one that requires continual reinvention to make sense of the changing world and country we live in.[6] Viewed thus, the Constitutional project becomes a long term project committed to transforming our country's political and social institutions and power relationships in a democratic, participatory, and egalitarian direction.[7]

It goes without saying that a very specific conception of the right to equality is required to give effect to this transformative vision. It requires first, a rejection of the traditional, liberal conception of equality that is based on the notion of sameness and similar treatment. Second, it requires the adoption of a more contextual or substantive conception of equality that measures equality and discrimination in terms of the *impact* of the act or omission on vulnerable sections of the community and asks whether the action or inaction complained of will have a specific negative impact on the more vulnerable and marginalized sections of the community. This means that the impact should, of course, be examined in relation to the prevailing social, economic and political circumstances in the country. The South African Constitutional Court has accepted this second vision of equality[8] and has recognised that it would have to examine the actual economic and social and political context in which claimants in our society

---

6   Klare "Legal culture and transformative constitutionalism' (1998) 14 *SAJHR* 146, 155.
7   Klare "Legal culture and transformative constitutionalism' (1998) 14 *SAJHR* 146, 150. The Constitutional text itself – particularly various sections of the Bill of Rights – alludes to this transformative nature of the obligations engendered by it. See e.g. s 1(a) (equality must be *achieved*; human rights and freedoms must be *advanced*); s 7(1) (the state must *promote* and *fulfil* the rights in the Bill of Rights); s 9(2) (to *promote the achievement* of equality, certain measures may be taken), s 26 (the state must take reasonable steps... in order to *achieve* the progressive realisation of the right of access to housing).
8   See *President of the Republic of South Africa v Hugo* 1997 4 SA 1 (CC), 729G, where Goldstone J remarks:

find themselves in order to determine whether the Constitution's commitment to equality is being upheld or not. Often, such an inquiry would reveal a world of systemic and pervasive group-based inequality, which needs to be taken into account in the formulation of jurisprudential approaches to equality rights.[9] Often, also, the enquiry will reveal that the failure of the state to act would perpetuate or reinforce patterns of disadvantage and harm. There might therefore be a constitutional duty on the state to take special measures to safeguard the most vulnerable sections of society. This might often require the state to take such steps as might be necessary to ensure that the very structures that prevent or inhibit marginalized and disadvantaged groups from realising their full potential are broken down.

This insight is significant for the discussion of the justiciability of social and economic rights in general and the right of access to housing in particular. Because the various rights in the Bill of Rights are interdependent and interrelated, any evaluation of the duties engendered by the equality provision of the South African Constitution will also have to take into account the other provisions of the Constitution, including the right of access to adequate housing.[10] For example, one could ask: given the Constitutional commitment to the right of access to adequate housing, does the specific action or policy by the government or other relevant actor (or their inaction and/or lack of any policy) impact negatively or

---

"We need, therefore, to develop a concept of unfair discrimination which recognises that although a society which affords each human being equal treatment on the basis of equal worth and freedom is our goal, we cannot achieve that goal by insisting on identical treatment in all circumstances before the goal is achieved."This view is already clear in the Court's endorsement of "human dignity" at the heart of equality jurisprudence, since it is based on the notion that all individuals have equal moral worth, not that all individuals are actually born free and equal.

9   In elaborating further on the Constitutional Court's substantive approach to equality – or what he called the "remedial" or "restitutionary" approach – Ackermann J stated the following in *National Coalition for Gay and Lesbian Equality and Another v Minister of Justice and Others* 1998 12 BCLR 1517 (CC):

"It is insufficient for the constitution merely to ensure, through its Bill of Rights, that statutory provisions which have caused such unfair discrimination in the past are eliminated. Past unfair discrimination frequently has ongoing negative consequences, the continuation of which is not halted immediately when the initial causes thereof are eliminated, and unless remedied, may continue for a substantial time and even indefinitely. Like justice, equality delayed is equality denied." (1546, par 60)

10 The non-discrimination aspect of the right to adequate housing is in line with international law. In *General Comment 4: The Right to Adequate Housing* (1991) CESCR UN Doc E/1992/23 the Committee on Economic, Social and Cultural Rights (CESCR) gave an authoritative interpretation of this obligation to adequate housing and asserted that:

"Individuals, as well as families, are entitled to adequate housing regardless of age, economic status, group or other affiliation or status and other such factors. In particular, enjoyment of this right must, in accordance with article 2 (2) of the Covenant, not be subject to any form of discrimination" (at par. 6).

disproportionately on a specific vulnerable group?[11] Because the equality provision of the Constitution prohibits both direct and indirect discrimination and hence because it is the impact of a specific action or inaction that might result in a breach of the equality guarantee, any state policy that disproportionately impacts on the poor and the homeless will become constitutionally suspect. If the policy impacts disproportionately on such a group, one may well be able to convince a court that this action or inaction constitutes an infringement of the equality guarantee, read with the guarantee of the right of access to adequate housing. This implies that the equality guarantee – just as much as the right of access to housing – places a duty on the state and other relevant actors to take steps that would assist social groups living in unfavourable conditions to obtain some form of access to housing by giving them particular consideration.[12]

This, I would contend, is a promising line of argument to be followed when trying to convince courts – also the South African Constitutional Court – to engage judicially with social and economic rights in a meaningful way. For example, if this line of reasoning were to be followed in a case like the one of *Grootboom v Oostenberg Municipality*,[13] it would go a long way to demonstrate that there exists in this case an "inherently justiciable" right not to be discriminated against regarding access to housing. In this case the applicants were constituted of men, women and children, families and individuals, all informal squatters, who were evicted from their shacks after a protracted legal battle. The materials from which their homes were built were destroyed during the evictions and they therefore found themselves homeless at the time when they brought their application to court. The respondents in the case contended that they could not be provided with access to shelter or housing because according to the housing strategy adopted by the national and provincial government resources were allocated only for the provisioning of formal housing. No resources were allocated by the relevant authority to

---

11 See generally Craven *The International Covenant on Economic, Social and Cultural Rights: A Perspective on its Development* (1995) Clarendon Press at 157.
12 *General Comment 7: The Right to Adequate Housing* (1997) CESCR UN Doc E/C.12/1997/4 further states that: "Women, children, youth, older persons, indigenous people, ethnic and other minorities, and other vulnerable groups all suffer disproportionately from the practice of forced eviction.... The non-discrimination provisions of articles 2.2 and 3 of the [ICESCR] impose an additional obligation upon Governments to ensure that, where evictions do occur, appropriate measures are taken to ensure that no form of discrimination is involved." (at para 11)
13 2000 (3) BCLR 277 (C).

provide access to any form of housing for destitute individuals who found themselves to be homeless with no reasonable prospect to gain access to formal housing and no special measures were put in place to deal with the issue of homelessness in general. At the time when the application was made, there was no reasonable prospect of applicants gaining access to formal housing provided by the state. The housing policy of the state therefore failed to take special measures necessary to protect one of the most vulnerable groups in society.[14] While this might well constitute an infringement of the right of access to housing – the Cape High Court decided that it did not[15] – it may also constitute an infringement of the equality guarantee. And because the right to equality is at the very heart of the Bill of Rights, it may well be easier for litigants to convince a court of their claim when they can show that not only the right of access to housing has been infringed, but also their right to equality.

South Africa's Constitutional Court has emphasised that vulnerable groups are particularly protected by the constitution.[16] It has also acknowledged that in specific contexts the poor[17] as well as children and the mothers of young children can be deemed to be vulnerable groups. According to the Court the latter group in particular had been the victims of discrimination in the past.[18] In the *Hugo* case O'Regan J. stated that: "The more vulnerable the group adversely affected by the discrimination, the more likely the discrimination will be held to be unfair. Similarly, the more invasive the nature of the discrimination upon the interests of the individuals affected by the discrimination, the more likely it will be held to be unfair."[19] If one reads the right to equality together with the right of access to housing, it would be possible to make a very strong argument that the state action or inaction in this case constituted "unfair discrimination" and was therefore an infringement of the equality guarantee in the Constitution.

---

14 *Grootboom v Oostenberg Municipality* 2000 3 BCLR 277 (C) 283-284.
15 *Ibid.*
16 See *S v Makwanyane* 1995 (6) BCLR 665 (CC) at 753 para 230 per Langa J; at 771 para 305 per Mokgoro J.
17 See *S v Makwanyane* 1995 (6) BCLR 665 (CC) at 692 para 49 fn 79 per Chaskalson P.
18 See *President of the Republic of South Africa and Another v Hugo* 1997 (6) BCLR 708 (CC) at 732 para 47 per Goldstone J.
19 At para 112. See also *City Council of Pretoria v Walker* 1998 (3) BCLR 257 (CC) at 279 para 45 where Langa DP endorsed this view.

3 NON-DISCRIMINATION OR CORE ENTITLEMENTS?

There will, of course, be situations where the right to equality will not be relevant or where it will be impossible to invoke it, but where the obligations on the state and other relevant actors to provide access to adequate housing will nevertheless be of such a nature that it may be subjected to court scrutiny. It is in such a situation, I would contend, that the concept of minimum core entitlements will be of particular assistance in the South African context to persuade courts to engage in a meaningful way with, say, the right of access to adequate housing. This is because, whatever the scope and content of this concept might be, in principle it signals that there are housing priorities that the state should begin to address as a matter of urgency. Although South African courts will be reluctant to plunge into an enquiry on the scope and content of the right of access to housing due to the perceived separation of powers problems, the identification of minimum core obligations in line with international law writings might persuade courts that there are ways to deal with this issue without getting involved with the intricate policy of housing that the court would feel would be better left to the legislature and the executive.

For example, in the field of the right of access to adequate housing, the concept of minimum core entitlements as developed in international law, includes an understanding that the state and other relevant actors have a primary responsibility to tackle the issue of homelessness. This means that the state will have a duty to address this issue as a matter of priority. This is clear from the comments of the Committee on Economic Social and Cultural Rights, who in General Comment 4 stated that:

> The Committee is of the view that a minimum core obligation to ensure the satisfaction of, at the very least, minimum essential levels of each of the rights is incumbent on every state. Thus, for example, a State party in which any significant number of individuals is deprived of essential foodstuffs, of essential primary health care, of basic shelter and housing, or of the most basic forms of education is, prima facie, failing to discharge its obligations under the Covenant. If the Covenant were to be read in such a way as not to establish such a minimum core obligation, it would be largely deprived of its *raison d'être*.[20]

---

20 See *General Comment 3: The nature of States parties obligations* (1990) CESCR UN Doc E/1991/23, para 10; See also "The Limburg Principles on the Implementation of the

It is submitted that use of the idea of the minimum core obligation regarding access to housing in the South African context might lead to an understanding that s 26, read with s 9 and 10 of the South African Constitution, creates a similar priority obligation on the state to provide at least basic shelter to the homeless. It was argued above that s 9, 10 and 26 are interrelated and that the duties engendered by s 26 must be interpreted in the light of the commitment to the core values of equality and human dignity enshrined in s 9 and 10 of the Constitution. This commitment places a duty on the state to ensure that especially vulnerable and disadvantaged groups – such as the poor, women and children – have access to at least the basic levels of shelter to preserve human life and dignity. Where the state fails to do this, it will constitute a failure to fulfil its obligations under s 9 and s 26. While individuals are deemed to be the subjects of their own social and economic development for the purposes of the realization of the right to housing, destitute people and groups subject to systematic patterns of disadvantage will in certain, limited, circumstances be unable to gain access to the right to housing through their own efforts and resources. It is in such cases where the state will have a core minimum obligation to take steps to ensure that such individuals gain access to housing or shelter.[21] In the context of the right of access to housing, the limited circumstances under which the state will face an obligation to provide at least basic shelter will, at the minimum, include those situations where particularly vulnerable groups have been evicted from their existing

---

International Covenant on Economic, Social, and Cultural Rights" (1987) 9 *Hum Rts Q* 122, para 72 and Van Boven, Flinterman, and Westendorp (eds) *The Maastricht Guidelines on Violations of Economic, Social, and Cultural Rights* (1989) Netherlands Institute for Human Rights, para 15(i) which refers to an obligation on the state to meet "generally accepted international minimum standards of achievement"; Liebenberg "Socio-economic Rights" in Chaskalson et al Constitutional Law of South Africa (Revision Service 5, 1999) Juta at 41-43 par 41.6(e)(v); De Vos "Pious wishes or directly enforceable human rights?: Social and economic rights in South Africa's 1996 Constitution" (1997) 13 SAJHR 67 at 97.) The UN Special Rapporteur on the Realization of Economic, Social and Cultural Rights, Danilo Türk, reiterated this at the fifth session of the CESCR where he stated that:

"States with specific legal obligations to fulfil economic, social and cultural rights are obliged, regardless of the level of economic development, to ensure respect for minimum subsistence rights for all." (See also "The New International Economic Order and the Promotion of Human Rights: Realization of Economic, Social and Cultural Rights: Progress Report Prepared by Danilo Türk" UN Commission on Human Rights, Sub-Commission on Prevention on Discrimination and Protection of Minorities, UN Doc E/CN.4/Sub.2/1991/17 at 18 par 52(d).

21 See Liebenberg "Socio-economic Rights" in Chaskalson et al *Constitutional Law of South Africa* (Revision Service 5, 1999) Juta at 41-43 par 41.6(e)(v); Eide "Economic, Social and Cultural Rights as Human Rights" in Eide, Crause & Rosas (eds) *Economic, Social and Cultural Rights: a Textbook* (1995) Martinus Nijhoff 21 at 37-38.

shelters and find themselves homeless. This is also in accordance with international law standards.

4 CONCLUSION

A deployment of the concept of minimum core obligations or minimum core content of the right of access to housing in the South African context will obviously not bring about miraculous results in the struggle to engage courts to advance the rights of homeless and inadequately housed people in South Africa. Perceived conceptual difficulties with the judicial enforcement of social and economic rights, and a deeply entrenched formalistic legal culture militate against such drastic results. There is, of course, also a danger that the concept of minimum core obligations would be used by the state and other relevant actors to escape their more fundamental duty to take not only the minimum steps associated by this concept, but to work towards the provision of adequate housing to all South Africans. Although I have sympathy for this view, this does not mean that the idea of minimum core obligations – sensitively and judiciously deployed – could not play a role in nudging the courts towards a more activist position regarding social and economic rights. I believe the inclusion of a full set of justiciable social and economic rights in the South African Bill of Rights presents an exciting opportunity for lawyers and judges to devise innovative solutions to the problems associated with the judicial enforcement of social and economic rights and in this, the concept of minimum core obligations might well play a significant role.

CORE OBLIGATIONS RELATED TO THE RIGHT TO HEALTH AND THEIR RELEVANCE FOR SOUTH AFRICA

Audrey R Chapman

1 INTRODUCTION

What does it mean to affirm a right to health? Is it possible to identify core obligations of the right to health applicable to all States parties that have ratified relevant international or regional human rights instruments or have constitutional recognition of the right to health or health care? And what is the relevance of the developing international jurisprudence, in particular a recent general comment on this topic adopted by the United Nations Committee on Economic, Social and Cultural Rights (hereafter the Committee or CESCR), for the interpretation of South African constitutional provisions on health?

The International Covenant on Economic, Social and Cultural Rights (hereafter ICESCR or the Covenant), generally considered to provide the most authoritative delineation, "recognizes the right of everyone to the enjoyment of the highest attainable standard of physical and mental health."[1] The inclusive conception in

---

1   Article 12, International Covenant on Economic, Social, and Cultural Rights, *opened for signature* 16 Dec 1966, *entered into force* 3 Jan 1976, 993 UNTS 3 (hereinafter ICESCR).

this instrument extends not only to the provision of timely and appropriate medical services in the event of sickness. It also encompasses the underlying determinants of health, such as access to safe and potable water and adequate sanitation, an adequate supply of safe food, healthy occupational and environmental conditions, and access to health-related education and information.[2] Put another way, the right to health in the Covenant includes both access to health care and health protection through various public health measures.

Thus, the approach to health in the Covenant bridges two different paradigms. The right to health care or health services focuses primarily on the health status of the individual, generally in the context of physical (and to a lesser extent mental) illness and disability. In contrast, public health is concerned with protecting the health of populations and ensuring the conditions in which people can be healthy.[3] Historically, health systems were developed on a medical or curative model of health. More recently, advances in epidemiological research have sensitised policy-makers to the importance of public health interventions and preventive strategies of health promotion.

In contrast, the health-related provisions of the South African Bill of Rights are framed within the narrower health care or medical paradigm. Section 27, which deals with several social and economic rights, including health, food, water, and social security, stipulates that "everyone has the right to have access to health services, including reproductive health care."[4] In regard to Section 27 rights, the Constitution directs that "The state must take reasonable legislative and other measures, within its available resources, to achieve the progressive realisation of each of these rights."[5] Another component of Section 27 is that "no one may be refused emergency medical treatment."[6] A related provision in the Bill of Rights states that children have a right to basic health care services.[7] Yet another section provides persons in state incarceration with a right to "adequate medical treatment" at state expense.[8]

Like the Covenant, the South African Bill of Rights anticipates that the state will only gradually fulfil the requirements of social

---

2   *Ibid* par 9.
3   Mann, Gostin, Gruskin, Brennan, Lazzarini, and Fineberg "Health and human rights" (1994) 1 *Health and Human Rights* 8.
4   The Constitution of the Republic of South Africa, 1996, section 27(1)(a).
5   *Ibid* section 27(2).
6   *Ibid* section 27(3).
7   *Ibid* section 28(1)(c).
8   *Ibid* section 35(2)(e).

and economic rights. The Covenant uses the language of "progressive realisation" within the context of the "maximum of available resources."[9] Nevertheless, progressive realisation requires a state to take steps or adopt measures towards the full achievement of the right in question. To qualify, such steps should be deliberate, concrete and targeted as clearly as possible towards meeting this goal.[10] Utilising a similar formulation, section 27(2) of the Bill of Rights mandates that "The state must take reasonable legislative and other measures within its available resources to achieve the progressive realisation of each of these rights." The dilemma is how to determine whether measures taken to implement the right to health are adequate to that purpose within the constraints of the available resources. As yet, no one has determined a methodology or formula by which to make such a complicated assessment, made all the more complex by the need to balance fulfilment of a series of human rights, or applied it to specific countries.

Herein is the importance of the concept of the core legal obligation of states that has developed from the jurisprudence of the United Nations Committee on Economic, Social and Cultural Rights, the treaty monitoring body for the International Covenant on Economic, Social and Cultural Rights. Core obligations, sometimes referred to as the minimum core, identify a set of key requirements that are of immediate effect and do not vary for states. By definition these obligations apply irrespective of the availability of resources or any other factors and difficulties. If a state cannot meet these requirements, it has the burden to justify why this is the case.

Of course this raises yet another set of issues.[11] Is this a reasonable approach? Is it possible to identify a meaningful and rea-

---

9   Article 2(1) of the ICESCR uses the language of progressive realisation as follows: "Each State Party to the present Covenant undertakes to take steps, individually and through international assistance and cooperation, especially economic and technical, to the maximum of its available resources, with a view to achieving progressively the full realisation of the rights recognized in the present Covenant by all appropriate means, including particularly the adoption of legislative measures."

10 On the interpretation of progressive realisation as defined in Article 2 of the International Covenant on Economic, Social and Cultural Rights see Alston "The International Covenant on Economic, Social and Cultural Rights" in *Manual on human rights reporting* (1991) United Nations Centre for Human Rights and United Nations Institute for Training and Research, 43.

11 The interpretation of the minimum core appears in para 10, *General Comment No. 3: The nature of States parties obligations* (1990) CESCR UN Doc E/1991/23 reprinted in *Compilation of General Comments and General Recommendations Adopted by Human Rights Treaty Bodies* (1992) UN Doc HR1/GEN1.

sonable set of obligations related to the right to health applicable even to poor countries with severe resource constraints? And given differences in the definition of the rights related to health in the international human rights instruments and the South African Constitution, are international interpretations of core obligations relevant for South Africa? This paper will explore these questions with particular reference to the framing of the core health requirements put forward in the CESCR's recent general comment on the right to health.[12]

1 INTERNATIONAL AND REGIONAL LEGAL AND CONCEPTUAL FRAMEWORK

The notion of a right to health emerged relatively recently. Historically, issues related to the health of populations and the availability of health care were not considered to be a major social or governmental concern. While health was valued as an important and beneficial asset, it was assumed to be in the private rather than the public or social domain. Moreover, until a century ago, little was understood about the causes of disease or effective prevention and treatment measures. Before the development of scientifically grounded medical technology, much of health care could be provided by lay people rather than by professionals. Therefore over the centuries care for the sick and dying remained the responsibility of families, private charities, and religious organisations rather than the public sector.[13] Broadened government responsibility for health care and other social services in many western European countries dates back to the second half of the nineteenth century. This development was originally motivated by the goal of achieving a more productive labour force and a healthier general populace and, in some cases, to ameliorate social unrest.[14]

The acknowledgement of a right to health or health care reflects a broadened sense of governmental responsibility for the welfare of its citizens and a more inclusive understanding of human rights.

---

12 *General Comment No. 14: The Right to the Highest Attainable Standard of Health* (2000) CESCR UN Doc E/C.12/2000/4.
13 President's Commission for the Study of Ethical Problems in Medicine and Biomedical Research, *Securing Access to Health Care: The Ethical Implications of Differences in the Availability of Health Services, Vol. One: Report* (1983) Government Printer 13.
14 President's Commission for the Study of Ethical Problems in Medicine and Biomedical and Behavioral Research, *Securing Access to Health Care*, 14-15.

Like other social and economic human rights, the concept of a right to health or health services evolved as a response to the deprivations of the great Depression, devastation of World War II, and atrocities of the Holocaust.

One of the first formulations of a right to health occurred in the preamble to the Constitution of the World Health Organization (WHO), adopted by the International Health Conference held in New York in 1946. The preamble states that "The enjoyment of the highest attainable standard of health is one of the fundamental rights of every human being without distinction of race, religion, political belief, economic, or social condition."[15] This document conceptualises health as "a state of complete physical, mental and social well-being and not merely the absence of disease or infirmity."[16]

While attractive in a number of ways, such a broad conceptualisation of the right to health is problematic. It implies that every person has a right to physical, mental, and social well-being. This is simply not an attainable goal. Nature itself imposes a series of limitations that make such a state of complete health unattainable. Moreover, as the basis for a human right, the WHO formulation seemingly requires a government to guarantee or provide complete physical, mental, and social well-being for all of its citizens. This is also an impossible goal.[17] Health status depends not only on state responsibilities, the focus of classical human rights interpretations, but also upon the actions of other individuals in the society and the behaviour of the individual himself or herself.[18] An individual's heredity, habits, and behaviour play an important role in shaping his/her health. Moreover, health status reflects a wide range of nonmedical factors. Levels of development, the nature of the environment, education, income, social status, housing, sanitation, and nutrition constitute key determinants of the state of health of an individual and a community. Studies have shown that not only do deprived people tend to

---

15 Pan American Health Organization "Constitution of the World Health Organization" in *Basic Documents* Official Document No 240 (1991) 23.
16 World Health Organization "Preamble to the Constitution" in *The First Ten Years of the World Health Organisation* (1958) WHO 11.
17 See Callahan *What kind of life: A challenging exploration of the goals of medicine* (1990) Touchstone Books 34-40; and Boyle "The concept of health and the right to health" (1997) 3 *Social Thought* 5-17.
18 Fuenzalida and Connor "Summary and analysis" in Fuenzalida-Puelma and Connor (eds) *The right to health in the Americas: A comparative constitutional study* (1989) Pan American Health Organisation 541.

have worse health than other people, but that health status is closely related to socioeconomic status.[19]

The first explicit mention of a right to health in an international human rights instrument occurs in the United Nations Universal Declaration of Human Rights (1948). The Universal Declaration of Human Rights states that "everyone has a right to a standard of living adequate for the health and well-being of himself and of his family, including food, clothing, housing, and medical care and necessary social services ..."[20]

The International Covenant on Economic, Social and Cultural Rights (1966), one of the two major international human rights instruments based on the Universal Declaration, is generally considered to be the most authoritative delineation of the right to health. Article 12 "recognizes the right of everyone to the enjoyment of the highest attainable standard of physical and mental health,"[21] and to the end, mandates that States parties to the Covenant undertake the following steps to achieve its full realisation:

- The provision for the reduction of the stillbirth-rate and of infant mortality and for the healthy development of the child;
- The improvement of all aspects of environmental and industrial hygiene;
- The prevention, treatment and control of epidemic, endemic, occupational and other diseases;
- The creation of conditions which would assure to all medical service and medical attention in the event of sickness.[22]

There are also provisions related to the right to health in other international human rights instruments. The International Covenant on Civil and Political Rights (ICCPR) recognises an inherent right to life.[23] The Human Rights Committee, which monitors compliance with this Covenant, has defined the role of the state in protecting human life to include obligations to undertake measures to eliminate epidemics.[24] In response to the Nazi

---

19   This was one of the major conclusions of a 1997 independent inquiry into inequalities in health set up by the British government. For a discussion of the Acheson Report see Marmot "Acting on the evidence to reduce inequalities in health" (1999) 18 *Health Affairs* 42-45.
20   Universal Declaration of Human Rights, UN GA resolution 217 A (III) of 10 December 1948.
21   Article 12, ICESCR.
22   *Ibid.*
23   Article 6, International Covenant on Civil and Political Rights, *opened for signature* 16 December 1966, *entered into force* 23 March 1976, 99 UNTS 171 (hereinafter ICCPR).
24   *General Comment 6: The Right to Life* (1982) Human Rights Committee, UN Doc A/37/40, para 5.

medical experiments with human subjects,[25] ICCPR also seeks to protect human subjects by affirming that no one shall be subjected without his (or her) free consent to medical or scientific experimentation.[26] Under the International Convention on the Elimination of All Forms of Racial Discrimination, States parties undertake to prohibit and eliminate racial discrimination in all its forms and to guarantee the right of everyone, without distinction as to race, colour, national or ethic origin, the enjoyment of the right to public health and medical care.[27] The Convention on the Elimination of All Forms of Discrimination Against Women directs States parties to take all appropriate measures to eliminate discrimination against women in the field of health care. It also mandates that States parties ensure equality of access to health care services, including those related to family planning, pregnancy, confinement, and the post-natal period, granting free services where necessary.[28] The Convention on the Rights of the Child extends provisions of the right to health enumerated in ICESCR to the child. The responsibilities of States parties under this instrument are to take appropriate measures to diminish infant and child mortality, ensure the provision of necessary medical assistance and health care to all children with emphasis on the development of primary care, combat disease and malnutrition, provide clean drinking water, and combat the dangers and risks of environmental pollution.[29]

Similar provisions appear in several regional human rights instruments. The European Social Charter recognises the right to the highest possible standard of health attainable[30] and a right to social and medical assistance.[31] The African (Banjul) Charter on Human and Peoples' Rights similarly affirms that every individual shall have the right to enjoy the best attainable state of physical and mental health and mandates States parties to undertake necessary measures to protect health and ensure that their people

---

25 Brody *Biomedical Technology and Human Rights* (1993) Dartmouth/UNESCO 23.
26 Article 7, ICCPR.
27 Article 5(e)(iv), International Convention on the Elimination of All Forms of Racial Discrimination, *opened for signature* 7 March 1966, *entered into force* 4 January 1969, 60 UNTS 195 (hereinafter ICERD).
28 Article 12(1), Convention on the Elimination of All Forms of Discrimination against Women, *opened for signature* 18 December 1979, *entered into force* 3 September 1981, 1249 UNTS 13 (hereinafter CEDAW).
29 Article 24, Convention on the Rights of the Child, *opened for signature* 20 November 1989, *entered into force* 2 September 1990, 28 ILM 1456 (hereinafter CRC).
30 Article 11, European Social Charter, *opened for signature* 18 October 1961, *entered into force* 26 February 1965, 529 UNTS 221 (hereinafter European Social Charter).
31 *Ibid*, Article 3.

receive medical attention when they are sick.[32] The Additional Protocol to the American Convention on Human Rights in the Area of Economic, Social and Cultural Rights defines the right to health as the enjoyment of the highest level of physical, mental and social well-being and directs States parties to adopt a series of measures to ensure realisation of this right.[33]

In 1977, the World Health Assembly affirmed that health is a basic human right and a worldwide social good essential to the satisfaction of basic human needs and the quality of life. It set the goal of "Health for All" by the year 2000, now extended until 2010, defined as the attainment of a level of health that will permit all citizens to lead a socially and economically productive life.[34] A year later, the Declaration of Alma-Ata further linked the "Health for All" goal with rectifying inequalities in health status of people both within and between countries. To address these inequities, the World Health Assembly called on member states to include equity-oriented targets in their national Health for All strategies related to improved health among disadvantaged groups such as women, the rural poor, inhabitants of urban slums, and people engaged in hazardous occupations.[35]

Constitutions of a number of countries articulate a right to health protection that focuses on the public health context of health status.[36] A right to health protection focuses on preventative measures, such as the provision of potable water and the improvement of environmental conditions. Sometimes the distinction is phrased as the right to health care when one is sick and the right to health protection to prevent the population from becoming sick. However, even with an explicit constitutional provision, the right to health protection is rarely interpreted to be an immediately enforceable individual entitlement. It is more likely

---

32 Article 16, African Charter on Human and Peoples' Rights, *opened for signature* 26 June 1981, *entered into force* 21 October 1986, 21 ILM 59 (hereinafter African Charter).

33 Article 10, Additional Protocol to the American Convention on Human Rights in the Area of Economic, Social and Cultural Rights (Protocol of San Salvador), *opened for signature* 17 November 1988, *not yet in force*, OAS Treaty Series No 69 cited in Fluss "International public health law" in Detels, Holland, McEwen, and Omenn (eds) *Oxford textbook of public health* (3d ed 1997) Oxford University Press 373; Tomasevski "Health rights" in Eide, Krause and Rosas *Economic, social and cultural rights: A textbook* (1995) Martinus Nijhoff 130.

34 World Health Organization, *Global Strategy Health for All by the Year 2000* (1985) World Health Organization.

35 On September 12, 1978 representatives of 134 nations participating in Alma-Ata (former Soviet Union) at an International Primary Health Care Conference agreed to this declaration. See Pan American Health Organization *Basic Documents* 548.

36 Fuenzalida-Puelma and Connor (eds) *The right to health in the Americas: A comparative constitutional study* (1989) Pan American Health Organization.

to be considered a programmatic or policy directive that articulates goals.[37]

Despite nearly a half century of enumeration in various forms in international and regional instruments, WHO documents, and state constitutions, there is still confusion and controversy about the nature and scope of the right to health and the concomitant obligations of States parties. A recent study on the subject concludes that "The problem with the right to health is therefore not so much a lack of codification, but rather the absence of a consistent implementation practice through reporting procedures and before judicial and quasi-judicial bodies – as well as an ensuing lack of conceptual clarity."[38] Perhaps even more problematic is the failure of most countries, even among the 136 states that have ratified the ICESCR, to utilise its norms as a framework for formulating health policy and to take their obligations seriously.

The WHO approach is all too typical. Despite the rhetorical commitment to a right to health in various documents, WHO, at least up to the time of this writing, does not understand this language as imposing specific requirements. Instead it emphasises that expressions such as "countries should" or "countries shall collaborate in ..." refer to the commitment voluntarily assumed by countries and "By no means whatsoever should be interpreted as the imposition of definite actions on countries, by a supra-national agency."[39]

3 INTERPRETATIONS OF THE RIGHT TO HEALTH BY UN HUMAN RIGHTS TREATY MONITORING BODIES

Each of the major international human rights instruments has a United Nations-appointed oversight body mandated to review periodically the performance of States parties, the countries which ratify a particular human rights instrument and are therefore bound by its provisions. Human rights treaty monitoring bodies, which are usually composed of experts, also have the authority to develop interpretations of the rights enumerated in their respec-

---

37 *Ibid* at 608.
38 Toebes *The right to health as a human right in international law*, Vol. 1, School of Human Rights Research (SIM) Series (1999) Intersentia, Antwerp, 346.
39 This point is made in and the citation taken from PROVEA *Health as a right: National and international protection framework of the right to health* (Caracas, manuscript copy made available to this author) 43.

tive conventions. As noted, the right to health is dealt with in several of these documents. However, the relevant human rights treaty bodies – the Committee on Economic, Social and Cultural Rights, the Committee on the Elimination of Discrimination Against Women, the Committee on the Rights of the Child, and the Committee on the Elimination of Racial Discrimination – have been slow to interpret the right to health. Moreover, there has been virtually no coordination among them in the manner in which they have conducted their evaluations of states' compliance with health-related obligations.

The Committee on Economic, Social and Cultural Rights should have taken a leadership role in interpreting the right to health, but it did not do so. It held a day of general discussion on the right to health in December 1993. Such days of general discussion with experts and representatives of nongovernmental organisations often give rise to a process of drafting a general comment. In this case, however, the presentations at the day of general discussion were very general and inconclusive,[40] and the Committee did not immediately go forward with efforts to develop a general comment. Also, in the 1990s the Committee did not generally spend much time in its country reviews dealing with health issues. And on those occasions when the Committee asked about a state's implementation of the right to health, it tended to do so in a somewhat haphazard manner.[41]

In 1999 this situation changed. The Committee on the Elimination of Discrimination against Women (CEDAW) adopted a general recommendation on women and health at its 1999 session.[42] That same year the CESCR also began work on a general comment on the right to health. I was one of several experts who worked closely with the rapporteur, Professor Eibe Riedel, a member of the Committee, and contributed a background resource for the process. *General Comment No. 14: The Right to the Highest Attainable Standard of Health* was adopted by the Committee in May 2000.[43]

---

40 This author wrote a background paper and participated in the day of general discussion. The problem was that presenters generally ignored the guidelines set by the Committee and made very general presentations affirming the importance of the right.
41 This point was made by Brigit Toebes in her book, *The right to health as a human right in international law*, Vol. 1, School of Human Rights Research (SIM) Series (1999) Intersentia, Antwerp, chapter three. I concur from my own observations of the Committee.
42 *General recommendation on article 12: Women and health* (1999) Committee on the Elimination of Discrimination Against Women CEDAW/C/1999/I/WG.II/WP.2/Rev.1.
43 *General Comment 14: The Right to the Highest Attainable Standard of Health* (2000) CESCR UN Doc E/C.12/2000/4.

General Comment 14 is an important contribution to interpreting the right to health. The approach taken is to be concrete and relatively expansive in identifying the specific state health-related obligations of States parties. As noted, the conception of the right to health includes both ensuring the availability of timely and appropriate health care and protecting public health through such measures as providing safe and potable water, adequate sanitation, healthy occupational and environmental conditions, and appropriate health-related education and information. The general comment emphasises the importance of the participation of the population in all health-related decision-making at the community, national, and international levels.[44]

The general comment identifies four standards or criteria – availability, accessibility, acceptability, and quality – by which to evaluate the attainment of the right to health.[45] Availability measures whether public health and health-care facilities, goods, services, personnel, and programmes exist in sufficient quantity. Accessibility has four overlapping dimensions – nondiscrimination; safe physical reach of all sections of the population, especially vulnerable or marginalised groups; affordability; and information accessibility, the right to seek, receive and impart information and ideas concerning health issues. Acceptability refers to the requirement that all health facilities, goods, and services be respectful of medical ethics and culturally appropriate. Quality is the parallel need for health facilities, goods and services to be scientifically and medically appropriate and of good quality.

Another important feature of the general comment is its emphasis on the need for a gender perspective and a comprehensive national strategy for eliminating discrimination against women.[46] The approach taken in the general comment is to update the text of Article 12 of the Covenant by utilising a variety of subsequent documents that recognise the need to take special measures to protect women's right to health. The general comment makes particular use of the 1999 general recommendation on health rights adopted by CEDAW. Like CEDAW's general recommendation, the text of General Comment 14 recommends that states integrate a gender perspective into their health-related policies, planning, programmes and research that takes into account the important role of both biological and socio-cultural

---

44   *Ibid* para 11.
45   *Ibid* para 12.
46   *Ibid* paras 20 and 21.

factors in influencing the health of women and men.[47] It also calls for states to develop and implement a comprehensive national strategy for promoting women's right to health throughout their life span. According to the text, a major goal should be reducing women's health risks, particularly lowering rates of maternal mortality and protecting women from domestic violence. It also notes the importance of removing the barriers interfering with women's access to health services, education, and information, including with regard to sexual and reproductive health.[48]

According to the text of the general comment, the obligation to respect the right to health requires the state to refrain from actions, policies, or laws that contravene the standards set out in article 12. The list of such prohibited activities set forth in the general comment is meant to be illustrative. These include the following: denying equal access for all persons (including prisoners or detainees, minorities, asylum seekers and illegal immigrants) to health services; refraining from marketing unsafe drugs and from applying coercive medical treatments; abstaining from enforcing discriminatory practices as a state policy and from imposing discriminatory practices related to women's health status and needs. The general comment also directs states to refrain from limiting access to contraceptives; from censoring, withholding or intentionally misrepresenting health-related education and information; and from unlawfully polluting air, water, and soil, for example, through industrial waste from state-owned facilities.[49]

The legal obligation to protect, according to the general comment, requires the state to adopt legislation or to take other measures to ensure that third parties comply with the standards set forth in the Covenant. The general comment identifies a series of specific measures including the following: ensuring equal access to health care and health-related services provided by third parties; controlling the marketing of medical equipment and medicines by third parties; ensuring that medical practitioners and other health professionals meet appropriate standards of education, skill, and ethical codes of conduct. The text of the general comment also specifies that states are obligated to ensure that harmful social or traditional practices do not interfere with medical care and to prevent third parties from coercing women to undergo traditional practices.[50]

---

47 *Ibid* para 20.
48 *Ibid* para 21.
49 *Ibid* para 34.
50 *Ibid* para 35.

According to the general comment, the obligation to fulfil requires States parties to give recognition to the right to health in the national political and legal systems and to adopt a national health policy with a detailed plan for realising the right to health. Among the other obligations it identifies are the following: states are obligated to ensure provision of health care, including immunisation programmes against major infectious diseases; to ensure equal access for all to the underlying determinants of health; to provide for sexual and reproductive health services, including those related to pregnancy and delivery; to ensure the appropriate training of doctors and other medical personnel; to provide a public, private or mixed health insurance system which is affordable for all; to promote health education, in particular with respect to HIV/AIDS, sexual and reproductive health, traditional practices, domestic violence, and the abuse of harmful substances; to adopt measures against environmental and occupational health hazards; to formulate and implement national policies aimed at reducing and eliminating pollution of air, water, and soil.[51]

The text goes on to explain that the obligation to fulfil (facilitate) requires states to take positive measures that enable and assist individuals and communities to enjoy the right to health. This includes providing the means to assure the realisation of a specific right contained in the Covenant in circumstances in which an individual or group is unable to do so themselves. Some of the responsibilities the general comment assigns to states under this category include fostering recognition of factors favoring positive health results; ensuring that health services are culturally appropriate; and disseminating appropriate information relating to healthy lifestyles, nutrition, harmful traditional practices and the availability of services.[52]

4 CORE OBLIGATIONS RELATED TO THE RIGHT TO HEALTH

Is it possible to define minimum essential levels of the right to health that apply to all States parties regardless of their economic development or social and political context? I believe that it is possible to do so. Carefully targeted policies with modest costs

---

51 *Ibid* para 36.
52 *Ibid* para 37.

can often make significant contributions toward realising specific human rights. A World Health Organization study, for example, identifies a minimum package of cost-effective public health and clinical interventions appropriate for low- and middle-income countries. Properly delivered, it is estimated that this package would eliminate 21% to 38% of the burden of premature mortality and disability in children under 15 years and 10% to 18% of the disease burden in adults. The package outlined for low-income countries would have a per capita cost of $12 per year. The version for middle-income countries would entail about $22 per capita. The minimum essential package of health services includes some of the interventions identified below as minimum state obligations related to the right to health, such as an expanded programme of immunisations, tobacco and alcohol control, AIDS prevention, prenatal and delivery care, and family planning. It also incorporates clinical services that go beyond the recommendations of this paper.[53]

It is important to note that there is not a direct correlation between societal resources and health outcomes or equity in access to health care.[54] Costa Rica and Uruguay, two middle income countries, have achieved near universal health care coverage while wealthier countries in Latin America, Mexico for example, lag far behind.[55] In 1997 the United States spent $3,925 per capita on health, 13.5 percent of gross domestic product, more than twice the median Organisation for Economic Cooperation and Development country. Yet the United States had the lowest percentage of the population with health insurance; some 43 million persons, one sixth of the total population, lack insurance and, as a consequence, access to reliable health care. Moreover, despite high levels of health spending, the United States generally compares unfavourably with other industrialised countries and occasionally even developing countries on many health outcome indicators.[56]

---

53   Bobadilla, Cowley, Musgrove, and Saxenian "Design, content and financing of an essential national package of health services" in Murray and Lopez (eds) *Global comparative assessments in the health sector: Disease burden, expenditures and intervention packages* (1994) World Health Organization171-180.
54   Leary "The right to health" Working paper prepared for the day of general discussion on the right to health, 6 December 1993, Committee on Economic, Social and Cultural Rights, ninth session, E/C,12/1993/WP20.
55   Mesa-Lago *Health care for the poor in Latin America and the Caribbean* (1992) Pan American Health Organization 192-193.
56   Anderson and Poullier "Health spending, access, and outcomes: Trends in industrialized countries" (1999) 18 *Health Affairs* 178-192.

While financial constraints have to be kept in mind, particularly in the poorest countries, South Africa is not among this group. Granted, South Africa has many economic problems and a very uneven distribution of wealth. Nevertheless, its per capita 1998 gross domestic product was measured at $3,918.[57] The United Nations Development Programme places South Africa in the medium development group on its human development index, which is[58] based on a life expectancy at birth, adult literacy, and educational enrolment ratios as well as gross domestic product. South Africa also has a far better health infrastructure and more trained health professionals than most developing countries. The issue in South Africa is more how scarce resources will be allocated, particularly between primary and tertiary health care and rural and urban areas, than the absence of funds.

5 THE CORE OBLIGATIONS OF STATE PARTIES AS DEFINED IN GENERAL COMMENT 14

General Comment 14 affirms that state parties have a core obligation to ensure the satisfaction of, at the very least, minimum essential levels of the right to health.[59] It addresses the topic of core obligations in far greater depth than any other of the Committee's general comments written to date. In the Committee's view, the core includes at least the following requirements:
- to ensure the right of access to health facilities, goods and services on a non-discriminatory basis, especially for vulnerable or marginalised groups;
- to ensure for everyone access to the minimum essential food which is sufficient, nutritionally adequate and safe, to ensure their freedom from hunger;
- to ensure access to basic shelter, housing and sanitation, and an adequate supply of safe and potable water;
- to provide essential drugs, as from time to time defined by WHO's Action Programme on Essential Drugs;
- to ensure equitable distribution of all health facilities, goods, and services;

---

57 United Nations Development Programme (UNDP) *Human Development Report 2000* (2000) Oxford University Press 180.
58 *Ibid.*
59 *General Comment 14: The Right to the Highest Attainable Standard of Health* (2000) CESCR UN Doc E/C.12/2000/4 paras 43-45.

- to adopt and implement a national public health strategy and plan of action, on the basis of epidemiological evidence, addressing the health concerns of the whole population; the strategy and plan of action shall be devised, and periodically reviewed, on the basis of a participatory and transparent process; they shall include mechanisms, such as right to health indicators and benchmarks, by which progress can be closely monitored; the process by which the strategy and plan of action is devised, as well as their content, shall give particular attention to all vulnerable or marginalised groups.[60]

In another paragraph, the Committee also includes the following as components of core health obligations:
- to ensure reproductive, maternal (pre-natal and post-natal) and child health care;
- to provide immunisation against the community's major infectious diseases;
- to take measures to prevent, treat and control epidemic and endemic diseases;
- to provide education and access to information concerning the main health problems in the community, including methods of preventing and controlling them;
- to provide appropriate training for health personnel, including education on health and human rights.[61]

Two other components of the core obligations of the state are implicit in the document. The first is that States parties will explicitly recognise the right to health and provide appropriate legal and administrative remedies should the right not be respected. The second is that the state will refrain from executing any laws, policies, or activities that will negatively affect realisation of this right.

6 RELEVANCE FOR SOUTH AFRICA

In a narrow legal sense, the South African government is not bound by General Comment 14. At the time of writing South Africa had not yet ratified the International Covenant on Economic, Social and Cultural Rights and was therefore not a State party to it.

---

60 *Ibid* para 43.
61 *Ibid* para 44.

In a broader sense though the developing international interpretation related to the right to health is relevant to understanding the legal implications of the health provisions in the South African Bill of Rights. The socio-economic rights in the South African Constitution, including its health provisions, have been modelled on the Covenant.[62] Section 39 of the Constitution recognises the relevance of international law in the interpretation of the rights in the Bill of Rights. Moreover, there are few other resources South Africa can draw upon.

Significantly, the Constitutional Court made explicit reference to General Comment 3 of the Committee on Economic, Social and Cultural Rights, including its concept of the minimum core obligations, in the decision in *Government of the Republic of South Africa v Grootboom*[63], defining the scope of the right to have access to adequate housing. In its opinion, the Court acknowledged the relevance of the concept of the minimum core for evaluating whether the measures taken by the state to realise the right are reasonable, but also underscored the difficulties in setting its content in a South African context. It is noteworthy though that in the case of the right to housing the Court did not have the benefit of a general comment outlining the core obligations. *Grootboom* opines that the Court did not have sufficient information to determine what would comprise the minimum core obligation in the context of the South African Constitution.[64]

In assessing the relevance of General Comment 14, it is important to note that the provisions on health are defined differently in the Bill of Rights and in the Covenant. The right to health in the Covenant is broad and multidimensional. The language refers to "the right of everyone to the enjoyment of the highest attainable standard of physical and mental health". To that end it directs States parties to undertake a series of steps, one of which is the creation of conditions that would assure to all medical service and medical attention in the event of sickness".[65]

In contrast, Section 27(1)(a) of the Bill of Rights refers to "the right to have access to health care services, including reproductive health care". The right to health care services is of course narrower than the right to health, and the addition of the clause "to

---

62 Pillay "South Africa's commitment to health rights in the spotlight" (2000) 2 *ESR Review* 1.
63 *Government of the Republic of South Africa & Others v Grootboom & Others* 2000 (11) BCLR 1169 (CC).
64 *Ibid* para 33.
65 Article 12(d), ICESCR.

have access" further circumscribes the right. Two other articles in the Bill of Rights are more categorical. Section 27(3) states that "no one may be refused emergency medical treatment." Section 28(1)(3) recognises the right of every child to basic health care services.

Nevertheless, I believe that too much should not be made of the difference in the scope of the rights to health in the Covenant and the Bill of Rights. Given South Africa's apartheid past, the implementation of any health-related rights must begin by addressing the access issue. Historically, the state played a dominant role in establishing and maintaining an inequitable health care system that resulted in significantly worse health outcomes for Africans, especially those living in the rural areas. Hence dealing with the access issue requires a fundamental structural reform of the health system that compensates for the historical disadvantages of the black majority.

The major documents setting the framework for the transformation of South Africa's health system recognise the centrality of the principles of equality and nondiscrimination, but achieving the right to have access to health will require something more closely approximating a commitment to affirmative action. Extreme differentials in income distribution, yet another legacy of apartheid, make private health care inaccessible to the vast majority of the population. At present only 20 percent of the population has private health coverage and those covered tend to be younger, healthier, and better remunerated.[66] Thus the public health system has the burden of covering the vast majority of the population, including those with the greatest needs, with only a fraction of the resources of private providers.

Furthermore, it is not possible to realise any right to health care services without placing this entitlement in a fairly broad context that includes some form of a right to health protection. Several years ago the Science and Human Rights Program of the American Association for the Advancement of Science (AAAS) undertook a project to explore the implications of recognising a right to a basic and adequate standard of health care and to assess the benefits and problems of doing so. Cognizant of the issues that had been raised about an inclusive right to health, the project decided to focus on the narrower right to basic health care. The

---

66   Ngwena "The recognition of access to health care as a human rights in South Africa. Is it enough?" (2000) 5 *Health and Human Rights* 30.

project proposed that the United States, then the only industrial democracy that failed to provide a legal entitlement to health care, recognise a right to a basic and adequate standard of health care consistent with the available level of resources.[67] In the course of the project, however, it became clear that the formulation of a right to health care had significant limitations. The project concluded that even in an affluent society the right to a basic standard of health care could not be achieved apart from wider issues of health protection. To quote from the AAAS document,

> Clearly there are regions of the world in which the most valuable steps toward improvement of health are not medical services but public health protection. Poor countries with limited resources would better improve health standards by investing scarce resources in clean water and environmental clean-up rather than by offering curative health care to a small fraction of the population. Moreover, even within an advanced industrialised country, health status will continue to deteriorate and health care costs will continue to escalate unless there is greater attention paid to promoting more favourable health conditions ... improvements in the standard of health depend on preventing health problems before they arise. Investments in curative health care make little sense unless they are accompanied by policies that deal with roots of public health problems. Moreover, the failure to do so contributes to the escalating cost of health care.[68]

Particularly in the face of an AIDS pandemic, South Africa is unlikely to achieve progress in improving levels of health unless it takes a broad construction of the right to health services. During the 1990s the percentage of infected adults jumped from about 1 percent to close to 20 percent of the South African population. Estimates made in 2000 suggest that one in nine South Africans and one in four adults are infected by HIV, and data show that infection is still spreading.[69] If the epidemic continues at this rate, HIV/AIDS will potentially affect 30 to 40 percent of the South African population.[70] South Africa's high prevalence rates consti-

---

67 For a discussion of the project, see Chapman *Exploring a human rights approach to health care reform* (1993) American Association for the Advancement of Science.
68 *Ibid* 19.
69 Swarns "Newest statistics show AIDS still spreading in South Africa" *The New York Times*, March 21, 2001, A8.
70 These figures are from a presentation by Dr. Desmond Johns, a member of the South African Mission to the United Nations, at a workshop on Trade in Pharmaceuticals and Human Rights, co-organised by UNCTAD and Rights and Humanity, Geneva, 28 November 2000.

tute a national emergency. If the epidemic continues, it will wreak both medical and economic devastation.

Therefore, many dimensions of the minimum core obligations set forth in General Comment 14, with some minor changes in wording, apply to South Africa. These include the obligation:

- to ensure the right of access to health facilities, goods and services on a non-discriminatory basis, especially for vulnerable or marginalised groups [disadvantaged by the distribution of health facilities during the apartheid regime];
- to [assure the availability of] essential drugs [related to South Africa's priority health needs at a reasonable cost];
- to ensure [a more] equitable distribution of all health facilities, goods, and services [by giving priority to investments that will raise the standards of those racial and geographic communities discriminated against during the apartheid period];
- to adopt and implement a national public health strategy and plan of action, on the basis of epidemiological evidence, addressing the health concerns of the whole population; the strategy and plan of action shall be devised, and periodically reviewed, on the basis of a participatory and transparent process; they shall include mechanisms, such as right to health indicators and benchmarks, by which progress can be closely monitored; the process by which the strategy and plan of action is devised, as well as their content, shall give particular attention to all vulnerable or marginalised groups.[71]
- to ensure [the availability of basic] reproductive, maternal (pre-natal and post-natal) and child health care;
- to provide immunisation against the community's major infectious diseases;
- to take measures to prevent, treat and control epidemic and endemic diseases, [particularly HIV/AIDS];
- to provide education and access to information concerning the main health problems in the community, including methods of preventing and controlling them;
- to provide appropriate training for health personnel, including education on health and human rights.[72]

An effort to achieve the minimum core obligations related to health rights will require the development of a detailed and com-

---

71 *General Comment No. 14: The Right to the Highest Attainable Standard of Health* (2000) CESCR UN Doc E/C.12/2000/4 para 43.
72 *Ibid* para 44.

prehensive national plan of action by the national and regional governments, according priority to improving the situation of the most disadvantaged. A meaningful plan to implement the right of access to health care will include the establishment of priorities with a timetable and appropriate resource investments scoped out in relationship to each goal. To be consistent with human rights requirements, the planning process should involve consultation with representatives of the disadvantaged groups and non-governmental organisations devoted to health care issues and rights. Associated monitoring protocols should be instituted to evaluate the extent to which the various governmental units have succeeded in reaching this goal.[73]

The obligation to rectify and redress the inequities of the apartheid period has several major implications for the health sector. First and foremost it means dismantling the racial discrimination that pervaded the institutions, practices, and allocation of resources in the health care system and enabled it to be used as an instrument to support white supremacy. A report prepared by the American Association for the Advancement of Science and Physicians for Human Rights at the request of the Truth and Reconciliation Commission characterises the legacy of the apartheid health sector as follows:

> racism was manifested in every aspect of health: rigid segregation of health facilities; grossly disproportionate spending on the health of whites as compared to blacks, resulting in world-class medical care for whites while blacks were usually relegated to overcrowded and filthy facilities; public health policies that ignored diseases primarily affecting black people; and the denial of sanitation, clean water supply, and other components of public health to homelands and townships. Health services were deliberately fragmented to perpetuate discrimination. Race bias infected health research and even the keeping of health statistics....Under apartheid, few blacks could become health professionals. Those who were trained were subjected to schools with inadequate resources and, when admitted to white institutions, were demeaned....[74]

---

73 On these points see the *Report of the Seminar on appropriate indicators to measure achievements in the progressive realisation of economic, social and cultural rights*, Geneva, 25-29 January 1993, A/CONF.157/PC/73, 20 April 1993, paras 205 and 206.
74 Chapman and Rubenstein (eds) *Human rights and health: The legacy of apartheid* (1998) The American Association for the Advancement of Science and Physicians for Human Rights in conjunction with the American Nurses Association and the Committee for Health in Southern Africa xix-xx.

Even as late as 1985, the white population received four times more in annual per capita health expenditures than African people, with Indian and coloured people having an intermediate position.[75] These inequities were reflected in racial disparities in health outcomes with respect to morbidity, mortality rates, life expectancy, and infant mortality.

Meaningful health care reforms require reversing the apartheid patterns so that the largest proportion of government funds are spent on meeting the basic health care needs of the majority black population. Core health obligations also necessitate paying far more attention to health conditions and needs in the hitherto seriously neglected rural areas. To do so will involve the adoption of new models reorienting the health sector from an emphasis on curative to preventative and primary health care so as to better meet the needs of the majority of the population. The central and regional governments have begun this process.

To date, the South African government has adopted a framework for the health system that incorporates many, but not all, of the elements specified in the minimum core. The principles of equality and non-discrimination are set forth in the White Paper for the Transformation of the Health System in South Africa (1997) and the Promotion of Equality and Prevention of Unfair Discrimination Act 4 of 2000. The White Paper on the Transformation of Health Services requires health service providers to assure an equitable distribution of health facilities, goods, and services. The government has also adopted an essential drug policy.[76] Understandably though, implementation has been very uneven, and sometimes highly problematic. Nor has the Ministry of Health set priorities with guidelines and a clear timetable for their realisation. Moreover, there is not a monitoring apparatus to evaluate the performance of the central and regional governments.

Given the unevenness of implementation of the socio-economic rights enumerated in the Bill of Rights, it is not surprising that there have been several court cases testing judicial remedies. The courts have been forthright that the state is required to respect, protect, promote and fulfil the rights included in the Bill of Rights,[77] but somewhat timid about how to enforce these rights in

---

75 "Institutional Hearing: The Health Sector" in *Truth and Reconciliation Commission of South Africa Report, Volume Four* (1998) CIP Book Printers 120.
76 Pillay "South Africa's commitment to health rights in the spotlight" (2000) 2 *ESCR Review* 3.
77 See for example *Government of the Republic of South Africa & Others v Grootboom & Others* 2000 (11) BCLR 1169 (CC), para 20.

a given case. The decisions reveal a particular reluctance to provide judicial remedies to enforce socio-economic rights conditioned by "progressive realisation" clauses. Instead the Justices appear more inclined to accord the government discretion over the allocation of resources.

To date there have been two Constitutional Court cases seeking judicial remedies for health-related rights. In the case of Soobramoney v Minister of Health (Kwa-Zulu Natal), the Constitutional Court turned down an appellant who sought dialysis from a state renal unit on the grounds of limited resources.[78] The appellant had based his claim on the right not to be refused emergency care and the right to life rather than the right of access to health care. In a second case, *B v Minister of Correctional Services*, a High Court ordered state prison authorities to provide expensive antiretroviral drugs to two HIV-infected prisoners.[79] This case, however, does not provide a clear precedent for implementation of a broader right to health care because the section of the Bill of Rights specifying the right of prisoners to adequate medical treatment at state expense is not qualified. Moreover, the manifest failure on the part of the respondent state organ to provide satisfactory evidence of lack of resources was a contributing factor in this decision.[80]

Of the Constitutional Court's initial socio-economic rights cases, *Grootboom* is the most significant effort to determine the state's core obligations. The decision reiterated that the state has a positive obligation to ameliorate the plight of the hundreds of thousands of people living in deplorable conditions throughout the country, including providing access to housing, health care, sufficient food and water, and social security.[81] It stated that "the Constitution requires the state to devise and implement within its available resources a comprehensive and coordinated programme progressively to realise the right to adequate housing."[82] Nevertheless, the Court did not recognise a right to claim shelter or housing immediately upon demand. However, the decision found that the state housing programme in the area in question

---

78 *Soobramoney v Minister of Health (Kwa-Zulu Natal)* 1997 (12) BCLR 1696 (CC).
79 *B v Minister of Correctional Services*, 1997 (4) SA 411 9(C), 1997 (6) BCLR 789 (C), (1997) 50 BMLR 206 SA HC.
80 Ngwena "The recognition of access to health care as a human right in South Africa: Is it enough?" (2000) 5 *Health and Human Rights* " 34-5.
81 *Government of the Republic of South Africa & Others v Grootboom and Others* 2000 (11) BCLR 1169 (CC) par 93.
82 *Ibid* par 99.

fell short of compliance with the standards noted above: "it failed to make reasonable provision within its available resources for people in the Cape Metropolitan area with no access to land, no roof over their heads, and who were living in intolerable conditions or crisis situations."[83]

By analogy, the courts may be willing to review whether health policies meet a core health care standard. Other countries, particularly in Latin America, have utilised judicial remedies to clarify obligations related to the right to health through a mechanism termed the *accion de amparo* (protection suit), a form of writ that includes and expands upon the Ango-Saxon writ of *habeas corpus*. In 1998, for example, the Argentine Center for Legal and Social Studies (more often known by its Spanish acronym, CELS) brought a suit on behalf of 3.5 million affected people to force the Argentine government to manufacture and distribute a vaccine against Argentine Hemorrhagic Fever. It argued that provision of the vaccine was the most effective means of combatting the disease in a population lacking easy access to medical services. In an historic ruling, the Court found that the state did have such an obligation.[84] Utilising a similar approach, the Venezuelan human rights group PROVEA filed an action in 1997 on behalf of 10 patients, complaining that drastically reduced public spending in public hospitals was producing unreasonable delays in waiting for brain surgery to be performed. The trial court ruled in favor of the plaintiffs and confirmed the obligations of the state as the guarantor of health care.[85]

Extrapolating from these examples, it might be possible to bring a suit related to the failure of government health policies to fulfil core obligations. The *Grootboom* case demonstrated that the Court was willing to direct the government to enforce a socio-economic right even in the face of budgetary constraints. And some issues derive more from failures of policy than from expenditure of funds. The problem that calls out for such a judicial review is the government's persistent mismanagement of the HIV/AIDS pandemic. South Africa's record compares very unfavourably with other African countries which have lower incomes and less developed health sector infrastructures. Uganda, Senegal, and Côte d'Ivoire, for example, have mounted far more effective AIDS prevention and treatment efforts.

---

83 *Ibid* par 99.
84 Ely Yamin "Protecting and promoting the right to health in Latin America: Selected experiences from the field" (2000) 5 *Health and Human Rights* 125.
85 *Ibid* 126.

The South African government has been much criticised for its ineptitude and mismanagement of the HIV/AIDS epidemic, including by many high level South Africans.[86] The first confirmed cases of AIDS in South Africa date from 1982. HIV rates rose slowly during apartheid and then surged after democratisation.[87] Since 1998, primarily due to governmental ineptitude bordering on willful neglect, South Africa has had the fastest growing HIV epidemic in the world and the highest numbers of people affected (4.7 million). Nevertheless, the government has yet to launch an aggressive campaign to mobilise resources and develop an appropriate infrastructure to prevent or treat HIV/AIDS. While in office, President Mandela did not make the AIDS epidemic a priority and rarely, if ever, addressed the topic. President Mbeki's public skepticism about the link between HIV and AIDS has created confusion among those at risk for HIV and demoralised and undermined the efforts of AIDS workers. Dr. Mamphela Rampele, the former vice-chancellor of the University of Cape Town, has characterised President Mbeki's position about the cause of AIDS, as "irresponsibility that borders on criminality".[88] While the President's disbelief about the etiology of AIDS is now being downplayed as official policy, he has yet to issue a categorical acknowledgement that HIV is a sexually transmitted viral infection.

President Mbeki has raised issues about whether commonly prescribed anti-AIDS drugs are safe, and the government has refrained from making such medications widely available. In contrast with other countries that have a high prevalence of HIV/AIDS, the South African government has been reluctant to adopt a cost-effective national programme to limit mother-to-child transmission of HIV through administration of a short course of antiretroviral medication. The government alternatively claimed that antiretrovirals were too toxic or too expensive. In a welcome change of policy, it was announced that beginning in March 2001 the government was launching a pilot programme to have public hospitals test pregnant women for HIV. To those who test positive, the Government will provide the anti-retroviral

---

86 Mr Justice Edwin Cameron, a justice of the High Court of South Africa, characterised governmental policy in his lecture at the XIII International AIDS Conference in South Africa in July 2000 as the "The deafening silence of AIDS." An edited version appears in (2000) 5 *Health and Human Rights* 5 7-24.
87 Whiteside and Sunter *AIDS: The challenge for South Africa* (2000) Human & Rousseau 47-51.
88 Her statement is quoted by Justice Cameron, *Ibid* 14.

drug Nevirapine, as well as a six-month supply of formula to prevent infection of babies through breast-feeding.[89]

Nor has the South African government established pilot programmes to make AIDS drugs widely available for AIDS patients. In March 2001 the South African government decided against declaring the HIV/AIDS epidemic a national emergency, even though such an action would have enabled the country to eliminate legal obstacles to importing and producing cheap, generic versions of patented AIDS drugs under World Trade Organization rules.[90] The government's reluctance apparently reflected fears that doing so might discourage foreign investment. Fortunately, one month later the 39 multinational pharmaceutical companies that had brought suit in 1998 to prevent South Africa from implementing a law allowing the government to import cheaper anti-AIDS drugs and other medicines, withdrew their legal suit. Even after this ruling, though, the health minister maintained that providing AIDS drugs to those infected with HIV was not a government priority.[91]

Clearly, the courts cannot ensure realisation of the right to health or to health care. In the end the fulfilment of core health obligations will depend primarily on the implementation of appropriate government policies in the health sector and beyond that to measures to eliminate poverty and promote greater economic and social equality. However, the courts may be able to provide a partial counterweight for manifest governmental failures to respect the requirements of core obligations related to constitutionally guaranteed human rights.

---

89 Jeter "South Africa relents on maternal HIV care" *The Washington Post*, February 1, 2001, A1.
90 Jeter "South Africa resists call for AIDS 'emergency'" *Washington Post*, March 15, 2001, A1.
91 Swarns "Despite legal victory, South Africa hesitates on AIDS drugs" *The New York Times*, April 21, 2001, A4.

SOUTH AFRICA'S COMMITMENT TO HEALTH RIGHTS IN THE SPOTLIGHT: DO WE MEET THE INTERNATIONAL STANDARD?

Karrisha Pillay

1 INTRODUCTION

In its endeavours to establish an appropriate, efficient and constitutionally sound framework for the realisation of health rights in South Africa, the South African government has adopted a broad range of measures. On the one hand it has sought to learn from the many international experiences, whilst, on the other hand, it has attempted to develop an innovative and original approach to reflect the realities and needs of our country.

On 11 May 2000 the Committee on Economic, Social and Cultural Rights (CESCR) adopted General Comment 14 on the Right to the Highest Attainable Standard of Health.[1] This General Comment aims to provide guidance on the implementation of the right to the highest attainable standard of health[2] in the In-

---

1 *General Comment 14: The Right to the Highest Attainable Standard of Health* (2000) CESCR UN Doc E/C.12/2000/4.
2 Article 12.

ternational Covenant on Economic, Social and Cultural Rights (ICESCR).[3]

This paper focuses on the content of General Comment 14 and some of its key recommendations in respect of health rights. Special attention is also given to the extent to which South Africa complies with some of these key recommendations.

2 WHAT IS THE RELEVANCE OF GENERAL COMMENT 14 FOR SOUTH AFRICA?

Apart from the fact that the recent adoption of General Comment 14 has given further impetus to the need for the South African government to ratify the ICESCR, it is also likely to be instructive in the interpretation of health rights in South Africa.

The fact that the right of access to health care services in section 27(1)(a) of the Constitution[4] is modelled on provisions of the ICESCR has necessitated some reliance on the interpretation given to the Covenant. The following concepts in section 27(1)(a) have been imported from the Covenant:
- the duty on the state to take reasonable legislative and other measures;
- to achieve the progressive realisation of the right;
- within its available resources.

However, in spite of these similarities between the ICESCR and the South African Constitution, there are also some important differences between both these documents. Most notable is the Covenant's recognition of a right to a highest attainable standard of health as opposed to the South African Constitution's recognition of a right of access to health care services.

Despite these differences, the potentially valuable role of international law in the interpretation of the rights in the Bill of Rights (which would clearly include the health rights) is explicitly recognised in the Constitution. Section 39 of the Constitution obliges a court, tribunal or other forum to consider international law when interpreting the Bill of Rights. The Constitutional Court has further confirmed that such consideration must be given to

---

3 International Covenant on Economic, Social, and Cultural Rights, *opened for signature* 16 Dec 1966, *entered into force* 3 Jan 1976, 993 UNTS 3.
4 Constitution of the Republic of South Africa, 1996.

both binding and non-binding international law.[5] This decision effectively means that despite the South African government's failure to ratify the International Covenant on Economic, Social and Cultural Rights, the interpretation given to health rights under this Covenant is nevertheless relevant to the interpretation of health rights within the South African constitutional context.

3 OVERVIEW OF GENERAL COMMENT 14

The adoption of this General Comment is a welcome initiative in the efforts to clarify the meaning and content of health rights. General Comment 14 covers a wide range of issues, which include:
- the normative content of the right to health;
- state obligations engendered by the right;
- violations of the right; and
- the implementation of the right at national level.

3.1 Normative content of Article 12

The General Comment recognises that the right to health must be understood as a right to the enjoyment of a variety of facilities, goods, services and conditions necessary for the realisation of the highest attainable standard of health.[6]

It notes that the right to health contains the following interrelated and essential terms, the precise application of which will depend on the conditions prevailing in a particular state party:
- Functioning public health and health care facilities, goods and services, and programmes which must be sufficiently available within the state party.
- Health facilities, goods and services have to be accessible to everyone without discrimination. This includes physical accessibility, economic accessibility (affordability) and information accessibility.
- All health facilities, goods and services must be presented in a manner that respects medical ethics and is culturally appropriate.

---

5   *S v Makwanyane* 1995 (6) BCLR 665 (CC).
6   Para 11.

- Health facilities, goods and services must be scientifically and medically appropriate and of good quality.[7]

Special attention is also given to the health needs of women, children and adolescents, older persons, persons living with disabilities and indigenous people.[8]

3.2 States parties' obligations

The General Comment highlights both general and specific legal obligations imposed by the right to health. In particular, it notes that there is an immediate obligation on states parties to guarantee that the right will be recognised without discrimination of any kind.[9] It also reaffirms that the progressive realisation of the right to health should not be interpreted as depriving states parties' obligations of all meaningful content. Instead, it makes clear that states parties have a specific and continuing obligation to move as expeditiously and effectively as possible towards the full realisation of the right.[10] It reiterates the strong presumption that retrogressive measures are impermissible.[11]

The specific legal obligations imposed by the right to health include the state duties to respect, protect and fulfil the right. The General Comment includes an illustrative list of what these specific duties entail.[12] As these obligations are echoed in section 7(2) of the South African Constitution,[13] this illustrative list is likely to prove useful.

The duty to respect health rights requires States parties to refrain from interfering directly or indirectly with the enjoyment of the right to health. The duty to protect requires that States parties take measures that prevent third parties from interfering with the guarantees of the right to health. The duty to fulfill, according to the General Comment, requires States parties to adopt appropriate legislative, administrative, budgetary, judicial, promotional and other measures towards the full realisation of the right to health.[14]

---

7   Para 12.
8   Para 21.
9   Para 18.
10 Para 31.
11 Para 32.
12 Paras 34 – 37.
13 7   (1) ...
      (2) The state must respect, protect, promote and fulfil the rights in the Bill of Rights.
14 Para 33.

The attention given to the core obligations of the right to health in the general comment is particularly interesting. It confirms that states parties have a core obligation to ensure the satisfaction of, at the very least, minimum essential levels of the right to health.[15] Departing from earlier general comments,[16] General Comment 14 states in unequivocal language that "a State party cannot, under any circumstances whatsoever, justify its non-compliance with the core obligations, ... which are non-derogable".[17] It highlights that states parties have core obligations in respect of the right to health to:
- ensure access to health facilities, goods and services on a non-discriminatory basis, especially for vulnerable or marginalised groups;
- ensure access for everyone to the minimum essential food which is sufficient, nutritionally adequate and safe, and ensures their freedom from hunger;
- ensure access to basic shelter, housing and sanitation, and an adequate supply of safe and potable water;
- provide essential drugs, as from time to time defined by the World Health Organisation's Action Programme on Essential Drugs;
- ensure an equitable distribution of all health facilities, goods, and services; and
- to adopt and implement a national public health strategy and plan of action, on the basis of epidemiological evidence, addressing the health concerns of the whole population. The strategy and plan of action should be devised, and periodically reviewed, on the basis of a participatory and transparent process. It should also include mechanisms, such as health indicators and benchmarks, by which progress can be closely monitored. The process by which the strategy and plan of action is devised, as well as their content, should give particular attention to all vulnerable or marginalised groups.[18]

It is worth noting that the list of core obligations that all states parties must comply with is fairly extensive. The list includes some of the underlying preconditions for health as well as the nature of the actual health care services that should be provided. This

---

15 Para 43.
16 For example *General Comment 3: The nature of States parties obligations* (1990) CESCR UN Doc E/1991/23, para 10.
17 Para 47.
18 Para 43.

should be seen in light of the fact that compliance with these core obligations is mandatory for all States parties regardless of their levels of development.

The core obligations outlined in the general comment raise serious questions regarding the extent to which they meet the actual health needs of all countries, and, accordingly, the extent to which they warrant prioritisation in all contexts. These core obligations within the context of the growing HIV/AIDS catastrophe (sometimes referred to as the medical holocaust) in sub-Saharan Africa is particularly questionable. The absence of any focus on preventative health care is equally concerning.

However, in spite of these shortcomings, an excursus through the South African legal framework indicates at least a theoretical commitment to these core obligations. Though not comprehensive, and sometimes subject to criticism in implementation, the following initiatives adopted by the South African government are illustrative:

- The principle of equality and non-discrimination underpins the entire health system. Support for this can be found in the White Paper for the Transformation of the Health System in South Africa[19] as well as the Promotion of Equality and Prevention of Unfair Discrimination Act.[20]
- Provision is made for minimum essential foodstuffs through a range of policies and programmes. The Primary School Feeding Scheme, which provides food to children in primary schools and the Infant and Young Child Feeding Scheme, which provides nutritional aid to infants in hospitals, are two such programmes.
- The Housing Subsidy Scheme is a key strategy through which the right of access to adequate housing is fulfilled.
- The National Water Act[21] is an example of legislative steps taken to give access to an adequate supply of safe and potable water.
- The Essential Drug Policy as well as the White Paper for the Transformation of the Health System in South Africa's commitment to ensuring that essential drugs, that are safe and of good quality, are available in all health facilities also indicates compliance with core obligations in the general comment.
- The White Paper for the transformation of the health system in South Africa is an example of the commitment to an equitable distribution of all health facilities, goods, and services.

---

19   April 1997.
20   Act 4 of 2000.
21   Act 36 of 1998.

In addition to the core obligations, the general comment confirms certain obligations that are of "comparable priority". It is unclear why these were not included in the list of core obligations, given that they are supposed to enjoy comparable priority. These include the obligations to:
- ensure reproductive, maternal (pre-natal as well as post-natal) and child health care;
- provide immunisation against the community's major infectious diseases;
- take measures to prevent, treat and control epidemic and endemic diseases;
- provide education and access to information concerning the main health problems in the community, including methods of preventing and controlling them; and
- provide appropriate training for health personnel, including education on health and human rights.[22]

3.3 Violations of States parties' obligations

The general comment further provides an illustrative list of possible violations by States parties. These violations are formulated in respect of each of the States parties' specific obligations.[23]

So, for instance, violations relating to the obligation to respect the right to health care may result from unfair discrimination in access to health services, facilities or goods.[24]

Examples of violations of the obligation to protect the right include:
- failure to prevent, stop or discourage medical or cultural practices that endanger health;
- failure to discourage production, marketing, and consumption of cigarettes, alcohol and drugs; and
- failure to protect women against violence or to prosecute perpetrators of such violence.[25]

Examples of violations of the obligation to fulfill the right include failure to recognise and/or meaningfully implement a right to health or to health care and failure to adopt a gender-sensitive approach to health.[26]

---

22 Para 44.
23 Paras 46 – 52.
24 Para 34.
25 Para 35.
26 Para 37.

3.4 Does South Africa meet the test?

South Africa's scorecard against General Comment 14 cannot be totalled without first asking the question: Does General Comment 14 reflect and meet the health needs of South Africa? In response I would argue that, whilst there are certain clear limitations inherent in General Comment 14, particularly given the absence of any explicit strategy to deal with or even acknowledge the HIV/AIDS pandemic, its value in clarifying health rights cannot be underestimated. Its clear exposition of the content and duties imposed by health rights is particularly encouraging. However, caution should be exercised in not limiting priorities in a country like South Africa exclusively to those articulated in the general comment. For instance, within the South African context, an indisputable priority is the need to address the HIV/AIDS epidemic effectively, an issue that is not canvassed in the general comment.

The South African government's inability to deal effectively with the HIV/AIDS crisis has been extremely disappointing and a severe constraint on the realisation of health rights. The ever-increasing statistics on HIV/AIDS are indicative of this ineffective preventative strategy. Ineffectiveness and confusion on this front are exacerbated by the South African President's recent statements challenging the link between HIV and AIDS. Limitations in its preventative strategy are also evidenced by the government's failure to provide anti-retroviral treatment to reduce mother-to-child transmission of HIV and to prevent infection of rape survivors. In addition, the government's proposed policy to make AIDS a notifiable disease, if adopted, would be a further shortcoming in effectively addressing the AIDS crisis. This policy's violation of the patient's rights to privacy and confidentiality as well as its potential to create an unsafe and threatening environment in which people are unlikely to voluntarily present themselves for HIV testing are particularly concerning.

The adoption of the White Paper for the Transformation of the Health System in South Africa clearly outlines the overall policy governing the realisation of health rights in South Africa. However, the absence of an overarching legislative framework for health rights poses a severe constraint for the realisation of this right. Three years have lapsed since the adoption of the health policy, yet the National Health Bill has still not been passed. The passage of this legislation is crucial as it is intended to give clear overall direction to health rights in South Africa.

However, despite these shortcomings, some credit must be given to the Department of Health for its adoption of a wide range of other measures aimed at making health rights a reality for all in South Africa.

Its commitment to equality and non-discrimination in the health sector lays a solid foundation for the realisation of health rights in South Africa. Its emphasis on affordable health care, particularly through its policies of free health care to pregnant women and children under the age of 6 and its attempts to access more affordable medication are encouraging. Its emphasis on accessible health care through the adoption of the primary health care approach is also positive. The government's progressive reproductive health laws relating to choice on termination of pregnancy and reproductive health are equally encouraging. Finally, South Africa's broader commitments regarding the realisation of all socio-economic rights is likely to create the underlying preconditions for a state of good health for all in South Africa.

4 WHERE TO FROM HERE?

In spite of certain shortcomings, General Comment 14 provides a useful framework for the realisation of health rights in South Africa. Its attempts at being comprehensive, and providing clarity on a range of complex issues relating to health are particularly impressive. Whilst it is crucial that an overall health strategy for any country must be "home-grown," South Africa can certainly learn from and advance its realisation of health rights through international standards such as those articulated in General Comment 14. Whilst the content of this General Comment can aid in the interpretation of health rights in South Africa, its role in the advancement of these rights can be significantly enhanced through South Africa's ratification of the ICESCR. Upon ratification, South Africa will be subject to the scrutiny of the CESCR through its reporting process.

Finally, it should be noted that the standards set out in General Comment 14 can and indeed must inform the domestic monitoring of health rights in South Africa. The South African Human Rights Commission, through its constitutional mandate to monitor the realisation of socio-economic rights, should use General Comment 14 to assess the realisation of health rights in South Africa.

Subject to the comments made above, the legislative and policy framework for the realisation of health rights in South Africa has to a large extent been developed. However, the challenges posed by the implementation of these rights must be acknowledged and addressed. In tallying the scorecard, it is vital that international standards as well as domestic standards (developed to reflect the health needs of South Africa) be taken into account.

THE RIGHT TO ADEQUATE FOOD: VIOLATIONS RELATED TO ITS MINIMUM CORE CONTENT

Rolf Künnemann

1 INTRODUCTION

Rights are a serious matter. They are much more than only justified claims on a desirable state of affairs. If the right to food meant nothing more than the claim that everyone should have enough to eat, then a violation of the right to food might sound trivial – as though the right to food would be violated simply when people do not have enough to eat. Taking rights seriously, however, entails thinking in broader terms: clarifying the normative content and state obligations, and identifying mechanisms, both within and outside the realm of the law, to realise the right. Violations then become identifiable acts and omissions related to the specific obligations of the duty-holder.

Human rights are an even more serious matter, as they concern states' obligations to vulnerable individuals and communities. If human rights are to be more than simply words, they have to exist in a conducive ethical environment, in which people subscribe to the principle that certain basic dimensions of life – including the economic, the social and the political – be enjoyed by everyone, that these basic human standards be respected by everyone in their interactions with others, and that states, both individually and collectively, respect these standards themselves, defend them against being destroyed by third parties, and fulfil them for people deprived of them.

Human rights exist in three spheres: in the minds of the people, in ethical codes governing states' performance and in similar super-positive realms of justice, and, ultimately, in national and international law.

Justice has much to do with reason, and reasoning on the basis of human rights principles is one of the basic tasks of this paper. Reasoning will clearly identify obligations that are still a long way from being recognised by many states. Reasoning will reveal that we are still far from the full realisation of the right to food. We still have a long way to go – not so much because of the excessive numbers of malnourished people in the world. Numbers are not very important in human rights. The presence of one single malnourished person in the world may indicate a violation of the right to food. No, we have a long way to go because we must establish states' obligations and ensure that they are implemented and realised. On the other hand, positive law concerning the right to food both domestically and internationally is already further developed than most people are aware, and it establishes a foundation for the full realisation of the right to adequate food.

2 THE RIGHT TO FOOD IN THE MINDS OF THE PEOPLE

The obligation to ensure that their people can feed themselves is one of the oldest obligations of communities and their leaders. It is an obvious obligation within families and kinship groups – in prehistoric times as much as today.

With the arrival of civilisation, this obligation began to extend beyond the limits of kinship to include all members of the state, and eventually of the community of states as well. The survival of the state required social cohesion at the level of the community and its inhabitants, as well as at the level of individuals and clans. The corresponding duties were concentrated in the rulers and regulated by law and custom. Although the welfare state is an achievement of the last century, rudimentary social policies and social legislation have been around to varying degrees since antiquity.

Two very important phenomena have appeared in recent decades. One has been the strengthening of states' obligations by introducing an individual right to food. The other is the broadening of states' obligations beyond their own territory to the international level. Both processes are at a relatively early stage and require further strengthening.

All of this is taking place at a time of crisis. The welfare state is under ideological attack, and economic globalisation further complicates the task of states and the international community in implementing the right to food. Human beings and the environment frequently suffer as a result of these developments. Differing cultural norms are coming into increasingly close contact and must be accommodated peacefully. There is an obvious and urgent need to find global answers to global problems. This calls for a common global and national legal framework based on human rights. The nation state is not only too small to solve the big problems, but also too big to solve the small ones.

The following study will take a close look at the core content of the right to adequate food – not as a moral demand, but as a legal right, providing the legal and political leverage to compel states and international governmental organisations to meet their obligations.

Before turning to the right to food as it is expressed in international law, it is important to understand that the right to food does not exist in the field of law alone or even primarily, but in the hearts and minds of people. The right to food is a key concept for those who refuse to accept the persistence of hunger and malnutrition in a world of plenty. The right to food is widely understood as the right to feed oneself, to have access to resources and work, to foster one's community and develop one's culture. Without the right to feed oneself, political participation, cultural identity and democracy lose their meaning.

Human rights are rights (of vulnerable individuals or communities) that recognise certain basic human standards and impose certain obligations on states and the community of states. Upon recognition as a human right, the related basic human standard can be called its "human rights standard." Therefore, an investigation of the normative content of the right to food must examine the basic human standard recognised and the obligations generated by this right.

The human rights standard is a certain quality of life manifest in certain situations (e.g., access to food, political participation, etc.) to which people normally aspire. When this standard is not met, the result is seen as a form of deprivation. In lax language the human rights standard is sometimes identified with the human right to which it is linked. A human right, however, is a relationship between vulnerable persons or communities and the state or community of states. And a human rights standard is a particular quality of life of a person or community recognised as something to be respected, protected and fulfilled.

Every single case of malnutrition is a deprivation of the human rights standard to be free from hunger. Does it also indicate a violation of this human right? Violations of human rights are always acts or omissions by states, using the term "violation" in the strict classical sense.[1] Violations are breaches of states' obligations. Although it is true that nonstate actors have responsibilities under human rights law, the distinction between violations (committed by national or international state authorities), and crimes (committed by nonstate actors) must be upheld in economic, social and cultural rights as much as in civil and political rights.

The human rights standard recognised by the right to adequate food is access to adequate food. For the right to freedom from hunger, it is the absence of hunger or malnutrition. Both standards are clearly linked: The absence of hunger or malnutrition requires access to food.

3 THE RIGHT TO FOOD IN INTERNATIONAL LAW

The principal instruments (in chronological order) establishing food as a human right in international law are:[2]
- The Universal Declaration of Human Rights 1948
  The Universal Declaration of Human Rights declares in paragraph 25 that "... everyone has the right to a standard of living adequate for the health and well-being of himself and his family, including food ...".[3]
- The Declaration of the Rights of the Child 1959
  In the principles 4 and 8 of the Declaration of the Rights of the Child, "The child shall have the right to adequate nutrition, housing, recreation and medical services. The child shall in all circumstances be among the first to receive protection and relief".[4]

---

1   For a further discussion of the reasons for taking a classical approach to violations, see Künnemann *Food and freedom: A textbook for human rights education* (1999).
2   A more comprehensive list with quotes can be found in Bekker (ed) A *compilation of essential documents on the rights to food and nutrition*, Vol 3, Economic and Social Rights Series, (2000) Centre for Human Rights, University of Pretoria.
3   Universal Declaration of Human Rights, GA Res 217A (III), UN Doc A/810 at 71 (1948).
4   Declaration on the Rights of the Child, GA Res 1386 (XIV), UN Doc A/4354 (1959).

- The International Covenant on Economic, Social and Cultural Rights 1966
  The International Covenant on Economic, Social and Cultural Rights clearly states in Article 11.1 the "right to an adequate standard of living including food, housing, clothing." Moreover it recognises in 11.2 the "fundamental right of everyone to be free from hunger".[5]
- The Universal Declaration on the Eradication of Hunger and Malnutrition 1974
  The Universal Declaration on the Eradication of Hunger and Malnutrition proclaims that "Every man, woman, and child has the inalienable right to be free from hunger and malnutrition in order to develop fully and maintain their physical and mental faculties".[6]
- The Rome Declaration on World Food Security 1996
  The Rome Declaration on World Food Security states in Article 1: "We the Heads of State and Government, or our representatives gathered at the World Food Summit at the invitation of the FAO, reaffirm the right of everyone to have access to safe and nutritious food, consistent with the right to adequate food and the fundamental right of everyone to be free from hunger."[7]
- The Plan of Action of the World Food Summit 1996
  The Plan of Action of the World Food Summit 1996 formulates as its objective 7.4:
  > To clarify the content of the right to adequate food and the fundamental right of everyone to be free from hunger, as stated in the International Covenant on Economic, Social and Cultural Rights and other relevant international and regional instruments, and to give particular attention to the implementation and full and progressive realisation of this right as a means of achieving food security for all.[8]

Moreover, there is no shortage of documents recognising certain states' obligations related to securing access to food. These include

---

5 International Covenant on Economic, Social, and Cultural Rights (hereafter ICESCR), opened for signature 16 Dec 1966, 993 UNTS 3 (entered into force 3 Jan. 1976), GA Res 2200 (XXI), UN Doc A/6316.
6 Universal Declaration on the Eradication of Hunger and Malnutrition, GA Res 3348 (XXIX), UN Doc E/CONF. 65/20, at 1 (1974).
7 The Rome Declaration on World Food Security, adopted 17 Nov. 1996, FAO, WFS 96/REP (Part I) (1997).
8 The Plan of Action of the World Food Summit, adopted 17 Nov 1996, FAO, WFS 96/REP (Part I) (1997).

(in chronological order) the Declaration on the Protection of Women and Children in Emergency and Armed Conflicts 1974,[9] the World Employment Conference 1976,[10] the Additional Protocol to the Geneva Conventions, Relating to the Protection of Victims of International and Non-International Armed Conflicts 1977,[11] the World Food Programme's fourth statement 1977,[12] the Declaration of Principles of the World Conference on Agrarian Reform and Rural Development 1979,[13] the Codex Alimentarius Commission of the Code of Ethics for International Trade 1979,[14] the International Code of Marketing for Breastmilk Substitutes 1981,[15] the General Assembly Declaration on the Critical Situation of Food and Agriculture in Africa 1984,[16] the Declaration on the Right to Development 1986,[17] the Convention on the Rights of the Child 1989,[18] the International Conference on Nutrition (ICN) World Declaration on Nutrition 1992,[19] and the World Food Summit's Rome Declaration 1996.[20]

Since the 1980s the right to food has continued to improve its standing in international law. In 1983 the Economic and Social Council (ECOSOC) of the UN appointed a special rapporteur to investigate and report on the right to adequate food. This was the first study ever undertaken in the UN system on a specific right in the International Covenant on Economic, Social and Cultural Rights. In 1987 the UN Human Rights Commission approved the

---

9 The Declaration on the Protection of Women and Children in Emergency and Armed Conflicts, GA Res 3318, 29 UN GAOR Supp. No. 31, at 146, UN Doc A/9631 (1974).
10 International Labour Organization World Employment Conference, Geneva, 1976, No WEC/CW/E.I (1976).
11 Protocol Relating to Victims of International Armed Conflicts, 8 June 1977, 1125 UNTS 3; Protocol Relating to Victims of Non-International Armed Conflicts, 8 June 1977, 1125 UNTS 609.
12 Target for World Food Programme Pledges for the Period 1979-1980, UN Doc A/RES/32/112 (1977).
13 Declaration of Principles and Programme of Action of the World Conference on Agrarian Reform and Rural Development, UN Doc E/ESCAP/AD/3/16 (1981).
14 Joint FAO/WHO Food Standards Programme, Code of Ethics for International Trade in Food, CAC/RCP 20-1979 (rev 1 1985) in 1 CODEX ALIMENTARIUS 15-22 (2d ed 1992).
15 The International Code of Marketing of Breastmilk Substitutes (1981), World Health Assembly, 24th Assembly, WHA Res 22, UN Doc A34/Vr/15 (1981), reprinted in 20 ILM 1004.
16 Declaration on the Critical Situation of Food and Agriculture in Africa, UN Doc A/RES/38/159 (1983).
17 Declaration on the Right to Development, GA Res 41/128, 4 Dec 1986.
18 Convention on the Rights of the Child [CRC], opened for signature 20 Nov 1989, 28 ILM 1448 (entered into force 2 Sept 1990), GA Res 44/25.
19 International Conference on Nutrition World Declaration on Nutrition, FAO/WHO (1992).
20 The Rome Declaration on World Food Security, adopted 17 Nov 1996, FAO, WFS 96/REP (Part I) (1997).

report.[21] In 1984 the International Law Association formed a Right to Food Committee. In June of the same year, the Netherlands Human Rights Institute sponsored an international conference in Utrecht on the right to food. In 1989 the UN Committee on Economic, Social and Cultural Rights (CESCR) held a day of general discussion on the right to food. In 1996 the World Food Summit in Rome called for a greater clarification of the right to food as a human right and asked the UN High Commissioner for Human Rights to provide "guidelines" for the implementation of the right to food. In response to the latter request several civil society organisations developed and published a draft Code of Conduct on the Right to Adequate Food in 1997.[22] Since then the Code of Conduct has been endorsed by hundreds of NGOs and some governments. In 1999 the UN Committee for Economic, Social and Cultural Rights issued its General Comment 12: The Right to Adequate Food (Article 11 of the Covenant).[23] This is currently the most authoritative interpretation of the right to food within the UN human rights system and reflects the present state of international law.

The following sections of the paper will guide the reader through the general comment. This paper should not, however, be seen as an interpretation of the general comment. The paper reflects the views and interpretations of the author. It follows the outline of the general comment, starting with some general observations, then proceeding to the normative content, obligations, and violations. In discussing these aspects of the right to food, special emphasis will be given to its minimum core content.

Article 5 of General Comment 12 states that:

> Despite the fact that the international community has frequently reaffirmed the importance of full respect for the right to adequate food, a disturbing gap still exists between the standards set in article 11 of the Covenant and the situation prevailing in many parts of the world. More than 840 million people throughout the world, most of them in developing countries, are chronically hungry; ... The Committee observes

---

21 Report on the right to adequate food as a human right submitted by Mr. Asbjörn Eide, Special Rapporteur, ECOSOC E/CN.4/Sub.2/1987/23, 7 July 1987.
22 FIAN, the international organisation for the right to feed oneself; WANAHR, the world alliance for nutrition and human rights; and the Institute Jacques Maritain. Available from FIAN, PO Box 102243, D-69012 Heidelberg, Germany; www.fian.org.
23 *General Comment 12: The right to adequate food*, Committee on Economic, Social and Cultural Rights (hereafter CESCR), UN Doc E/C.12/1999/5.

that while the problems of hunger are often particularly acute in developing countries, malnutrition, undernutrition and other problems which relate to the right to adequate food and the right to freedom from hunger, also exist in some of the most economically developed countries. Fundamentally, the roots of the problem of hunger and malnutrition are not lack of food, but lack of access to available food, inter alia because of poverty by large segments of the world's population.

According to Article 5, hunger, "malnutrition, undernutrition and other problems which relate to the right to adequate food" are due not to a lack of resources, but to the poverty of the deprived groups. They are in particular not technical or resource problems. This important point was recognised in the 1974 Universal Declaration on the Eradication of Hunger and Malnutrition: "Every man, woman and child has the inalienable right to be free from hunger and malnutrition. . . Society today already possesses sufficent resources, organisational ability and technology and hence the competence to achieve this objective."[24] There is no need for more food in the world – other than in the hands (and the fields) of the poor. Hunger and malnutrition are problems of people lacking the freedom to feed themselves, of people lacking the power to influence the political and economic decisions that would give them access to food in dignity. A significant development in recent years is that the right to adequate food has begun to be operationalised as a human right: States' obligations (as well as the duties of third parties) have begun to be clearly defined, and many of these obligations are potentially justiciable.

4 THE NORMATIVE CONTENT OF THE RIGHT TO ADEQUATE FOOD

The right to adequate food as a human right is enshrined in Article 11 of the International Covenant on Economic, Social and Cultural Rights. Article 11 can be seen as a codification of the earlier norm contained in Article 25 of the Universal Declaration of Human Rights of 1948.

Article 11 contains two rights: "the right of everyone to an adequate standard of living ... including adequate food ..." in

---

24 Universal Declaration on the Eradication of Hunger and Malnutrition, GA Res 3348 (XXIX), UN Doc E/CONF. 65/20, at 1 (1974).

Article 11.1, and the "fundamental right of everyone to be free from hunger" in Article 11.2. Freedom from hunger is the only right in the Covenant termed "fundamental".

The first norm is obviously much broader than the second. Strictly speaking, the right to freedom from hunger recognises only the justified claim to food in order to prevent hunger and imposes the corresponding obligations. The right to adequate food, on the other hand, is part of the right to an adequate standard of living. Article 6 of General Comment 12 warns that "[t]he right to food shall therefore not be interpreted in a narrow or restrictive sense which equates it with a minimum package of calories, proteins and other specific nutrients." This sentence refers to the part of the normative content that is linked to the right to adequate food in the preceding sentence of Article 6: "physical and economic access at all times to adequate food or means for its procurement."

The concepts of "access" and "adequacy" are key to understanding the full scope of the normative content of the right to food. General Comment 12 develops these concepts in Articles 8–13.

"Accessibility" refers to both economic and physical accessibility.[25] Food is economically accessible if an individual or a community has access to food as a result of their economic activities in the widest sense. These economic activities can include direct food production based on access to natural productive resources (e.g., land, water, forest, pastures, fishing grounds) or other resources and means of production. Economic activities also encompass work, for both the self-employed and wage-employed. Economic accessibility "applies to any acquisition pattern or entitlement through which people procure their food."[26] "Availability refers to the possibilities either for feeding oneself directly from productive land or other natural resources, or for well-functioning distribution, processing and market systems that can move food from the site of production to where it is needed ..."[27] The income generated must be sufficent to provide an adequate standard of living, which includes food and other basic needs. According to para 13, "[e]conomic accessibility implies that personal and household financial cost associated with the acquisition of food for an adequate diet should be at a level

---

25 *General Comment 12: The right to adequate food*, CESCR, UN Doc E/C.12/1999/5, para 13.
26 *General Comment 12: The right to adequate food*, CESCR, UN Doc E/C.12/1999/5, para 13.
27 *General Comment 12: The right to adequate food*, CESCR, UN Doc E/C.12/1999/5, para 12.

that the attainment and satisfaction of other basic needs are not threatened or compromised".

In contrast to economic accessibility, physical accessibility emphasises the simple question of immediate access. "Physical accessibility implies that adequate food must be accessible to everyone ..." Physical accessibility of food is unconditional, just as the right to an adequate standard of living in Article 11 is unconditional. Physical access to food is not conditional upon economic activities or specific merits (whether or not people "deserve" aid). If an individual can buy food, then clearly, food is accessible. If someone cannot buy or otherwise gain access to food, or can do so only under conditions of unacceptable hardship affecting the enjoyment of other human rights, food is not physically accessible to this person. Such a situation would trigger the states' obligations described below.

Physical access is an entitlement for everyone. The human right to adequate food, however, entitles one to more than just physical access. An individual, group or community also has a right to economic access to food, that is, access to food as a result of economic activities. Thus, paragraph 6 defines the normative content of the right to food as "... physical and economic access at all times to adequate food or means for its procurement." Without the means to procure food, economic access is impossible. The normative content of access to food, therefore, implies access to the means to procure it. These include natural and other resources, for example, skills, knowledge, and markets.

The access to food of some groups is especially threatened. Among them are "socially vulnerable groups such as landless persons and other particularly impoverished segments of the population," "indigenous groups whose access to their ancestral lands is threatened," and "victims of natural disasters."[28] To fulfil their access to food, these vulnerable groups may require special programmes. Although physical access is often the most immediate need, economic access must be available as well. Some groups, including infants and young children, the elderly, people with disabilities, people with terminal illnesses and people with persistent medical problems, including mental illness, are unlikely to be able to make use of economic access. For them, physical access must be ensured.

General Comment 12 places particular emphasis on sustainability,[29] echoing the Special Rapporteur's report, stipulating that

---

28 *General Comment 12: The right to adequate food*, CESCR, UN Doc E/C.12/1999/5, para 13.
29 *General Comment 12: The right to adequate food*, CESCR, UN Doc E/C.12/1999/5, para 8.

"[a]ccess to food must be sustainable over time."[30] This is an ecological as well as an economic requirement. "The notion of sustainability is intrinsically linked to the notion of adequate food or food security, implying that food will be accessible for both present and future generations." In addition, "... sustainability incorporates the notion of long-term availability and accessibility."[31] Whereas long-term availability points to the ecological limitations of food production and distribution, long-term accessibility underscores the importance of ensuring that the access to food itself must not be risky but continual over time – even over a long period of time.

Moreover, food is to be "accessible in a manner which does not destroy one's dignity as a human being".[32] General Comment 12 builds the normative content of the right to adequate food around the concepts of accessibility and adequacy. The General Comment also specifies the quantity and quality of the food. Food must be "sufficient to satisfy the dietary needs of individuals, free from adverse substances, and acceptable within a given culture."[33] Each of these aspects is further detailed in paragraphs 9, 10 and 11 of the General Comment. Dietary needs require a mix of nutrients for "physical and mental growth, development and maintenance." The mix will vary depending on factors such as occupation, gender, or age. Food must be free from adverse substances. Adverse substances include naturally occurring toxins, as well as those that originate from contamination or adulteration of the food chain. Cultural acceptability refers to non-nutrient based values attached to food and food consumption, as well as to informed consumer concerns regarding the food supply.

It should not be surprising that the right to adequate food has a fairly comprehensive normative content. Food is perhaps the single most important determinant of human health in every part of the world.[34] Moreover, food has deep cultural and spiritual

---

30 Report on the right to adequate food as a human right submitted by Mr. Asbjörn Eide, Special Rapporteur, ECOSOC E/CN.4/Sub.2/1987/23, 7 July 1987, para 135.
31 *General Comment 12: The right to adequate food*, CESCR, UN Doc E/C.12/1999/5, para 7.
32 *Report on the right to adequate food as a human right*, submitted by Asbjörn Eide, Special Rapporteur, para 52, ECOSOC E/CN.4/Sub.2/1987/23, 7 July 1987.
33 *General Comment No. 12, The right to adequate food*, CESCR, UN Doc E/C.12/1999/5, para 8.
34 General Comment No.14, on the right to health, mentions among the core obligations under the human right to health the obligation "to ensure access to the minimum essential food which is sufficient, nutritionally adequate and safe, to ensure freedom from hunger to everyone." *General Comment No. 14, The right to the highest attainable standard of health*, CESCR, UN Doc E/C.12/2000/4. Even beyond mere freedom from hunger, adequate food is a key determinant of health.

meaning. All of these aspects of the normative content are important. In some situations it may become necessary to think about which parts of the normative content of the right to adequate food should receive priority in the allocation of resources.

5 THE MINIMUM CORE CONTENT OF THE RIGHT TO ADEQATE FOOD

In a situation of scarce resources insufficient to protect and fulfil the full normative content of the right to food, some priority content of the right to adequate food has to be met first. This priority-setting applies also to states that may not be resource-poor, but that have so far failed to implement the full normative content of the right. There is general agreement that the priority content should be directed to those who are most deprived with respect to the human rights standard at issue. The concept of core content is still debated, and the terminology is still somewhat unclear. Sometimes the terms "core content" and "minimum core content" are used interchangeably. "Core content" is often used to describe the "key part" of the normative content, containing the central elements of the normative content, and serving as a kind of "archetypical" understanding of the right. That is the sense in which the term is used in this paper. Core content would, of course, encompass the minimum core content.

In its General Comment 3, the Committee on Economic, Social and Cultural Rights offers as an example of the minimum core content of a right, a state party "in which any significant number of individuals is deprived of essential foodstuffs," and says that such a state is *"prima facie* failing to discharge its obligations under the Covenant."[35]

This example indicates that the Committee sees "access to essential foodstuffs" as part of the minimum core content of the right to adequate food. This coincides with the extraordinary emphasis placed on "the fundamental right to freedom from

---

35 *General Comment No. 3, The nature of states parties obligations,* 5th Sess. (1990), CESCR, reprinted in *Compilation of general comments and general recommendations adopted by human rights treaty bodies* (hereafter *Compilation of general comments*), Annex III, UN Doc HRI\GEN\1\Rev.1, para 10 at 45 (1994). The introduction of vague statistical concepts like "significant number" may be debated. Statistical concepts are not used in civil and political human rights to define a violation and should not be used in economic and social human rights either. Human rights are first of all fundamental claims of individuals. The existence of just one malnourished person in a country of plenty indicates that (most probably) the obligation to fulfil access to food for everyone was breached.

hunger" in Article 11 of the Covenant, showing that the core content of the human right to adequate food includes freedom from hunger as its baseline and minimum core content.

According to paragraph 8 of General Comment 12, the Committee defines the core content of the right to food as "[t]he availability of food in quantity and quality sufficient to satisfy the dietary needs of individuals, free from adverse substances, and acceptable within a given culture; the accessibility of such food in ways that are sustainable and that do not interfere with the enjoyment of other rights."

The Committee has a dynamic view of core content. Core content should not be set off or separated from the rest of the normative content. The core content of the right to adequate food is also much broader than freedom from hunger. According to General Comment 12, "[t]he right to adequate food shall therefore not be interpreted in a narrow or restricted sense which equates it with a minimum package of of calories, proteins and other specific nutrients".[36] The fact that freedom from hunger belongs within the core content is implied by the last sentences of paragraphs 6 and 14: "However, States have a core obligation to take the necessary action to mitigate and alleviate hunger as provided for in paragraph 2 of Article 11, even in times of natural or other disasters."[37] And, "[e]very State is obliged to ensure for everyone under its jurisdiction access to the minimum essential food which is sufficient, nutritionally adequate and safe, to ensure their freedom of hunger".[38] This gives rise to a minimum core content, even though the General Comment itself does not use this term. The question of minimum core obligations will be addressed in section 6 of this paper.

6 STATES' OBLIGATIONS UNDER THE RIGHT TO ADEQUATE FOOD

A judgment whether a case of malnutrition results from a violation of the right to freedom from hunger has to be based on an analysis of the specific obligation that was breached: for example, certain legislation that is missing or discriminatory; certain programmes not carried out by the authorities; or certain officials fail-

---

36 *General Comment 12: The right to adequate food*, CESCR, UN Doc E/C.12/1999/5, para 6.
37 *General Comment 12: The right to adequate food*, CESCR, UN Doc E/C.12/1999/5, para 6.
38 *General Comment 12: The right to adequate food*, CESCR, UN Doc E/C.12/1999/5, para 14.

ing to do their duty. This analysis should start with the generic obligation to take steps toward full realisation as quickly as possible and with maximum available resources. It should go beyond the well-known three-part framework of obligations to respect, protect and fulfil access to food, into the details of implementation.

Implementation provides tools (implements), which vulnerable groups need in order to realise their rights. These tools are typically programmes, legislation or some other framework, with clearly delineated access and procedures. The process of providing such implements is called "implementation". Under Article 2.1 of the Covenant, full implementation, realised progressively and to the maximum of available resources, is a state obligation, since it is the key ingredient in full realisation of the right to food. Paragraph 21 of the general comment requires states to put in place a national implementation strategy with benchmarks to monitor progress.

Economic and social rights, including the right to food, are rights on the same basis as other human rights. Sometimes, however, they are dealt with as though they are only policymaking principles. Policies are important, but without concrete programme measures and clear implementation, the individual guarantees under the fundamental right to freedom from hunger cannot be achieved. Victims should be able to sue states for noncompliance with their obligations under the right to freedom from hunger in national or international courts.

A violation of a right is defined as a breach of obligations under this right by the respective duty-holder(s). In the case of human rights the duty-holders are states.[39] For the human right to food, as for any human right, there has to be a clear understanding of the corresponding states' obligations.

The full realisation of the right to adequate food need not be achieved immediately. It must, however, be pursued progressively to the maximum of available resources. "This imposes an obligation to move as expeditiously as possible toward this goal".[40] Obligations that can be met right away are incumbent upon states immediately. This includes all obligations to respect economic and physical access to adequate food. Taking steps progressively, rather than immediately, is only permissible if resources are lacking. Lack of resources is applicable only with respect to the obliga-

---

39 For a further discussion of the reasons for taking a classical approach to violations, see Künnemann *Food and freedom: A textbook for human rights education* (1999).
40 *General Comment 12: The right to adequate food*, CESCR, UN Doc E/C.12/1999/5, para 14.

tions to fulfil and (to some extent) the obligation to protect. The obligation to respect, that is, to refrain from destroying people's access to adequate food, does not require resources. Similar resource issues are found in the Covenant on Civil and Political Rights, when it comes to the obligation to fulfil. The difference between Article 2 in both Covenants is not a difference in the rights themselves, but rather, a difference in emphasis. The Covenant on Civil and Political Rights puts more emphasis on the obligations to respect, whereas the Covenant on Economic, Social and Cultural Rights puts more weight on obligations to fulfil. However, civil and political rights must be fulfilled also, and economic, social and cultural rights must be respected.

What does it mean to be without access to adequate food? It should be clear that a person without access is a person who wants access, but lacks it. Someone who makes a conscious decision not to use available access is, of course, a person who does have access. When "an individual or group is unable, for reasons beyond their control, to enjoy the right to adequate food by the means at their disposal, States have the obligation to fulfil (provide) the right directly."[41]

This obligation entitles the target group to a mix of programmes that provide physical access to food and programmes providing economic access. Some people may choose not to make use of their economic access. Even in this situation, physical access must be assured. Economic access to food results from producing food for oneself or obtaining food in return for economic activities. People should be able to choose freely among the various economic activities that will procure food. Whatever their choice may be, people need access to resources, such as natural and capital resources, skills and technologies, markets and/or work. This second type of programme can therefore be referred to as "resource programmes". Access to land can be provided through agrarian reform, access to skills and technologies through training programmes, and access to work through employment programmes. These programmes do not have to be new activities; they may redistribute existing work, or recognise, pay for or improve existing activities of the target group that benefit the community and society as a whole.

For economic access to be sustainable, various kinds of limitations must be taken into account. First, there are the environmen-

---

41 *General Comment 12: The right to adequate food*, CESCR, UN Doc E/C.12/1999/5, para 15.

tal impacts of economic activities. Economic activities and their consequences can easily use (and use up) resources, making them ultimately unsustainable. Secondly, the access to resources provided by the programmes must be economically sustainable. They must be geared to and embedded in a framework of economic policies that take into account whether the economic activities generated by these programmes satisfy actual needs, so that their economic value will be recognised and maintained by society and/or markets in the long run. Only if a programme for economic access addresses real needs will it enable the target group to feed itself on a sustainable basis even after the programme ends.

The obligation to fulfil (provide) needs further explanation. Why does the General Comment use the term fulfil (provide) instead of simply "fulfil?" According to paragraph 15, the Committee considered adopting an intermediate level of obligation, "to facilitate." It decided, however, to maintain the three levels of obligation found in the Maastricht Guidelines. General Comment 12 therefore considers the obligation to fulfil as having two different dimensions. "The obligation to fulfil (facilitate) means that states must engage proactively in activities intended to strengthen people's access to and utilisation of resources and other means to ensure their livelihood."

The obligation to fulfil (facilitate) access to food is directed at people who have access but whose economic access needs strengthening. The state's obligation to people who lack access to food is to fulfil (provide) them with access. For this second group, facilitation is not enough. It is perhaps for this reason that the "obligation to facilitate" was designated an "intermediate" level. The Committee had good reason not to create an intermediate level of state obligation. Such an obligation would introduce a second threshold into the theory of human rights. For the purpose of analysis here we can say that there are two categories of persons and groups: those who enjoy the full normative content of the right and those who do not. The new target group (for facilitation) would consist of people who are intermediate in the sense that they are not truly deprived, but they are not fully enjoying the normative content of the right either. They would have to be clearly distinguished from people who are truly able to enjoy the right. Instead of a yes/no situation, the categories would be yes/almost/no. This does not add to the clarity of the concepts. The usual pragmatic way to deal with borderline situations is to decide on a case by case basis, accepting the serious cases as valid and rejecting the rest. Even though it is natural for sensible governments promoting human rights to strengthen the position of the "less serious" cases, this distinction need not be carried into the system of human rights law.

After rejecting this new category, the Committee tried to incorporate it into the obligation to fulfil by means of an internal differentiation: fulfil (provide) for truly deprived persons/groups and fulfil (facilitate) for persons/groups whose access to food is limited but not nonexistent. This does not help much: The second threshold is still around, although now it has become an internal distinction within the obligation to fulfil. Moreover, it presents an additional conceptual problem, because internal differentiations tend to be overlooked. This would lead to unacceptable consequences for human rights: Should slaves be helped by "facilitating freedom from slavery"? What if states facilitated job creation, to enable slaves to earn the money to buy their freedom? Would it help victims of torture or persons at risk of torture, if authorities facilitated courses for them on how to persuade their (prospective) torturers to behave properly? States are obligated to ensure freedom from torture and slavery. They are also obligated to ensure freedom from hunger and malnutrition. Simply facilitating the normative content is not sufficient.

It should therefore be clearly understood that the terminology fulfil (facilitate) was not meant to modify the binding nature of the obligation to fulfil, which can be described as follows: For persons or groups not in a position to enjoy the normative content of the right in question, states are obligated to implement programmes and policy measures providing immediate enjoyment of the normative content. States also have a duty to take measures to provide a framework for economic, social and cultural, civil and political life, so that people can enjoy, if they wish, the normative content of the right without further recourse to such programmes.

States parties undertake to guarantee that the right to food will be exercised without discrimination on account of property or social origin. General Comment 12 elaborates on the question of discrimination in paragraph 26, calling for "particular attention for the need to prevent discrimination in access to food or resources for food", and demanding "guarantees of full and equal access to economic resources". Paragraph 18 prohibits discrimination on a number of grounds, including property: "any discrimination in access to food, as well as to means and entitlements of its procurement on the grounds of ... property ... nullifying or impairing the equal enjoyment or exercise of economic, social and cultural rights constitutes a violation of the Covenant." These paragraphs are highly significant as they relate the right to food and the means for its procurement to the question of property, and imply that resources and means of production cannot be treated as a separate domain. Resources and means of production belong to the common heritage of humankind. They are to be used in the first instance by the people whose ability to feed themselves depends on them.

> The most appropriate ways and means of implementing the right to adequate food will inevitably vary significantly from one state party to another. Every state will have a margin of discretion in choosing its own approaches, but the Covenant clearly requires that each party take whatever steps are necessary to ensure that everybody is free from hunger and as soon as possible can enjoy the right to adequate food. This will require the adoption of a national strategy to ensure food and nutrition security for all, based on human rights principles that define the objectives, and the formulation of policies and corresponding benchmarks.[42]

Also, "states should consider the adoption of a framework law as a major instrument of the national strategy concerning the right to food."[43]

The margin of discretion will be limited by the general nature of the human right to food as an individual right and the structure of obligations and related programmes detailed above. Obligations to respect are (or can be made) easily justiciable. The framework law will have to outline the system of programmes necessary to make the obligation to fulfil operational and justiciable for those not enjoying the normative content of the right. The obligations to protect will occupy an intermediate position. Priority should be given to meeting the state's minimum core obligations, as outlined below.

The *raison d'être* for the framework policies is to promote and secure realisation of the right to adequate food as an individual right. This means that, like any human right, its realisation can be pursued in court, if necessary. Justiciability of the right to adequate food may be a long way down the road for some states. For others it is just around the corner.

---

42 *General Comment 12: The right to adequate food*, CESCR, UN Doc E/C.12/1999/5, para 21.
43 *General Comment 12: The right to adequate food*, CESCR, UN Doc E/C.12/1999/5, para 29.

To keep framework policies targeted to the implementation of the right to food, monitoring is important. According to the General Comment, "[s]tates parties shall develop and maintain mechanisms to monitor progress towards the realisation of the right to adequate food for all, to identify the factors and difficulties affecting the degree of implementation of their obligations, and to facilitate the adoption of corrective legislation and administrative measures ..."[44]

The General Comment provides for compensation and remedies, including judicial remedies and adequate reparation for victims of right to food violations.[45] This reminds us that the right to food belongs in essence to the legal category, not to the category of political principles or morals. The right to food is not about food policies or developmental economics, but about individual persons or groups (perhaps hungry or malnourished) who turn up here and now, claim to be victims of violations of the right to food and ask for remedy and reparation. They will not be helped much by judges ordering states to carry out policies or programmes that might ten years from now increase their statistical access to food, if indeed they are still alive by then. Remedies must be provided in the present and for this particular claimant, through judicial or other procedures. Remedies should include the provision of physical or economic access to adequate food, compensation for the suffering caused by the violation, and programmes providing economic access to food, and enabling victims to feed themselves in the future. Only in this situation can we talk about the right to food being realised as a human right.[46] People without access to adequate food realise their right by means of programmes and institutions established to provide remedy and reparation, using judicial, quasi-judicial or other procedures.

Besides remedy and rehabilitation, additional legal consequences should follow upon a violation of the right to food. Just as with other human rights, the impunity that violators of the human right to food currently enjoy is a matter of concern. Remedies should be in place at the national and international levels.[47] This is particularly important when it comes to interna-

---

44 *General Comment 12: The right to adequate food*, CESCR, UN Doc E/C.12/1999/5, para 31.
45 *General Comment 12: The right to adequate food*, CESCR, UN Doc E/C.12/1999/5, para 32.
46 People eating do not "realise their right to food" while eating, people who get food from their salaries as teachers don't "realise their right to food through teaching". This is inappropriate and inflationary use of human rights terminology; they just eat, they just teach.
47 *General Comment 12: The right to adequate food*, CESCR, UN Doc E/C.12/1999/5, para 32.

tional obligations. With respect to international respect-bound and protection-bound obligations, states have an obligation to prevent the destruction of access to food in other countries. Some people in State B may be threatened by hunger and malnutrition because State A contributed to the destruction of their livelihoods, for example by failing to intervene to halt the destructive activities of a third party. Even if State B itself has respect- and protection-bound obligations, this does not release State A from the duty to act in situations in which it can have a decisive impact in protecting access to food in other countries. Such situations are increasingly common in the context of globalisation.

The General Comment reminds states of the importance of international cooperation:

> States parties should take steps to respect the enjoyment of the right to food in other countries, to protect that right, to facilitate access to food, and to provide the necessary aid when required. In international agreements, states parties should, whenever relevant, ensure that the right to adequate food is given due attention and consider the development of further international legal instruments to that end.[48]

The second sentence demonstrates the Committee's concern that international human rights law could be undermined by international agreements that ignore human rights standards. A similar concern was voiced by the Subcommission on the Promotion and Protection of Human Rights during its August 2000 session when it recalled the primacy of international human rights law over other international agreements in the context of intellectual property rights.[49]

General Comment 12 also calls on states not to take actions that would destroy access to adequate food of people in other countries, for example, by taking part in food embargoes or the practice of "dumping" in international trade.[50] An international obligation to assist in fulfilment is "to cooperate in providing disaster relief and humanitarian assistance in times of emergency, including assistance to refugees and internally displaced persons."[51] The Committee also urges international financial institu-

---

48 *General Comment 12: The right to adequate food*, CESCR, UN Doc E/C.12/1999/5, para 36.
49 *The realization of economic, social, and cultural rights: intellectual property rights and human rights*, UN Doc E/CN.4/Sub.2/2000/7.
50 *General Comment 12: The right to adequate food*, CESCR, UN Doc E/C.12/1999/5, para 37.
51 *General Comment 12: The right to adequate food*, CESCR, UN Doc E/C.12/1999/5, para 38.

tions, especially the International Monetary Fund and the World Bank to pay greater attention to the human right to food in their lending policies and "in international measures to deal with the debt crisis." Structural adjustment programmes should ensure that human rights, including the right to food, are protected.[52]

7 MINIMUM CORE OBLIGATIONS: SOME VIOLATIONS RELATED TO THE MINIMUM CORE CONTENT

7.1 What is special about minimum core obligations?

The right to freedom from hunger holds unconditionally; it is independent of participation in economic activities. Everyone has the right to an adequate standard of living, including food. This is commonly achieved by means of an adequate income.[53] Often, in the absence of minimum income provisions, violations of the right to freedom from hunger result from violations of the right to work.

Human rights and their resulting obligations are universal. Every obligation that a state has the means to meet, must be met. However, under certain circumstances, some obligations cannot be met even by the best state in the world. In these situations one can ask whether such a norm can still be called an obligation. One can only be obliged to do something that one has the capacity to accomplish. Nevertheless, it is a good practice to retain the term "obligation", realising that for some obligations, one must determine on a case by case basis whether the state is in a position to meet the obligation, and therefore, whether this obligation is incumbent upon the state. It does not make sense to accuse a state of having violated a human right by breaching an obligation that it could not possibly have met.

These issues arise with all human rights – civil and political rights, as well as economic, social and cultural rights – as soon as the obligation to protect or the obligation to fulfil involves scarce

---

52 *General Comment 12: The right to adequate food*, CESCR, UN Doc E/C.12/1999/5, para 41.
53 What is an adequate standard of living? The UN report on the Right to Adequate Food suggests that "adequacy" is dependent upon cultural variables. Because of the universality of human rights, the degree of dependence on these variables must be the same for each country, although the content of an adequate standard of living will vary from country to country.

resources. These analytical difficulties can be avoided by restricting oneself to obligations to respect, as often occurs in the field of civil and political rights. Respect-bound obligations can always be met because they do not draw on scarce resources; hence, every breach of a respect-bound obligation violates the corresponding human right.

The only two circumstances that can relieve a state from meeting certain positive obligations are lack of resources and lack of time to take measures. The determination of the incumbent obligations under the right to adequate food will therefore depend upon judgments about the availability of resources, as well as on how expeditiously certain measures (for example, legislation, orders or programmes) can be taken. Any person with reasonable experience of the proper functioning of the state and the rule of law can determine whether the executive, judicial or legislative branch has taken measures promptly, or is really not interested in the matter. Judgments concerning the availability of resources, however, are more difficult.

Lack of resources is a favourite argument used by many states to avoid obligations under the human right to adequate food. It is the only argument that is possibly valid, and it deserves serious consideration. In these situations a judgment concerning violations of the right to food (especially for fulfilment-bound obligations) would also necessitate a judgment about whether a state has violated the generic obligations in Article 2.1 of the Covenant by not taking measures to the maximum of its available resources. A state claiming that a certain obligation is not incumbent upon it carries the burden of proof.

The Committee subscribes to this argument, at least for certain minimum obligations of the right under consideration. According to General Comment 12:

> Violations of the Covenant occur when a State fails to ensure the satisfaction of, at the very least, the minimum essential level required to be free from hunger. In determining which actions or omissions amount to a violation of the right to food, it is important to distinguish the inability from the unwillingness of a State party to comply. Should a State party argue that resource constraints make it impossible to provide access to food for those who are unable by themselves to secure such access, the State has to demonstrate that every effort has been made to use all the resources at its disposal in an effort to satisfy, as a matter of priority, those minimum obligations. ... A

state claiming that it is unable to carry out its obligation for reasons beyond its control therefore has the burden of proving that this is the case and that it has unsuccessfully sought to obtain international support to ensure the availability and accessability of the necessary food.[54]

What are these resources and how can a state prove their lack? The availability of resources has to be judged on the basis of the society of which the state is a part. It cannot mean the given budgetary resources of the state (except in short-term emergency situations). Otherwise states could simply avoid obligations by reducing their income (for example by tax reforms) until they can claim inability to comply. Moreover, resources must be available now. Projected economic growth is irrelevant to the realisation of right to food, just as it is for any other human right.[55]

Two norms are always incumbent on states. These are the obligation to respect and the principle of nondiscrimination, because neither is affected by resource constraints. Any breach of the obligations to respect or any case of discrimination can be identified immediately as a violation. In addition, states have breached a positive obligation if they do not demonstrate within a reasonable period of time that they are unable to take the required measures because of lack of resources.

That an obligation is incumbent upon a state does not by itself qualify it as a minimum core obligation. Freedom of hunger is often mentioned as a minimum level for access to adequate food. However, the core content, as defined in General Comment 12, encompasses much more than freedom from hunger. In the following discussion, minimum core obligations are considered to be the obligations affecting freedom from hunger. The fundamental human rights principle of non-discrimination should be considered a minimum core obligation of the right to adequate food as well.

Identifying violations related to the minimum core content means identifying breaches of minimum core obligations and discriminatory or unsustainable practices in implementing and en-

---

54 *General Comment No. 12, The Right to Adequate Food*, CESCR, para 17, UN Doc. E/C.12/1999/5.
55 "The obligation of progressive achievement exists independently of the increase in resources; it requires effective use of resources available". "The Limburg Principles on the implementation of the International Covenant on Economic, Social, and Cultural Rights" (1987) 9 *Hum Rts Q* 122 at 23.

forcing these obligations.[56] A minimum core obligation is incumbent upon a state if the state cannot prove lack of resources or time to implement it. Unless and until such a proof has been provided, anyone deprived of the minimum core content is prima facie seen as a victim of a violation of a human rights violation, in this case of the right to adequate food.[57]

The following list of sample violations related to the minimum core content of the right to adequate food is organised according to the type of obligation breached.

7.2 Minimum Core Obligations to Respect and Protect

A breach of a minimum core obligation to respect occurs if a state[58] destroys a person's physical access to food, thereby putting this person at risk of hunger and malnutrition.

State-induced dismantling of access to food is only permitted if physical access to essential food is maintained by compensatory measures. In the larger context of core content, economic access must be maintained as well. This means that proper rehabilitation measures for the affected person/community must be guaranteed. In any event, destruction of current access to food should be considered acceptable only if the victims agree to it or its avoidance would cause undue hardship to the general public. The argument that measures that destroy livelihoods may lead to economic growth or are otherwise in the national interest is insufficient.

A breach of a minimum core obligation to protect occurs if a state fails to prevent the destruction of an individual's or a community's physical access to essential food by a third party, such as a large landlord or a corporation, without proving that it lacked the time or resources to do so. Dismantling the current form of

---

56 Further reflections on the core content and violations of the right to food can be found in Künnemann, "Comment" in The *right to complain about economic, social and cultural rights* (1995) Netherlands Institue of Human Rights, SIM Special No.18.

57 This echoes *General Comment 3: The nature of states parties obligations*, 5th Sess (1990), CESCR, reprinted in *Compilation of general comments*, no 10, UN Doc HRI\GEN\1\Rev.1 at 45 (1994).

58 Whether and how the community of states—for example, their specialised agencies and financial institutions may also be counted among potential violators—is a matter for debate (cf Van Boven, Flinterman, and Westendorp (eds) *The Maastricht Guidelines on violations of economic, social, and cultural rights*, (1998) Netherlands Institute of Human Rights, SIM Special No. 20, para 19). Intergovernmental organisations cannot violate the Covenant as they are not party to it. If the fundamental right to freedom from hunger is seen as part of general international law, however, intergovernmental organisations have the corresponding obligations under international law.

physical access to food is only permitted under the conditions described above.

More specifically, states breach minimum core obligations to respect or protect if they commit or permit the following acts, to the extent that these acts destroy an individual's or community's physical access to essential food:
- destroying an individual's or community's food-producing resources through the effects of activities such as predatory mining, oil exploration or industrial fishing;
- destroying an individual's or community's food-producing resources by polluting or withholding water, or by destroying people's access to other essential inputs, such as seeds;
- destroying an individual's or community's food supplies;
- forcibly evicting peasants, nomadic people, fisherfolk, or indigenous people from their land, fishing grounds or forests;
- preventing or destroying access to markets for people depending on this access for their livelihoods;
- blocking food transports into vulnerable areas or for vulnerable people (for example, as a result of war or through sanctions);
- dumping food or other products on a local market of vulnerable producers;
- destroying a future generation's food-producing resources and food security;
- dismantling a fulfilment-bound programme or legislative act by means of a retrogressive measure, unless forced to do so by lack of resources;
- destroying community- or family-based systems of social security.

7.3 Minimum core obligations to fulfill

Minimum core obligations to fulfill apply in situations in which an individual, group or community is deprived of physical access to essential food and is threatened by malnutrition and hunger. In terms of core content, access to food also means economic access; hence, it cannot be separated from access to productive resources or work. Economic access automatically results in physical access. If economic access is not used or is not feasible, physical access is to be secured by a transfer of funds or food guaranteed by the state (but possibly provided by a community, a family or others).

Framework policies cannot fulfil freedom from hunger for each individual or community. Specific programmes are essential. According to the concept of accessibility as developed in General Comment 12, such programmes must entail physical access (or income) programmes, and economic access (or resource) programmes. Resource programmes must guarantee access to productive resources, including natural resources, capital resources, knowledge and skills, work, and minimum wages. Such resource programmes include specific self-employment or wage-employment programmes, or agrarian reforms providing access to land, water, and other necessary inputs. Resource programmes should offer vulnerable persons or groups the possibility to feed themselves in the future without further recourse to such programmes. The corresponding framework policies should enable these persons to feed themselves over time. Another aspect of these resource programmes should be a minimum wage programme, sufficient to provide a decent standard of living, including adequate food.

Minimum core obligations to fulfil are less demanding. They require, however, that, at the least, physical access to essential food be fulfilled for each deprived person as expeditiously as possible. This does not mean that only income programmes need to be considered. Although resource programmes may not be absolutely mandatory because minimum core obligations focus only on freedom from hunger, the right to freedom from hunger should not be seen in isolation from the right to adequate food. Therefore, the question of economic accessibility should be considered. Resource-poor states may prefer to place people in resource rather than income programmes, since the former would be less costly and would improve the chances that vulnerable groups would gain sustainable access to food and would not have to continue relying on such programmes. The minimum core obligation of freedom from hunger does, however, impose certain requirements on these resource programmes.

Freedom from hunger imposes requirements on wages. In a number of states parties, large numbers of workers, including agricultural or informal sector workers, are not covered by minimum wage laws. Even where minimum wage laws exist it may be difficult to enforce them. Workers may be hesitant to insist on their rights if they are completely dependent on an employer for their essential food. To address these difficulties, the enforcement of minimum wages must be treated as a specific component of resource and income programmes.

Moreover, freedom from hunger is often affected by discriminatory practices. Gender discrimination is inherent in many societies.

Women and children often bear the brunt of hunger and malnutrition. Discrimination in ensuring freedom from hunger can affect various victim groups. In the examples below women serve as key example of discriminated persons, and indigenous peoples are an example of communities suffering discrimination. The violations described below can, of course, be suffered by any other discriminated persons or communities as well. One often overlooked group that is subject to discrimination is future generations. Future generations will suffer as a result of damage to environmental sustainability. Ecological sustainability[59] can be thought of as a human rights principle to prevent discrimination against future generations.

A breach of a minimum core obligation to fulfil occurs, therefore, if hunger or malnutrition results from any of the following omissions (unless the states can prove that these omissions are due to lack of resources):

(a) *In resource programmes:*
- Resource programmes do not secure immediate physical access to essential food.
- Resource programmes, including agrarian reforms and other serious attempts to offer self-employment or wage employment to each interested person, do not provide sustainable access to essential food.
- Minimum wage programmes either do not exist or are inadequate to provide essential food or meet the family's other basic needs.
- The international community, in a situation in which a state has proven its inability to meet the minimum obligation to fulfil, fails to provide sufficient matching funds to secure the operation of fulfilment-bound programmes, at least to the extent of providing physical access to essential food for each person in the territory of the state.

(b) *In income programmes:*
- A state does not establish or maintain income programmes that provide each person threatened by hunger and malnutrition with access to food.

---

59 The Vienna Declaration and Programme of Action of the World Conference on Human Rights 1993 established in Article 11 the principle that the developmental and environmental needs of present and future generations must be met equitably. Vienna Declaration and Programme of Action, UN Doc A/CONF.157/24, adopted at Vienna, 14-25 June 1993, reprinted in 32 ILM 1661 (1993). Moreover sustainability of access is mentioned in the Report on the right to adequate food as a human right submitted by Mr. Asbjörn Eide, Special Rapporteur, ECOSOC E/CN.4/Sub.2/1987/23, 7 July 1987.

- The income provided by income programmes (in cash or in kind) is insufficient to provide access to food.
- An income programme's coverage is reduced, for example, if retrogressive measures in these programmes lead to hunger and malnutrition.
- Persons in prisons or other state custody are not provided with adequate food.
- Persons are excluded from income programmes.
- The international community in emergency situations fails to provide emergency funds to secure physical access to food for each person in the territory of the state.

(c) *Through discriminatory practices*
- Food-producing resources (land, water, genetic resources) are not protected against ruinous use, such that physical and economic access to adequate food is jeopardised with respect to the food security of future generations (lack of ecological sustainability).
- In a situation of threatening hunger, the access to food of women and girls is less protected against actions by third parties or is less fulfilled in resource or income programmes than the access of males.
- In a situation of threatening hunger, the access to food of indigenous communities is less protected against actions by third parties or less fulfilled in resource or income programmes than the access of mainstream communities.

The examples listed above under the obligation to fulfil emphasise programmes and their proper maintenance with respect to freedom from hunger. For fulfilment-bound obligations, it is in the context of these programmes that individuals can realise their right to food and seek remedies through courts as required by the right to adequate food. The role of framework policies to ensure freedom from hunger, important as they are, can only be properly focused and discussed in connection with the development and proper functioning of these programmes.

THE MINIMUM CORE CONTENT OF THE RIGHT TO FOOD IN CONTEXT: A RESPONSE TO ROLF KÜNNEMANN

Danie Brand

1 INTRODUCTION

Rolf Künnemann has in his paper done much more than simply mapping out the minimum core content of the right to food. In the space of a few pages he has given an overview of the nature and content of the right to food in general terms, and the obligations imposed by it, its recognition in international law and detailed examples of its violation. He has also taken care to humanise the theory he preaches, pointing out the abstract and therefore often inadequate nature of statistics as indicators of human rights violations and emphasising that human rights entail a complex and dynamic relationship between vulnerable persons and a state or other powerful entities.

The two concerns I raise in my response to his wide-ranging paper are not directly relevant to his ideas alone (they would seem to apply to the theme of the conference in general terms) and arise from a difference in perspective rather than a disagreement in principle. As was the purpose with this conference, Rolf

Künnemann in his presentation analysed the right to food and the idea of a minimum core content of the right to food from the perspective of international human rights law. This is of course the perspective from which the idea of a minimum core content, or minimum core obligations, of socio-economic rights developed in the first place.

The normative development of international human rights law, as is the case with any system of law, is conditioned and constrained (also) by the institutions through and manner in which it is, or it can be, enforced. Within the United Nations human rights system human rights are enforced not through judicial, but at best through quasi-judicial processes. For the greater part the most effective enforcement mechanisms are still non-judicial state reporting and other monitoring systems. This is particularly true of the enforcement of socio-economic rights. Despite recent developments to the contrary[1] the only effective enforcement mechanism for socio-economic rights at the international level remains the state reporting system created through Articles 16 and 17 of the International Covenant on Economic, Social and Cultural Rights (ICESCR).[2] This reporting system has been so manipulated in practice by the United Nations Committee on Economic, Social and Cultural Rights (CESCR) as to become one of the most effective state reporting systems in the United Nations human rights structure. However, it still suffers from the limitations inherent in any state reporting system: It still depends for its success on the effective participation of states (that is rarely forthcoming) and it has no real sanction attached to it to ensure compliance in the final instance. Most importantly, by its very nature, such a reporting system is general rather than specific in its focus. It considers the acceptability in general terms of state policies and their outcomes, tested against generalised, abstract

---

1   I refer here to the recent drafting by the United Nations Committee on Economic, Social and Cultural Rights (hereinafter cited as the CESCR) of an Optional Protocol to the International Covenant on Economic, Social and Cultural Rights (hereinafter cited as the ICESCR) creating a system for receiving individual complaints and to the recently developed practice of the CESCR to send missions to states parties to investigate and report on specific alleged violations of rights in the ICESCR. Unfortunately the draft Optional Protocol has not as yet been and is unlikely to be adopted by states and the practice of sending missions to countries has been limited to the right to housing.

2   International Covenant on Economic, Social, and Cultural Rights, *opened for signature* 16 Dec 1966, *entered into force* 3 Jan 1976, 993 UNTS 3. In terms of this reporting system, states parties to the ICESCR have to submit reports to the CESCR once every five years on their domestic implementation of the provisions of the ICESCR. The CESCR considers these reports and drafts a set of Concluding Observations containing its observations and recommendations regarding a particular state report.

norms and standards, and, in the words of Matthew Craven, is unable "to respond to specific individual claims that might arise in relation to the enjoyment of rights in particular states."[3] In short, the reporting system is neither judicial, nor *quasi*-judicial in nature. This to me has an inevitable consequence for the norms the system enforces.

In a warped sense, those who deal with socio-economic rights on the international level have the "luxury" to think normatively about these rights in generalised, rather than specific terms. The enforcement structures with which they are blessed require the development of generalized rather than specific norms. International human rights lawyers therefore tend to describe the basic standards set by the minimum core content of socio-economic rights in general or universal and fixed terms, as they do with the minimum entitlements and obligations implied by the core content. They do so partly because such general standards and such general or universal entitlements and obligations are the most useful within their institutional framework.

In South Africa, with regard to our domestic constitutional law, we are in a different position. We are obviously fortunate in the sense that economic and social rights have been given the edge of reality and therefore of particularity for us. The right to have access to food, as the rights to have access to water, health care services, social security and assistance, housing, education and land are justiciable rights in our constitution.[4] This good fortune bears also a sharp edge. We have to be concrete and practical in our thinking about a right such as the right to food, because our ideas are likely, at on time or another, to be tested under the white light of judicial scrutiny by a not altogether sympathetic judiciary.[5] More pertinently, because the institutions through and manner in which socio-economic rights are to be enforced in South Africa differ from those on the international level, we have to be far more specific, particular, concrete, context-sensitive and flexible in our thinking about basic standards, core entitlements and minimum obligations. Claims for the enforcement of socio-economic rights in our context will always arise from specific and

---

3   Craven "Introduction to the International Covenant on Economic, Social and Cultural Rights" in Blyberg and Ravindram *Circle of rights. Economic, social and cultural rights activism: A training resource* (2000) International Human Rights Internship Programme/Asian Forum for Human Rights and Development 49 at 55.
4   See sections 26, 27, 29(1), 28(1)(c) and 35(2(e) of the Constitution of the Republic of South Africa, 1996 (hereinafter the constitution).
5   See discussion in part 3 below, particularly the references in notes 19 and 20.

concrete individual situations. It is against this background and from this perspective that I raise my first concern with the idea of a minimum core content of the right to food and of socio-economic rights generally.

2 NORM SETTING

Thinking about the minimum core content of socio-economic rights such as the right to food essentially has to do with norm setting. The proponents of the minimum core concept aim to define and describe the minimum level of satisfaction of socio-economic rights, so as to answer critics who point to the vague and undefined nature of these rights and so as to be able to hold forth a basic level of state obligation or responsibility which cannot be obscured behind the ICESCR's dual qualifiers of resource constraints and progressive realisation.[6] On the international level, they tend to do so in abstract and generalised terms, because this is what the system requires.[7]

Rolf Künnemann has explained to us that a human right such as the right to food is not simply a basic standard against which the living conditions of people can be tested. The right to food, as all other human rights, implies a relationship of entitlements and duties, particularly obligations of conduct, between a vulnerable person or group and a powerful entity such as the state. He also made the point that, although it is relatively straightforward to identify the standard set by the minimum core content of the right to food (he identified it as freedom from hunger) it is more difficult, but in practical terms far more important to think of concrete entitlements and obligations of conduct created by that standard. I agree that this is where the most important inquiry lies, but I question whether it is possible to describe, in concrete terms, these entitlements and obligations in a way that would be helpful in a process of adjudication.

The right to food, as any other right, is indeed a relationship or rather it is potentially countless different relationships.[8] Every

---

6 Article 2(1) of the ICESCR describes the duties imposed by rights entrenched in the ICESCR as duties that states have to implement only "to the maximum of...available resources, with a view to achieving progressively the full realisation of the rights recognized in the present Covenant..."
7 See for instance the contribution of Fons Coomans in this volume, where he argues that "universal" minimum obligations should be formulated.
8 The idea of rights as relationships rather than boundaries has been current mostly in constitutional theory for the last three decades and is usually associated with the work of

time there is the possibility of a violation of a right such as the right to food it would have occurred in a particular relationship. This relationship would exist between a particular, concrete person or group of persons, and a particular, concrete duty holder, usually the state, all within a particular set of circumstances. Within such a particular relationship, the entitlements and duties at play would also be context specific. Within each such particular relationship, the entitlements and duties implied by the minimum core content of the right to food will be different, determined by the particular parties involved, their capabilities and vulnerabilities and the particular circumstances of the case.

To illustrate this point I thought it might be worth while to speculate about the entitlements and duties implied by the minimum core content of the right to food in the context of the real situations of South Africa's 20th century history. I recently read South African social historian Charles van Onselen's wonderful book *The seed is mine. The life of Kas Maine, a South African sharecropper*.[9] The book, a powerful treatise on South African 20th century economic, social and political history, traces the life of one Kas Maine, a black sharecropper[10] who lived from 1894 to 1985, experiencing the rise and to some extent the fall of apartheid. It narrates his personal history, and tells the story of his gradual conversion, by the economic and political developments of his time, from an economically independent (and food self-sufficient) farmer to a destitute old man, largely dependent for his survival on handouts from the state and his family.[11] At different stages in

---

Jennifer Nedelsky. See Nedelsky "Reconceiving rights as relationships" (1992) 30 *Alta Law Rev*; and Nedelsky "Law, boundaries and the bounded self" (1990) 30 *Representations* 162. For an earlier use of a different but related metaphor, that of rights as conversations, see Simon "The invention and reinvention of welfare rights" (1985) 44 *Maryland Law Rev* 1 at 14 – 15.

9   Van Onselen *The seed is mine. The life of Kas Maine, a South African sharecropper 1894 – 1985* (1996) Hill and Wang.

10 Sharecropping agreements in the South African context were verbal agreements in terms of which an independent but landless black farmer and a (landed) white farmer agreed to share the harvest from the white farmer's farm in proportion to the economic inputs made to the farm. The agreements fulfilled a need for both parties. White farmers were generally rich in land but poor in labour, implements and draught animals with which to farm the land. Black farmers could not own land but could offer the labour, experience, implements and draught animals needed.

11 Although the ravages of apartheid eroded Kas Maine's self-sufficiency, eventually almost completely, it is important to keep in mind that he never became (only) a victim. As Van Onselen points out: "In an industrialising state founded on mineral wealth, which for the first fifty years of its existence devoted most of its effort to rendering African labour cheap, docile and plentiful, Kas Maine retained his economic independence. Kas worked for no man – black or white." Van Onselen *The seed is mine. The life of Kas Maine, a South African sharecropper 1894 – 1985* (1996) Hill and Wang at 3.

his life the minimum core content of the right to food of Kas and his family was threatened in different ways, within the context of different relationships. At different stages in his life he would have held different minimum entitlements against the state and others and they would have borne different minimum obligations.

In the early stages of Kas's economically active life, when the state had not yet intruded to the extent it would later,[12] the only threat to the minimum core content of Kas and his family's right to food (apart from the ravages of nature) was the possibility that a white farmer with whom he had entered into a sharecropping agreement would renege on the agreement before the harvest was in, without an alternative channel of access to food being available. The minimum entitlement implied by the standard of freedom from hunger that Kas had within his sharecropping relationship with different farmers at this stage was simply an entitlement that their agreement be honoured, so that he could gather his harvest and benefit from his share of it. The only minimum entitlement Kas had at this stage against the state in terms of the minimum core content of his right to food was perhaps an entitlement to a legal remedy he could use to protect his position should an agreement fail. A further, "non-core", entitlement would have been an entitlement that the state facilitate access to capital and other resources that would have enabled him to become an independent farmer, not bound to sharecropping agreements for his survival. The only minimum core duty incumbent on the farmers in these relationships was the duty to honour their agreements with Kas – a negative duty (borne by a private party). The minimum core duty incumbent on the state in these relationships was, I suppose, a duty to protect: to provide the necessary regulatory framework and legal remedies to protect the sharecropping agreements (a positive duty borne by the state). More generally there was a ("non-core") duty on the state to provide access to resources that would have enabled Kas to stand on his own feet, free from the dependence on white farmers (again a positive duty).

Later in Kas's life the state intruded directly into his ability to produce food for himself and his family by actively prohibiting

---

12 Although the practice of sharecropping had by this time already been prohibited on the statute books (by the Black Land Act, 1913) the practice was widespread in more marginal agricultural areas and the prohibition was not enforced in the WesternTransvaal were Kas farmed until the late 1930s.

the kind of sharecropping agreements that constituted Kas's only opportunity to generate his own access to food.[13] The minimum core entitlement at play between Kas and the state here was the entitlement to be left alone to exercise his capacity to produce food for himself through the sharecropping agreements. In addition, the background entitlement to access to resources and legal entitlements that would secure Kas's agricultural independence remained. The minimum core duty on the state is the obligation to refrain from interfering with an existing channel of access to food, without providing an alternative source, essentially a negative duty. The non-core positive duty to provide access to resources and entitlements so as to ensure agricultural independence remains.

During the latter stages of Kas's life, when he had become too old to farm effectively for himself and had anyway been relegated to the fringes of South African society by apartheid land and agricultural laws and policies,[14] the entitlement duty relationship implied by the minimum core content of the right to food changes again. Kas now has the entitlement, a positive one, to the provision of food or the means to gain access to food (social assistance grants, for example). The minimum core duty incumbent on the state is the duty to provide food or provide assistance – a positive duty. Alternatively, or in addition, a minimum core obligation lies against Kas's family to provide assistance. The background duty on the state, to facilitate access to resources that would make Kas self-sufficient, now disappears, as there is little self-sufficiency to support in this way.

The point is that I find it difficult to conceive of a way in which we can define in abstract terms the minimum core content of a right such as the right to food so that it has practical worth, particularly when we move within the confines of domestic judicial enforcement of socio-economic rights where rights operate in individualised, context specific arenas. What actually matters in this context are the specific entitlements and specific duties of conduct implied by the minimum standard of freedom from hunger, in real-time, specific situations. These entitlements and duties are not, and cannot be fixed. They are determined by the specific relationship within which they operate, the position of the parties involved in that relationship and the surrounding cir-

---

13 Active efforts to eradicate the practice also in the areas in which Kas farmed had commenced by this time.
14 This would be the period from the mid-1970s to the mid-1980s.

cumstances determining the nature of that relationship, by issues of dependency and self-sufficiency, distribution and relative entitlement, capability and functioning. Every time Kas's personal situation changed, whether because of external circumstances of a political or economic nature, or because of his own waning abilities, the minimum assistance to gain access to food that he could as of right expect from the state changed (qualitatively and quantitatively). If the current South African constitution had been in force during Kas's life and he had brought a claim before a court based on his right to food, the minimum duty that he would have attempted to enforce against the state (or against private actors?) would have been something different at different stages of his life. In South Africa, where the right to food is now justiciable and liable to judicial enforcement in specific, individualized cases, the core content is of necessity a shifting concept.

The idea that a certain basic level of satisfaction of socio-economic rights, its minimum core content, has to be met by the state as a matter of absolute priority is certainly very useful also on the domestic level. The attempts to describe and define that minimum core content and particularly minimum core obligations and entitlements in the abstract are not as useful as they have undoubtedly proven to be on the international level. That is my first point.

3 STRATEGIC CONCERNS

My second point is strategic rather than principled in nature and is aimed, I suppose, at lawyerly activists. It is a point which has been raised by others,[15] in another context (that of international human rights law), but I raise it here because I think it is a particular concern within the framework of judicial enforcement of socio-economic rights inside South Africa.

One of the major aims with the development of the idea of minimum core obligations has been to insulate some part of socio-economic rights from the handy excuses of limited available resources and time constraints allowed states by Article 2(1) of the ICESCR.[16] The South African constitution subjects its socio-eco-

---

15 Bolivar and Gonzalez "Defining the content of economic, social and cultural rights" in Ravindran and Blyberg (eds) *Circle of rights. Economic, social and cultural rights activism: A training resource* (2000) International Human Rights Internship Programme 151 at 156.
16 Article 2(1) requires states to take steps "to the maximum of [their] available resources with a view to progressively achieving the full realisation" of the rights in the Covenant.

nomic rights to limitations similar to those found in the ICESCR.[17] Commentators on the international level have pointed out that defining a minimum core content as somehow subject to a heightened, prioritised level of enforcement might persuade governments that they need only realise the minimum core content of rights and hold no further responsibility for the full realisation of the right. Although this possibility has, I think, been overstated in the international arena, I believe it presents a peculiar danger in the South African context.

Contrary to early rhetoric,[18] South African courts have proven very reticent in their approach to enforcing socio-economic rights. In a series of early decisions the courts have fashioned an inordinately deferential approach to the review of government decisions and policy implicating socio-economic rights.[19] Courts have also consistently opted for a limited rather than a generous interpretation of the scope of provisions entrenching socio-economic rights where a more generous interpretation was a viable alternative.[20]

The conservatism of courts in their approach to socio-economic rights was to be expected – in fact we are forewarned about it by

---

17 Sections 26(2) and 27(2) require the state to take steps "within its available resources" to attain the "progressive realisation" of the rights entrenched in sections 26(1) and 27(1) (the rights to have access to adequate housing, health care services, sufficient food and water, social security and social assistance).

18 See *In re: Certification of the Constitution of the Republic of South Africa, 1996* 1996 (10) BCLR 1253 (CC) 1289C – 1290C in which the Constitutional Court held that the inclusion of socio-economic rights in the Constitution did not violate the principle of separation of powers and that socio-economic rights were at least negatively enforceable against undue invasion from the state.

19 In *Soobramoney v Minister of Health KwaZulu-Natal* 1997 (12) BCLR 1696 (CC), adjudicating a claim indirectly based on the right to have access to adequate housing, the Constitutional Court held that it would require only that a plan be rationally conceived and honestly executed – on a limited interpretation hardly a standard of scrutiny at all. This decision was followed by the Cape High Court in *Grootboom v Oostenberg Municipality* 2000 (3) BCLR 277 (C) in the context of the right to have access to adequate housing. An even more deferential approach was followed by the Cape High Court in *Van Biljon v Minister of Correctional Services* 1997 (4) SA 441 (C) in which the Court held that it had no power to question allocational decisions made by medical experts working within the executive branch.

20 See for instance *Soobramoney v Minister of Health, KwaZulu-Natal* 1997 (12) BCLR 1696 (CC) in which the Constitutional Court held that section 27(3) of the constitution imposed no positive duty on the state to provide emergency medical treatment to the respondent; *Jooste v Botha* 2000 (2) BCLR 187 (T) in which the Transvaal Provincial Division of the High Court intimated that children's right to family, parental or appropriate alternative care (section 28(1)(b) of the constitution) imposed "primarily" negative duties to refrain from interference in existing care on the state, and no positive duties on parents; and *Van Biljon v Minister of Correctional Services* 1997 (4) SA 441 (C) in which the Cape High Court managed to read a resource constraint qualifier into the right of detained persons to adequate medical treatment, despite the fact that no such qualifier is to be found in the text of the constitution.

one of our fellow presenters at this conference, Pierre de Vos.[21] Whatever the cause, South African courts seem intuitively to want to play a rather limited role in the enforcement of socio-economic rights. Against this background I would argue that to introduce the concept of minimum core obligations related to socio-economic rights, as somehow immune to the limitations imposed on the duty to realise other, non-core obligations related to these rights, provides an easy way out for courts already hesitating to enforce the rights. South African courts might "inappropriately latch onto the notion of minimum core content as being the content of an ESC right that is justiciable, and leave the other components to government policies".[22] Strategically it would be wiser to avoid the idea of an "absolute" minimum core content as opposed to a "qualified" rest and rather to focus on the requirement that is expressly posed by the constitution, that the state take reasonable steps to realise socio-economic rights.[23] A standard of reasonableness against which to test government conduct is sufficiently flexible to incorporate the basic normative idea behind the formulation of a minimum core content, that certain basic needs should enjoy preference over more advanced elements of the realisation of socio-economic rights. However, it would do so without ghettoising the remaining elements of the rights.

---

21 Pierre De Vos warned in an early article on socio-economic rights in the South African constitution that it is "by no means assured that the various role-players will truly engage with" the challenge of formulating "innovative and even unorthodox approaches to the enforcement" of socio-economic rights. (De Vos "Pious wishes or directly enforceable human rights?: Social and economic rights in South Africa's 1996 constitution" (1997) 13 *SAJHR* 67 at 68).
22 Bolivar and Gonzalez "Defining the content of economic, social and cultural rights" in Ravindran and Blyberg (eds) *Circle of rights. Economic, social and cultural rights activism: A training resource* (2000) International Human Rights Internship Programme 151 at 156.
23 Section 26(2) (referring to housing), section 27(2) (referring to health care services, food, water and social security and assistance) and section 29(1)(b) (referring to further education) all require that the state take "reasonable measures" to realise the various rights progressively, within available resources.

SOCIAL SECURITY AS A HUMAN RIGHT

Lucie Lamarche

1 INTRODUCTION

Article 9 of the International Covenant on Economic Social and Cultural Rights (ICESCR)[1] provides for everyone's right to social security, including social insurance. The ICESCR's preparatory works are silent about the history of this article and social security is a highly technical domain too often neglected by human rights activists. The very basic question of giving a content to the right to social security has not been addressed by the human rights literature.

In fact, since the adoption of the ICESCR, the implementation and promotion of the right to social security has been seen as the unique task of a specialised agency: the International Labour Organisation (ILO). This paper argues that Article 9 of the ICESCR provides for a more inclusive approach to this right than ILO conventions, although the ILO conventions remain at the center of the process of defining the right to social security.

The first part of this paper offers a normative approach to the right to social security. The second part outlines a more contemporary normative content and proposes a minimum content of

---

1 International Covenant on Economic, Social, and Cultural Rights, *opened for signature* 16 Dec 1966, *entered into force* 3 Jan 1976, 993 UNTS 3 (hereafter the ICESCR).

the right to social security. This analysis suggests that a human rights approach to social security provides indicators that can be used when the time comes to depart from the traditional economics of social protection, in favour of a perspective on the need for social protection that is more consistent with human rights standards. The indicators treat issues related to social security systems, state accountability, and benefits in a modern world where wages can no longer be seen as the universal link to social security. After presenting a proposal for the content of the right to social security, the paper finally looks at clear violations of this right, using actual examples taken from the current context of social exclusion, privatisation and new state commitments to social security as a commodity.

By providing this information and offering these proposals, this paper hopes to stimulate debate concerning the issue of the opportunity for NGOs and civil society, at the local and national levels, to seriously consider social security as a significant way to ensure everyone's right to an adequate standard of living as guaranteed by Article 11 of the ICESCR.

2 AN HISTORICAL PRESENTATION OF THE RIGHT TO SOCIAL SECURITY

When social security is considered,[2] the ILO's work and the standards it has developed remain the most important source of interpretation and definition of the right to social security. This section introduces readers to the right to social security, as it has evolved through the adoption of numerous ILO conventions since the beginning of the 20th century. The purpose here is not to provide an exhaustive analysis of all the conventions but to emphasize the more significant ones in order to highlight the classic meaning of the right to social security. This presentation will be preceded by a brief introduction to the ILO's mandate, mission and methods of work, as well as to the importance of social security conventions in the universe of 183 different conventions and 191 recommendations so far adopted[3] by the ILO. These conventions and recommendations form the body of international law adopted by the ILO since its creation in 1919.

---

2   The expression "social security" must be distinguished from other expressions such as "social protection" or "social assistance". We will come back to this issue later.
3   Through July 2001.

2.1 ILO and the Right to Social Security

The ILO was born out of a concern that is of great relevance today. As the First World War ended, states, as well as unions and employers' representatives, recognised that peace could not be achieved without sufficient attention to conditions for social justice. Part XIII of the Treaty of Versailles constitutes the foundation of the ILO. The originality of the ILO is that at all decision-making levels, Member States, as well as employer and union representatives, were given voting seats. As provided in Article 3 of the ILO Constitution, the International Conference on Labour (the legislative body of the ILO), is composed of four representatives from each member state: two of them are state delegates, and the other two represent employers and workers. This structure, unique at the international level, is known as the ILO tripartite structure.

The first generation of conventions adopted by the International Labour Conference concerned labour conditions. Soon, however, the Conference adopted a group of conventions aimed at committing States to engage themselves in the creation and improvement of national mechanisms protecting workers from industrial and social risks.[4] The notion of "social risk" itself is well defined by those first conventions: sickness and medical care, unemployment, old age benefits, workers' compensation, family and maternity benefits, disability, and survivor's benefits. The right to social security was developed in a context in which industrial work predominated in Europe and the male industrial worker, as the family breadwinner, was seen as the first direct beneficiary of this right. It should be noted that social insurance is different from social security; social insurance refers to a technique of providing social security benefits to workers and their families at the national level. We will return to the nature of states' obligations by examining the basic reference in the field of social security: Convention 102 on Social Security (minimum standards) adopted in 1952.

---

[4] See ILO Conventions 17 and 18 on Workmen's Compensation adopted in 1925, Conventions 24 and 25 on Sickness Insurance adopted in 1927, Conventions 35 and 40 on Old Age, Invalidity and Survivor's Insurance adopted in 1933 and Convention 44 on Unemployment Provision adopted in 1934. On-line at:
http://ilolex.ilo.ch:1567/public/english/docs/convdisp.htm .

2.2 The Nature of ILO Social Security Conventions

The ILO has so far adopted 183 conventions. None of them has been widely ratified, and some have been given a more fundamental status than others. Because each convention is the result of a specific initiative based on a consensus concerning the urgency of addressing a particular labour issue, all ILO Conventions theoretically have equal value. Nevertheless, a careful reading of the ILO's mission shows a more complex reality. The Constitution affirms that freedom of expression and association constitute the fundamental principles on which the ILO is based. These principles are supported by others, including the well-known principle that "labor is not a commodity" and an affirmation of the need to launch a war against want to promote the common welfare.

2.3 The Right to Social Security According to the ILO

Convention 102 on Social Security (minimum standards), adopted by the ILO in 1952, does not provide a single definition of social security. This definition must be construed from various parts of the Convention, each one addressing one of the nine social risks that it covers. In order to ratify Convention 102,[5] an ILO Member State is obliged to comply, at the time of ratification, with at least three of the following parts of the Convention: medical care, sickness benefits, unemployment benefits, old age benefits, workers' compensation, family, disability, maternity and survivors' benefits. From among these enumerated risks, at least one provision concerning unemployment, old age, workers' compensation, disability or survivors' benefits must be accepted. Each part of the Convention provides specific standards aimed at guaranteeing the benefit of social protection to protected classes of persons, as well as a certain level of benefits. In all cases, a ratifying Member State must comply with certain general parts of the Convention, including Part XI, which provides for periodic payments of social security. Since the adoption of Convention 102,

---

5 Up to now, 40 States have ratified Convention 102, including more recently Congo (1987), Slovenia (1992), Slovakia (1993), Croatia (1991), Bosnia and Herzegovina (1993), the Czech republic (1993), Portugal (1994), the former Republic of Macedonia (1991) and Cyprus (1991). Mexico and Peru ratified the Convention in 1961.

subsequent international and regional social security instruments[6] have revolved around those three basic concepts: enlarging the protected classes of persons or workers, upgrading the level and duration of benefits, and guaranteeing the need, except in the case of medical care, for periodic social security payments.

Convention 102 was enriched by the subsequent adoption of some specific social security conventions, such as Convention 128 on Invalidity, Old Age and Survivors' Benefits (1967) and Convention 130 on Medical Care and Sickness Benefits (1969). Those conventions are aimed at raising the requirements for the categories of protected persons as well as the level of protection provided by national social security schemes covering these specific risks. This is why, for example, Article 44 of Convention 128 on Invalidity, Old Age and Survivors' Benefits states that the ratification of this Convention constitutes *ipso iure* a denunciation of previous conventions concerning the same social risk, provided that the relevant part of Convention 128 has been accepted. Article 74 of Convention 102 states that this Convention may not be regarded as a revision of any convention adopted previously. To the contrary, Convention 102 provides a general framework, to be enriched by the adoption of subsequent conventions related to specific risks. It can only be revised by subsequent conventions adopted and ratified by the same Member State.

In view of the level of development in some less industrialised countries in the 1950s, Convention 102 was designed to be a flexible human rights instrument. Article 3 of Convention 102 allows a state, in the case of insufficient financial or medical capacity, to ratify the Convention and avail itself of temporarily less stringent conditions, concerning the duration of benefits and categories of protected persons. The requirement of periodic payments is not affected.

(a) *Protected classes of persons*
In order to ratify Convention 102, an ILO Member State must be able to demonstrate for each provision of the Convention that it accepts, that a certain percentage of specified population groups is already protected from the accepted social risk. The categories are as follows: prescribed classes of employees constituting a certain percentage of all employees; prescribed classes of the economically

---

6   Except for Convention 168 on Employment Promotion and Protection against Unemployment (1988). See below, sub-section 4.2.

active population, including their wives [sic] and children, constituting a certain percentage of all residents, OR all residents according to a means test if the benefit meets the level stated in the Convention. In the second case, the programme or scheme must not deprive the beneficiary and his wife or children of what is necessary to maintain health and decency. For example, Convention 102 specifies that in the case of sickness benefits, it is deemed sufficient if the total amount of benefits paid exceeds by at least 30 percent the amount obtained by paying a percentage of unskilled labourers' wages in benefits when the state uses as a reference the economically active population.

All social security conventions adopted by the ILO show a constant tension between Member States and the organisation with regard to defining protected classes of persons. In the process of drafting a convention, the ILO has always tried to expand the categories of persons covered in order to reach the ultimate goal of social security conventions, which is universal coverage. Member States for their part have always succeeded in limiting the prescribed categories to a percentage of waged workers or residents.[7]

For example, Section 15 of Convention 102 states that sickness benefits are to be made available to prescribed categories of workers, representing 50 percent of all workers, OR to prescribed categories of the active population, representing 20 percent of all residents, OR to all residents according to a means test. Section 29 of the Convention, which provides for old age benefits, stipulates nearly the same requirement of coverage except that it does not apply a lower limit for benefits to a system that would satisfy the Convention requirement on the basis of a means test.

Convention 130 on Medical Care and Sickness Benefits and Convention 128 on Invalidity, Old Age and Survivors' Benefits rely on the same system but increase the level of protection. For example, Convention 130 provides that ALL paid workers, OR prescribed categories of the economically active population representing 75 percent of this population, OR all residents, subject to a means test, should benefit from sickness benefit insurance. Convention 128 contains the same requirement for old age benefits.

---

7   See, for example, the discussion that preceded the adoption of Convention 128 about the prescribed percentage of the population to be covered for the purpose of ratifying the Convention; Report V(I), 50th Session, 1966, at 12-13 and Report V(2) at 25-27. These reports and discussions also clearly illustrate that even at the time, States preferred a system based on prescribed categories of workers to any other, as it authorized them to not consider in their calculations atypical, marginal and part-time workers. But again, this strategy does not mean that social security schemes, in order to respect Convention 102 requirements, can be designed to only benefit workers.

Articles 15(d) and 27(d) of Convention 102 reduce the population coverage requirement for less developed countries. Let us recall that these exceptions, aimed at facilitating the ratification of the instrument, never affect the general obligation of the ratifying State to offer periodic benefits to the persons protected by a social security programme.

The assumptions under which Convention 102, as well as previous and subsequent international and regional social security conventions, was designed must be stressed here. First, social security conventions are "male" conventions, women often being described as the "wife of". Although women workers may of course be included in categories of workers used to establish classes of protected persons, the constant reference to the male industrial worker for various technical reasons, such as the level of benefits, clearly "leaves the women at home". Second, the method favoured by many states to establish levels of coverage – declaring that a national scheme protects a certain percentage of workers – permits the state to avoid the problems of atypical and part-time work, which is often gendered in industrial societies.

Thirdly, in cases in which Member States opt for the "all residents" coverage calculation for the purpose of ratifying Convention 102, the adequacy of the coverage would then be assessed by reference to industrial wages to determine the number of beneficiaries to be included, to ensure that a regime meets the standard of Convention 102. Finally, this Convention, as well as many other social security conventions at the international and regional levels, establishes a specific benchmark aimed at determining the capacity of a social security scheme to cover the needs of an industrial male worker and his family, calculated as a percentage of the industrial wages of either a skilled or unskilled labourer.

The goals of Convention 102 as an international standard for the right to social security must be kept in mind: the nine identified social risks for which social security benefits were to be provided are all aimed at realising a person's right to live a healthy life in decent conditions. The highest level of implementation of the right to social security means that this right must be effectively accessible to all. Social security's ability to provide the elements of a decent standard of living remains a clear advantage over other possible approaches aimed at realising the latter right.

Now that the working environment has changed, and the social exclusion process has started to appear everywhere in the world, Convention 102 might represent a useful benchmark describing the minimal or core content of the right to social security. However, its structure shows how difficult it is to conceptualise social security outside the industrial framework, unless a system relies on the lower option provided by Convention 102, which is the "all residents" category.

(b) *The level of benefits*
The technique used by Convention 102, as well as by subsequent social security conventions, is to make the level of benefits dependent on the category of the population covered. For example, Section 16 of Convention 102 provides that, when employees or the economically active population are chosen as a reference, the periodic health benefit will cover at least 45 percent of previous earnings (including family allowances) if those earnings are not lower than the wages of a male skilled manual worker.[8] If the category is the economically active population, the benefit must correspond to at least 45 percent of the wages of an unskilled worker deemed to have a wife and two children in his charge. If the reference base is all residents, the benefits must be calculated in a manner that will ensure decent living conditions for the beneficiary's family. These conditions cannot correspond to less than 45 percent of the wages of the ordinary adult male labourer. This level was increased from 45 to 60 percent by Articles 22, 23 and 24 of Convention 130 on Medical Care and Sickness Benefits (1969).

In the case of old age benefits, Article 29 of Convention 102 provides a benefit (based on certain conditions of contributing periods that provide the right to the benefit), of 40 percent, either of previous wages or of the average wages of skilled or unskilled workers, depending on how the protected classes of persons are determined.

In many ways, Convention 102 answers the question of what constitutes a social security benefit guaranteeing a decent standard of living. The proposal, though, is two-tiered and depends on the basis on which the coverage of a specific social risk is designed: whether by categories of workers (e.g., civil servants, industrial or service workers), or all by residents. The latter formulation guarantees a benefit level much closer to a basic income, while the former allows for a flexible level of benefits calculated on the basis of average industrial gains (skilled and unskilled). In both cases, wages rather than needs are considered, as it is

---

8   See Article 65 of Convention 102.

assumed that negotiated wages are already related to the needs of a working family.

Although the objection may be raised that, in a growing number of situations, the reference to wages for the purpose of guaranteeing a decent level of existence is not appropriate, Convention 102 provides a legal model aimed at avoiding the consequences of political interference over the definition of what is appropriate. The reference to wages, even in the case of regimes covering all residents against some social risks, is seen as a long-term and stable legal commitment that member states must respect. In Convention 102 wages are a means of implementing a social right as well as a guarantee against the ad hoc re-definition of the content of a right. The same cannot be said in regard to concepts such as social indicators or other benchmarks that offer no stable or binding approach to the implementation of a right.[9] Finally, in choosing to use wages as a reference, the model does not limit the requirements of a decent living to the satisfaction of basic needs.

2.4 Choice of Social Security Systems

Sections 71 and 72 of Convention 102 list the conditions a national social security scheme must meet in order to qualify as an acceptable system for the purpose of ratifying the Convention. Section 71(1) requires that the costs of benefits and administration be borne collectively through insurance contributions or taxation in a manner that avoids hardship to persons of limited means; section 71(2) states that the total of insurance contributions borne by employees must not exceed 50 percent of the total of a protected employee's financial resources; section 71(3) provides for a Member State to accept general responsibility for the due provision of benefits.

Many different systems aimed at providing social protection may be considered social security systems in accordance with Convention 102, even though they are not social insurance programmes. Sections 71 and 72 of the Convention put much greater emphasis on the characteristics of such a system than on the type of system itself. Four components must be respected: 1) costs to

---

9   For a critique of these tools, see Barsh *Measuring human rights : Problems of methodology and purpose* (1993) 15 *Hum Rts Q* 87.

the employees (through contributions or other means) must not be excessive; 2) responsibility must be taken by the public authority for the economic health of the system and its administration; 3) beneficiaries must participate in the administration of the system; and 4) the system must provide for the right to appeal in case of disagreement.

In addition, and for the purpose of verifying compliance with the different parts of the Convention, with the exception of workers' compensation and family benefits, coverage provided by non-compulsory insurance may be taken into account[10] (Section 6) if this means of insurance is supervised by public authority, jointly administered by employees and employers, and it covers a substantial number of low-waged workers. All State Parties to Convention 102 are bound by all sections of Part XIII of the Convention. Guarantees provided in this Part are thus unavoidable, and aimed at protecting beneficiaries, the better-off as well as the less-privileged ones, if the chosen method for describing the protected classes of persons includes categories other than workers or members of the active population.

The human right to social security requires a system of social benefits supervised, if not managed, by public authorities that does not disproportionately put at risk beneficiaries' available income, and that guarantees a family a decent living. For this guarantee to be effective, payments must be periodic. These requirements, although simple, are nevertheless at the heart of the privatisation process now underway in many countries, especially in the case of pensions.

2.5 Conclusion

One of the major problems surrounding social security instruments is not so much their lack of relevance for less developed – or transitional – countries, but the potential of these conventions for social exclusion. Indeed, a state may declare that its national scheme protects an acceptable percentage of protected classes of workers, but this leaves out many categories of the population such as female atypical workers, non-industrial workers, the self-employed and workers in the informal sector, who often exercise survival economic activities. Social security conventions contain

---

10 See Article 6 of Convention 102.

their own potential for discrimination, as is widely acknowledged. As developed by social security instruments, the right to social security can be described as a paradox: designed to eventually attain universality of coverage, it authorises ratifying members to halt progress at the threshold of modern forms of exclusion. On the other hand, it must be said that only social security conventions incorporate technical benchmarks aimed at guaranteeing the content of an economic right (level of benefit and duration of benefit). This is a useful safeguard, since it prevents states from claiming that any solution offered as a strategy to fight poverty and exclusion contributes to the implementation of the right to social security.

Although international social security conventions have never been widely ratified, they have influenced all developments related to social protection during the last century. This raises two questions: may social security instruments be considered when assessing, in a modern context, the right to social security as guaranteed by more universal instruments such as the ICESCR? And if so, what benchmarks can they usefully provide in doing so? The following section more specifically addresses these questions by focusing on the right to social security as articulated in Section 9 of the ICESCR.

3 VIOLATIONS OF THE RIGHT TO SOCIAL SECURITY: AN OPERATIONAL FRAMEWORK

Violations of the right to social security can only be identified by means of a common understanding of the content of this right. This is why a sub-section looking more specifically at Section 9 of the ICESCR will be preceded by some proposals aimed at determining the right to social security in the broad context of this universal human rights instrument. We will also examine the issue of the minimum content of this right. In doing so, we seek to demonstrate that ILO Conventions on social security, although a central source of interpretation, do not limit a broader conceptualisation of this right. But before addressing such issues, we must distinguish between the concepts of social security and social protection in a more universal context.

3.1 Social Security, Social Protection or Social Assistance?

In 1995, the International Social Security Association effectively summarised contemporary problems confronting the model of social security.[11] Cutbacks in benefits, privatisation of systems, the need for efficient protections in transitional countries, and the impact of structural adjustment programmes in developing countries were amongst them. The Council of Europe recently completed its Human Dignity and Social Exclusion Project (HDSE) and issued its final report.[12] This report, which takes into account realities in Western as well as Eastern European countries, emphasises the fact that social exclusion is not only the result of exposure to a set of social and economic risks. It is also about the uncertainty that characterises the present time (globalisation, transition, technical change) in a context in which the individualisation of responsibility regarding social risks produces negative effects and puts into question the "Triple A" social security model.[13] In any case, an analysis that examines the mechanisms of social security may show how the characteristics of this historical answer to social protection can be revisited.

This analysis, however, does not take into account the reality for those who are excluded from any benefit simply because of the way social security programmes are too often designed. These groups include workers in the informal sector, self-employed women, and other marginalized groups.

In this last case, as well as in the case of extreme poverty, many experts and international associations are tempted to talk more about the need for social protection than the need to consider efficient social security programmes. Social protection has been the historic goal of social security regimes, which are seen as a specific means of promoting social protection. The increasing poverty around the world governs the quest for a comprehensive approach to both social protection and social security. Such an

---

11 See Association internationale de sécurité sociale, 25ième Assemblée générale, novembre 1995, Nusa Dua, *Développements et tendances de la sécurité sociale dans le monde, 1993-1995, La sécurité sociale dans les années quatre-vingt-dix: la nécessité du changement.* Rapport I.

12 *The Human Dignity and Social Exclusion Project (HDSE) – Research opportunity and risk : trends of social exclusion in Europe* (April 1998) Katherine Duffy (De Montfort University, Leicester, UK) Director of Research for the Council of Europe – Project on Human Dignity and Social Exclusion, on line: http://www.coe.fr/dase/en/cohesion/inclus/freport.htm.

13 "Triple A" stands for accountability, affordability and accessibility of social security protection.

approach would facilitate social cohesion and inclusion and protect individuals from social risks. As a human right, social security can contribute to social protection by providing useful benchmarks to assess how the economic, political and ideological initiatives arising from the need for social protection contribute to respect for human rights, including the right to social security.

The connection between social protection and social security is crucial, since some international institutions, such as the World Bank, do not recognise social protection as a human right. Even when international financial institutions are willing to admit how detrimental economic restructuring programs have been, the successive adjustment programmes that followed the era of the Washington Consensus barely paid lip service to the concept of social protection:

> The Washington Consensus has supported social policies that rely on three main pillars: growth-led poverty reduction, targeting, and private sector participation in the delivery of private services. This strategy showed some loose ends. [...]. Social safety nets are needed in periods of macroeconomic crisis leading to high unemployment cuts in real wages and decline in real income of the poor. The social safety nets may comprise policies such as emergency employment programs, food distribution to children and vulnerable groups and schemes of minimum income support.[14]

This approach obviously confuses charity and human rights. In addition, it shows a total disdain for social protection and social security as tools capable of providing comprehensive answers to these same problems. It is worth comparing such a brutal neglect of the need for reliable social protection systems with the ILO's proposal for social protection systems that work for all. Since the beginning of the 1990s the ILO Social Security division has been given a mandate by the International Labour Conference to search for solutions that can include "other workers" in a social protection device. Naturally, the ILO used the principles of social security as a human right to govern its work.[15] Wouter Van Ginneken's proposal shows how flexible the right to social security can be when

---

14 See World Bank Policy Research Working Paper WPS 2091, December 1998, *Beyond unequal development: An overview*, Andrés Solimano at 28-29.
15 See Van Ginneken *Social security for the informal sector: Issues, options and tasks ahead* (1996) ILO, on-line at: http://www.ilo.org/public/english/110secso/techmeet/wouter2.htm.

confronted by the need for social protection. At the same time, it shows how useful the social security model is when social protection is faced with the need for human rights safeguards.

First, the ILO expert proposes an inclusive definition of social security that addresses principles as well as needs. The model suggests the following characteristics as forming the essentials of social security in a universal context:
- the provision of benefits to households and individuals;
- through public or collective arrangements;
- aimed at protecting against low or declining living standards;
- and arising from a number of basic risks and needs.

These characteristics are nothing new, as they express the basics of ILO Convention 102 without the reference to wages as a benchmark for implementation.

Next, the Social Security Division identifies the following social security needs as they are perceived by informal sector workers:
- health care costs (not only to help them meet large expenditures but also to improve the cost effectiveness of current expenditures);
- survivors' benefits (including funeral costs);
- disability benefits;
- maternity and child care benefits.

These represent four of the risks already provided for by Convention 102. Their novelty probably resides in the subjective hierarchy amongst all risks as established by beneficiaries themselves.

The Social Security Division then identified two fundamental requirements for setting up a successful social insurance scheme:
- the existence of an association based on trust;
- an administration that is capable of collecting contributions and providing benefits.

It is worth noting the crucial importance of the collective aspect of the solutions sought as well as the emphasis placed on the competence of any administrative system responsible for providing benefits.

Lastly, van Ginneken's team proposes benchmarks for evaluating existing schemes in the light of criteria previously established:
- Improving access to basic health services by means of a government-financed supply of services, in terms of type of

service (prevention, promotion and health care) in an equitable manner (access) which considers the extent of co-payments (formal and informal).
- Promoting self-financed social insurance[16] after having identified the limits and the viability of public and private insurance schemes.
- Evaluating existing programmes in terms of administrative costs per beneficiary. This concerns horizontal (percentage of the poor covered) as well as vertical (percentage of the poor covered within the total group of beneficiaries) efficiency.
- Analysing the cost-effectiveness of social security programmes, compared to other anti-poverty programmes, such as employment guarantee schemes and food subsidies to consumers.
- Analysing the role of social assistance programmes and their relationship to other anti-poverty measures.
- Extending formal sector social security schemes.

These criteria address issues larger than those initially considered when Convention 102 was adopted. They are aimed at paying attention to the "haves" as well as the "have nots". As the recent Initiative launched by the International Social Security Association suggests,[17] social security is about strengthening the "security" in social security. Implicit in the analysis suggested by van Ginneken is a multi-tiered approach to social security that may seriously depart from Convention 102 in some aspects with respect to protecting workers in the informal sector or all members of the population.

The new call to draw on private and community capabilities to promote human rights, such as the right to health or social security, is experimental. Nevertheless, once again the issue of the "haves" and the "have nots" is at stake, this time at the local level. Because it is not clear whether these micro models are promoted by default or by choice, the question is again raised how the more deprived elements of a community can be taken care of, when privatising social security at the local level is viewed as an answer to the limited public capability to do so. Are we not then back to

---

16 See, for example, *The social security program of the Self-Employed Women's Association*, Ahmedabad, India, on-line: http://www.ilo.org/public/english/110secso/step/frame.htm.
17 See International Social Security Initiative, *Strengthening the security in social security*, International Social Security Association (ISSA), on-line at: http://www.issa.int/engl/homef.htm.

solutions as ineffective as the current anti-poverty programmes promoted by the international financial institutions, which are seen as solutions of last resort for the local poor? No one has ever claimed that social security, as prescribed by Convention 102, works everywhere around the world. But it is not at all clear that the market can do better.

Supplementary initiatives aimed at providing what formal social security schemes cannot put at risk the more central state commitment that Convention 102 requires: public supervision, for which user participation and management are a substitute. From a human rights perspective, the problem is not so much the promotion of private or community initiatives as the fact that these initiatives are evolving in an environment without legal standards. Legal analyses, as well as analyses of the Bamako and Abidjan initiatives, show that participants in all cases recognise the need for legal support. The type of support needed is like the safeguards in place for commercial law and consumer protection. In the event that such an approach becomes viable, the question then becomes: what about public accountability for those who are already excluded from any insurance benefit? Returning the "have nots" to the law of contracts and corporations seems a bit odd, as further analysis of privatised pensions plans will show in Section 3. This creates an even bigger conceptual challenge for human rights monitoring bodies.

Proposals to uncouple the state – the body ultimately responsible for implementing the right to social security – from the local market tend to eliminate the variety of options provided by Convention 102, such as minimum protection for all members of the population. These proposals should consider reconnecting micro markets and the state by means of laws or guidelines guaranteeing non-discrimination in these new initiatives, as well as human rights accountability.

Often, developments in the field of social security do not come to the attention of human rights activists and experts. In view of these realities, what does Article 9 of the ICESCR mean?

3.2 Article 9 of the ICESCR and the Right to Social Security

Much has already been said about the structure of the ICESCR, although one important issue must be raised again here. Article 2 of the ICESCR provides for a general undertaking by States parties

for continuous improvement of the level of realisation of each right guaranteed by the Covenant, while simultaneously measuring the different levels of realisation against the available resources at the national level. When applied to Article 9 of the ICESCR, which guarantees the right to social security, the commitment articulated in Article 2 presents quite a challenge. Indeed, and at the risk of oversimplifying issues related to social protection around the world, the problems that revolve around the realisation of the right to social security can be classified into four different categories. There are:

- countries where social security regimes simply do not exist and never did;
- countries where existing social security regimes are crumbling because of their inability either to pay the statutory benefits or ensure the essential mechanisms aimed at guaranteeing such benefits (insufficient contribution basis, for example);
- countries where the social security system itself has been partially or totally transferred to the private sector (especially in the case of pension benefits), leading to more exclusion and uncertainty for beneficiaries; and
- finally, in the more developed countries, cases in which social security systems and functions are being fundamentally transformed, thereby generating fewer cash benefits, and more exclusion and poverty.

In this last case, the changes are strongly influenced by the economic and ethical ideology of a need for more active social protection measures, implying that the passive right to cash benefits is the wrong strategy. If in general, states claim that they can no longer afford the cost of social security benefits, the evidence shows that an increasing percentage of available social security funds is being spent on measures other than cash benefits. Some countries even claim that by doing so, they consider the right to vocational training or education, for example, to have a higher priority than the right to social security. From a human rights perspective, even the most optimistic analysis of this strategy would lead one to conclusions about the transitory nature of the right to social security. The transitory nature of unemployment was once a reality as well but we know that is not the case anymore. As for other benefits, such as pensions, a strange coincidence often occurs. States claim that they cannot afford the cost of the current defined benefits provided by statutory regimes, while simultaneously allowing private companies to operate with an increasing amount of savings made available through tax schemes aimed at facilitating retirement.

Articles 2 and 9 of the ICESCR must address non-realisation of the right to social security, as well as its progressive regression, or transformation and regression. Many scholars and activists express doubts about the legal feasibility of making progressive realisation of all rights guaranteed by the Covenant the central commitment of states parties. In the case of social security, experience shows that this basic commitment can serve to illustrate the different forms of regression or to examine through a human rights lens the objectives and the results of the transformation of social security systems.

Together with Article 11 of the ICESCR, Article 9 expresses a central dimension of social protection schemes at the national level. In many cases, States parties to the ICESCR claim that, although social security programmes do suffer from regression, states still comply with Article 11 of the Covenant by offering a variety of ways to implement everyone's right to an adequate standard of living. This proposal brings us back to the old social security/social assistance debate, as raised at the ILO and the Council of Europe. It is well to remember that resistance to the social assistance model was largely based on the lack of procedural or substantive guarantees attached to its exercise, causing it to be seen as a residual right.

An increasing number of NGOs report to the CESCR on human rights violations stemming from social protection systems. Typically, the Committee will request additional information from the state party, or will criticise the state for tolerating the prejudicial effects resulting from the cutbacks and transformations. Often, the criticism will be based on the following:

- cuts and transformations in the field of social protection lead to highly discriminatory and exclusionary results;
- these transformations of social protection systems often constitute a violation of the state's general obligation to achieve progressively the full realisation of all rights guaranteed by the Covenant; and
- new forms of social exclusion are an expression of numerous violations of everyone's right to an adequate standard of living for oneself and one's family, including adequate food, clothing and housing, and to the continuous improvement of living conditions, as stipulated in Article 11 of the Covenant.[18]

---

18 See, for example *Concluding observations of the Committee on Economic, Social and Cultural Rights: Canada*. 10/12/98,E/C.12/1/Add.31 10 December1998.

In certain cases, specific references to violations of the right to social security will be raised.[19]

In fact, addressing specific violations of the right to social security more frequently would be of strategic interest because the right to social security, as opposed to the right to an adequate standard of living in Article 11 of the ICESCR, contains its own set of technical, although flexible, standards aimed at guaranteeing the right. In other words, many technical characteristics of the right to social security provide effective benchmarks for interpreting a state's obligation to protect, promote and fulfil the right to an adequate standard of living in a non-regressive manner, and many existing social protection regimes show characteristics of a social security regime. As an indicator, it may be said that only purely private protection or systems that only provide for means-tested benefits clearly fall in the category of social assistance programs. In developed countries, these programs, although still in force, are rapidly declining and are being replaced by tax benefits or credits for the poor. In developing countries, a risk-by-risk approach is now favoured, although not always in a manner that respects the right to social security.

The Maastricht Guidelines[20] broadly identified actions or omissions of states that qualify as economic and social rights violations. Based on these principles, the classification that follows intends to contribute to a future discussion on public decisions that constitute violations of the human right to social security. This classification issues from the "obligation of conduct/obligation of result" model in the Maastricht Guidelines:

(a) *Positive Obligation of the State Parties to the ICESCR to Promote the Right to Social Security as an Obligation of Conduct:*
- States must maintain a comprehensive social security regime regulated by statute and supervised by a participatory public body at the national level;
- States are to make progress toward a mixed system of social security made up of public, autonomous or semi-public regimes dedicated, inter alia, to informal and self-employed workers;

---

19 Such as in the case of Peru. See *Concluding observations of the Committee on Economic, Social and Cultural Rights: Peru*.16/05/97. E/C.12/1/Add.14 (Concluding Observations/Comments), para 40, relating to the system of pensions.

20 See «The Maastricht Guidelines on Violations of Economic, Social and Cultural Rights», (1998) 20 *Hum. Rts. Q.* 691.

- States must guarantee through all available means that such regimes (public, mixed, community-based or private) never, as a consequence of their interdependency, exclude basic social risks as seen by the beneficiaries themselves and identified by the ILO: basic health services and sickness benefits, survivors' benefits and maternity benefits.

(b) *Positive Obligation of the State Parties to the ICESCR to Promote the Right to Social Security as an Obligation of Result*
- States must foster the existence, at the national level, of an independent bureau or service whose mandate is to monitor the efficiency of strategies aimed at protecting persons against social risks at the national, professional and local levels. Data must be made available on such questions as who contributes, the frequency of contributions, the minimal contributions needed to guarantee benefits in the event of occurrence of the risk, and the groups (for example, based on national origin, sex or age) who have reduced or no access to the system;
- When implementing new laws aimed at partially or totally promoting community or privatised social security schemes, states must adopt appropriate legal standards guaranteeing that beneficiaries who contribute to these schemes on a voluntary or compulsory basis will not be deprived of the effective protection of anti-discrimination standards provided in the constitution or the law or of their right of access to justice on grounds of discrimination;
- If a state passed a statute aimed at privatising social insurance schemes or devolving the responsibility to deliver social security services to the regional or local level, in order to respect human rights, the statute must include a provision creating a public regulatory body that will, in addition to auditing the insurance or trust funds, propose and monitor regulations providing for a core care or core benefits coverage with which all service providers will comply, whether they are providing cash benefits or services.

This model provides useful safeguards against the regressive movement observed in the field of social security. But it does not directly address the issue of progressive implementation. This suggests a preliminary question that must be asked. Is it relevant to continue to conceptualise social security risk by risk, at the cost of

of adding newly identified social risks, if necessary? We believe that the risk-by-risk approach is still appropriate. Methodologically, this traditional ILO approach to risk reinforces the human rights analysis by raising questions for each risk concerning the appropriate system and the role of the State in maintaining these systems, democratic participation in the management of these systems, the appropriate method for contributing to social funds, and finally, the adequacy of the benefits provided. In addition, a risk-by-risk approach facilitates control of discriminatory effects.

Finally, the risk-by-risk approach increases state accountability because it cannot be claimed or assumed that more general patterns of social assistance, tax credits or basic income implicitly cover all costs related to human dignity. The "risk by risk" model, therefore, contributes to the progressive implementation of the right to social security.

The risk-by-risk approach is derived from existing social security models or initiatives, whether public or community-oriented. It clearly rejects the private model or, more precisely, suggests that the "for profit" model offers little or no business interest when designed in a manner that respects the human rights framework. The case of *terra incognita* still has to be addressed. What about extremely poor countries or those countries in which social security patterns do not benefit from legal or administrative tradition or a strong economic foundation? The question in these cases is: shall we renounce Article 9 of the ICESCR, or does the right to social security have a minimal content subject to immediate realisation or immediate commitment from a state, as provided by General Comment 3, adopted by the CESCR in 1990?

3.3 The minimum content of the right to social security

What are the minimum state obligations with respect to the right to social security? First, it must be stressed that the right to social security, as guaranteed in the ICESCR, makes no reference to the ILO conventions on social security. Although it is important not to depart from its historic roots to understand this right, it is nevertheless possible to offer a minimal definition that is more flexible than the one proposed in ILO Conventions. This flexibility would respect the urgency, as well as the limited means, of States with obligations to implement the right to social security. As well, by clarifying the minimal content of the right to social security, a useful framework is made available to financial institutions, donors, human rights agencies and NGOs working in the field. It seems to us that five guiding principles should influence the definition of the minimal and immediate content of the right to social security in such a context:

- **the model:** social security, as a human right and not a commodity, relies on collective funding. This can be of different types: public, professional, community, private (if risks are assessed on the basis of a determined group and benefits paid to this group) or even mixed. In all cases, it is a basic and minimal requirement of the right that it be supervised by an independent, participatory and regulated body;
- **contributions and benefits:** notwithstanding how small or minimal the benefit is, it must be defined in advance, along with contributions that do not exceed a reasonable percentage of available income, whatever its source. Social security as a right reflects the human need for predictability and security;
- **risks:** according to the principle of the interdependency of all human rights and in order to implement the right to social security as well as the right to an adequate standard of living in Article 11 of the ICESCR, risks related to health care, sickness benefits, survivors' benefits and maternity benefits should be part of a priority basket of protected risks;
- **coverage:** states are to undertake negotiations with civil society aimed at guaranteeing social security for all, including the self-employed, rural workers, and workers in the informal sector. Provision must be made for periods of time when the insured person, family or group is not able to contribute to the system. In all cases, social security programmes should be subject by law to such a requirement;
- **discrimination:** in accordance with General Comment 9, adopted by the CESCR,[21] and in view of the fundamental nature of the right to be protected from discrimination, states will:
  - create an advisory body whose mandate is to identify direct and indirect discriminatory effects of the social security system and to suggest ways of implementing more inclusive patterns;

---

21 See *General Comment No. 9: The domestic application of the Covenant* (1999) UN Doc E/C.12/1998/24.

- guarantee that human rights codes will apply to all dimensions of the social security system. The right to benefit equally from social security will include protection from discrimination based on source of income.

The feasibility of this minimal social security scheme relies heavily on the state's ability to respect the principles of sound governance. But the causal link between good governance and respect for all human rights is obvious in all cases. The case of social security is perhaps more of a challenge, as more and more members of civil society are tempted to believe that the private sector (both profit and non-profit) can deliver "social risks" products more efficiently than the state. Therefore, they conceptualise social protection *en marge* of the state. No convincing evidence has been produced so far to show the viability of this approach. Finally, it must be remembered that the role of the State is, above all, regulatory. The State does not have to, and in many cases, cannot, implement social security schemes by itself. The choices are numerous and to be nationally determined.

3.4 Conclusion

As we have said, many different systems of social protection in fact show characteristics of social security systems. Accordingly, and keeping in mind the complexity of Article 2 of the ICESCR, in order to qualify as a human rights tool aimed at guaranteeing human dignity, these systems should least meet the standards set forth in the preceding section. If not, we suggest that the absence of these characteristics should be described as a core violation of the right to social security. In the same manner, non-existent systems or systems that can be seen as social assistance programmes (means-tested or charity-driven) will be seen *a priori* as constituting an obstacle to the implementation of the right to social security. Finally, in the case of extremely poor countries, attempts made by the civil society to introduce income protection mechanisms, as well as basic health care systems, could take inspiration from the proposal regarding the minimum content of the right to social security when looking for local solutions aimed at fighting social exclusion and poverty.

We have also suggested that the notion of progressive implementation provided in Article 2 of the ICESCR should be given due attention, as it provides a dynamic approach for dealing with cases in which social security regimes have suffered significant regression. In this last case, the concept of obligations of conduct and obligations of result in the Maastricht Guidelines can be helpful in demonstrating how changes in national social protection strategies may be human rights violations.

A vague statement about the need for an effective social protection system is not enough to save social security as a human right from becoming a commodity amongst others. Some recent transformations clearly illustrate this danger, as the last section of this paper will try to demonstrate.

4 VIOLATIONS OF THE RIGHT TO SOCIAL SECURITY

The previous sections of this paper tried to describe a positive and effective right to social security, based in part on ILO Conventions and in part by adapting the ILO model to fit universal situations that require flexible answers. By briefly exploring three different examples of real or potential violations, this section hopes to illustrate the need for effective content to the right to social security. These examples take their inspiration from current debates surrounding social security issues but they serve different purposes: (1) the well-known and often cited case of pension privatisation in Chile shows the importance of respecting the essential requirements of any social security scheme, as they are outlined in section 2; (2) ILO Convention 168 on Employment Promotion and Protection against Unemployment illustrates how a more general guarantee of the right to social security as provided for in Article 9 of the ICESCR can protect against the negative effects of the economic and ideological "hijacking" of a social security instrument; and finally, (3) a brief survey of potential discrimination, including gender discrimination, issuing from social security models will be presented in order to show the centrality of equality and nondiscrimination in realising the right to social security.

4.1 The Chilean Pension Model

The privatised Chilean pension system is well known[22] and often cited as an expression of the proposed three-pillar model that the World Bank has been promoting.[23] Essentially, Chile shifted from a public, PAYG (Pay as you go) defined benefits (DB) plan to a privately funded, defined contributions (DC) system in 1981. Participation is optional for those already enrolled in the state system but mandatory for new labour market entrants. Only workers contribute to the plan but employers must add to their paycheques nearly the equivalent of their previous contributions. The worker's contribution is equal to 14 percent of gross salary, 10 percent of which is a contribution and 3 to 4 percent are commissions to the *Administadora de Fondos de Pensiones* (Pension Fund Administrator, AFP). Pensioners bear the income risk in its entirety. With the Chilean model, however, it is easy to see that the government is still significantly involved in this risk as far as the guarantee of a minimal pension and the transition costs are concerned.

The defined contributions Chilean pension plan is highly regulated, which invites criticism from the financial markets. Essentially, regulation was and is aimed at financing the transition costs, supervising and regulating the AFPs, and, last but not least, guaranteeing minimum benefits. New pensions will eventually be topped off by public money if the accumulated capital does not provide for a

---

22 See Gillion and Bonilla *Analysis of a national private pension scheme: The case of Chile*, (1992) 131 *International Labour Review* 171; Conte-Grand ILO Equipo Técnico Multidisciplinario de Santiago, *Regimenes de seguridad social en America Latina, reformas, desafios pendientes*, paper presented at "Economic integration, labor law and social security in the Americas", Viña del Mar, Chile, April 14 and 15, 1998 [unpublished]; see also Conferencia Interamericana de Seguridad Social, Serie Estudios 16, *Administracion publica y privada de los seguros sociales en America Latina*, 1996, 223-267 and Serie Estudios 22, *Current pension systems evolution*, 1996, 101-147; Holzmann *Pension reform, financial market development and economic growth: Preliminary evidence from Chile*, 44 IMF Staff Papers, no 2, June 1997, 149-179. See Chilean Decreto Ley 3.500 Reforma Previsional (1980) as amended by Leyes 19.398, 19.404 and 19.415.

23 See *Averting the old age crisis: Policies to protect the old and promote growth* (1994) The World Bank, Oxford University Press. For a critique of this proposal see Beattie and McGillivray "A risky theory: Reflections on the World Bank Report averting the old age crisis" (1995) 48 *International Social Security Review* 5 and Singh "Pension reform, stock market, capital formation and economic growth: A critical commentary on the World Bank's proposal" (1996) 49 *International Social Security Review* 21; Gillion, Turner, Bailey and Latulippe *Social security pensions: Development and reform* (2000) ILO; *Le point sur la réforme des pensions* (2000) 53 *Revue internationale de sécurité sociale* 3; *The privatization challenge: A strategic legal and institutional analysis of international experience* (1997) World Bank 73 and ff.; Tamburi *Motivation, Objet et Processus de la réforme des pension* (1999) 52 *Revue internationale de sécurité sociale* 17.

minimum pension.²⁴ But the Chilean government is also financially liable for some other aspects of the system. First, the reform honored the government's implicit pension liabilities for those who had already retired and for those who chose not to switch to an AFP. In addition, recognition certificates *(bonos de reconocimiento)* were issued for those who changed plans. Fiscal surplus permitted the Chilean government to adopt such an attractive strategy in 1981.

According to Chilean data from 1996,²⁵ 3.8 million workers, representing 80 percent of the labour force, were registered with an AFP. Sixty percent of affiliates were under 35 years old. Although the self-employed can contribute voluntarily to the system, only 50,000 had registered by 1989.

The *Instituto de Normalización Previsional* (INP), the public pension administrator, still pays out approximately 900,000 pensions and manages contributions for 400,000 workers. It is estimated that this specific function of the INP will go on for another 40 years, gradually decreasing in importance over time.

As for the reality, studies and data show that:
- A majority of highly paid workers contribute regularly and significantly to their AFP account;
- Nearly 30 percent of young workers, mainly from the domestic services industry or part-time workers, contribute less than the required amount for minimum wage earners;
- Between 20 and 50 percent of affiliates do not contribute regularly. Of this percentage, 19 stopped contributing for less than a year, and another 19 percent stopped contributing for more than a year;
- According to some studies,²⁶ the government will be called upon to supplement the equivalent of $60 million US for annuities made available by accumulated AFP contribution in the coming years. At present, the basic pension is $55 to $60 per month, whereas the minimum wage is $71.²⁷

As a vulnerable group under this privatised pension plan, young people are obviously at risk. It also takes a lot of perseverance to

---

24 There are numerous possibilities for withdrawing this capital on retirement; indexed annuities seem to be preferred by pensioners.
25 See Conferencia Interamericana de Seguridad Social, Serie Estudios 16, *Administracion publica y privada de los seguros sociales en America Latina* (1996) at 233.
26 See Ortuzar "El deficit previsional: recuento y proyecciones" in Baeza and Manubens (eds) *Sistema privado de pensiones en Chile* (1988) Centre de Estudios Públicos 105-142.
27 See section 75 of Decreto Ley 3.500 of 1980.

find data relating to the discriminatory impact of this reform. Some data have recently been made available in the case of women.[28] What they reveal is not surprising:
- Women rely disproportionately on the public pension system because of their interrupted periods of contributions to AFPs;
- Women are disproportionately affected by the obligation to pay commissions to an AFP to remain affiliated, independent of whether they are actually contributing to a pension account;
- Women must contribute more to receive an annuity equivalent to that of men because of their longer life expectancy. This puts a disproportionate burden on women and reduces their available income;
- Women are also excluded in greater numbers from the public pension plan because of the requirement of a minimum of 20 years of contributions.[29]

Finally, the residual social assistance plan works on a closed budget in Chile. This means that local agencies manage growing waiting lists and often have to supply basic necessities, such as food in kind. For fiscal year 1991, the global public expenditure for welfare represented 0.41 percent of the Chilean GDP, while family allowances and public health expenditures amounted to roughly 2 percent.[30]

What the Chilean experience tells us is that:[31]
- waged work cannot be used as a contribution basis for the purpose of providing social protection: This mechanism, although it has been favoured and successful in a near full-

---

28 See Elter "La situación de la Mujer en el Sistema Previsional Chileno" in SERNAM *Igualdad de oportunidades para la Mujer en el Trabajo* (1996) and Instituto de la Mujer-Foro de Mujeres Sindicalistas, *Las Trabajadoras: por un sistema de seguridad social mas justa* (1997).
29 Compared to the Peruvian labor market, for example, the Chilean labor market is highly formalized. The situation is the same for women as for men, although there has been a significant shift to part-time and seasonal work since the Chilean economy is becoming more export-oriented. This is particularly true in the agro-industrial and fisheries processing sectors. See *Latin American Women, Compared Figures* (1995) FLASCO (Spain) and Diaz "Mujeres Trabajadoras Y Modelo Economico" in Asociacion Nacional de Centros CMP Flora Tristan, CUSO and OXFAM-UK *Las Mujeres En El Mundo Del Trabajo, Viejos Problemas En Nuevos Escenarios* (1996) at 23.
30 See Conferencia Interamericana de Seguridad Social, Serie Estudios 22, *Current pension systems evolution* (1996) 143.
31 For a more detailed analysis, see Lamarche "Social security at the end of the XXth century: Market-oriented or human needs oriented? Some examples from Canada and Chile" in *The New Yalta: Commemorating the 50th Anniversary of the Declaration of Human Rights in RBEC region* (1998) United Nations Development Program (UNDP), Regional Bureau of Europe and the CIS at 78-83.

employment context, clearly excludes large social groups and women in developed, less developed and transitional countries;[32]
- the State must ensure its financial capacity not only for benefits but also for preventive pro-active measures: Experience reveals that when a State moves toward the privatisation of social risks and social rights, its remaining capacity to guarantee the availability and quality of public goods diminishes;
- in the case of policies providing for non-public or privatised social security products, regulation of the fundamental dimensions of the plans must be high and binding: Minimal content of coverage, corrective measures fr discriminatory aspects of contribution rules, and actuarial rules are some examples of aspects needing such regulation.

Like many other states, Chile has not ratified ILO Convention 102. But Chile did ratify the ICESCR. In such a case, the concept of a core content of the right to social security would enable the CESCR, as well as NGOs, to monitor Chile's compliance with its obligations under Article 9 of the ICESCR. In fact, a recent proposal by the ILO would support such an approach.[33]

4.2 The Case of Unemployment Benefits and ILO Convention 168 on Employment Promotion and Protection against Unemployment

In 1934, the ILO adopted the Unemployment Provision Convention 44. This Convention reproduced the British model of unemployment insurance, which had been in force since 1907. As an instrument belonging to the first generation of social security conventions adopted by the ILO, Convention 44 is notable for the absence of any technical determination of what constitutes an acceptable and minimal level of income replacement in the case of involuntary unemployment. Adopted in the post-Depression economic context, Convention 44 nevertheless expresses the great difficulty of bringing states to recognise the need for a certain

---

32 On the proposal for a fourth pillar of social security for non-waged workers see Gillion and Bonilla *Analysis of a national private pension scheme: The case of Chile* (1992) 131 *International Labour Review* 161.
33 See Gillion *The development and reform of social security pensions: the approach of the International Labour Organisation*, on-line: http://www.ilo.org/public/english/110secso/bibliol.htm.

level of income replacement in cases of unemployment or underemployment. This is usually seen as a different social risk because it is closely connected to the issue of work discipline and viewed from the perspective of the economic pressure on wages. These themes reemerged in the 1980s.

Part IV of Convention 102 provides for prescribed categories of protected workers as well as for a level of benefits in the case of unemployment. Article 69 of Convention 102 reproduces the principles on which the initial British Unemployment Act was based: benefits may be suspended if a person neglects to make use of employment services,[34] loses employment as a direct result of a work stoppage due to a trade dispute, or voluntarily leaves a job without just cause. Unemployment is not a social risk like the others. Its initial temporary nature, as well as the intimate connection between work and the loss of work, caused many problems when the ILO tried to protect unemployment by reference to the broad logic of social risks coverage established in social security Conventions.

In 1988, the ILO adopted Convention 168 on Employment Promotion and Protection against Unemployment, which revises Convention 44.[35] This Convention,[36] although sparsely ratified, clearly illustrates a shift in the design of social security conventions whereby they simultaneously attempt to tackle modern issues related to the transformation of employment and the expansion of atypical labour contracts.[37] The pursuit of two apparently incompatible goals led to a paradigmatic change in social security, expressing the willingness of Member States to acknowledge some transformation of the functions of social security. In fact, Convention 168 draws inspiration from what the OECD would call a more active (as opposed to passive) approach to unemployment as a social risk. This active strategy assumes that the right to an income replacement measure can be superseded by

---

34 ILO conventions have never totally prohibited private employment services. Employment services can be private as well as public. In the former case though, they must be supervised by a public authority.
35 See Article 31 of Convention 102.
36 Six countries, including Brazil in 1993, ratified this Convention. But in 1966 countries like Canada adopted an Employment Act that reforms the Unemployment Act in accordance with the principles established in Convention 168.
37 See Lamarche "Le droit international des droits économiques de la personne et le quart monde occidental: a-t-on parlé pour ne rien dire?" (1993-1994) 8 *Revue québécoise de droit international* 34 and Lamarche "Le droit au travail et à la formation: enjeux et doutes du droit international" dans *Emploi précaire et non-emploi: droits recherchés*, Actes de la 5e Journée en droit social et du travail, sous la direction de Lucie Lamarche, Yvon Blais éditeur, Montreal, 1994, p. 59-89.

employment strategies aimed at shortening the stay on unemployment and encouraging the acceptance of work, despite lack of interest in and/or low salary offered by the available jobs.

This shift is illustrated in a fairly technical manner in Convention 168. More specifically, and as opposed to the principles of social security conventions, Article 11(3)(a) of Convention 168 provides for the possibility of any ratifying Member State to limit the percentage of covered workers to 85 percent of prescribed categories of workers and even to reduce this percentage to 50 percent.[38] Article 15(1) of the Convention provides for a percentage of benefits representing at least 50 percent of previous gains, but Article 15(2) states that this percentage may be reduced to 45 percent of those gains if the workers'[39] capacity to meet their basic needs is not affected. Although most modern unemployment regimes provide for a minimum duration of benefits of about one year (except in North America), Convention 168 establishes a period of 39 weeks as an acceptable duration, which may be reduced to 13 weeks, even in developed countries.[40] Many sections of the Convention clearly encourage social security regimes to provide for the maintenance of partial benefits if an unemployed person accepts part-time or occasional work during a period of unemployment. Historically, the possibility of derogation from technical standards that a Member must meet in order to ratify a social security convention has been limited to the less developed countries. But with Convention 168, derogations are, in fact, a disguised way of transforming the coverage of a social risk into an active employment strategy by pledging lower benefits.

This low requirement approach is even more obvious in the case of Part IV of the Convention, which provides protection for atypical workers or newcomers to the labour markets.[41] Member

---

38 In this case, any State, when reporting according to section 22 of the ILO Constitution, must provide information as to how it intends (a) to cover the contingency of partial unemployment; (b) to increase the number of persons protected; (c) increase the amount of the benefits; (d) reduce the length of the waiting period; (e) extend the duration of payment of benefits; (f) adapt statutory social security schemes to the occupational circumstance of part-time workers; (g) endeavour to ensure the provision of medical care to persons receiving unemployment benefits and their dependents; (h) endeavour to guarantee that the periods during which such benefit is paid will be taken into account for the acquisition of the right to social security benefits and, where appropriate, the calculation of disability, old-age and survivors' benefits. For the purpose of unemployment regimes, a worker is an active worker with a job. Long-term and short-term unemployed are not considered to be workers.

39 The reference to the worker's family is not specified in Convention 168.

40 See Articles 19(2) and (4) of Convention 168. Canada and the United States objected to the inclusion of a period of benefits in the Convention.

41 Women, the young, migrants, ex-prisoners, students, etc.

States can simply ratify Convention 168 without accepting Part IV. In the same manner, the commitment to establish or maintain a national unemployment regime that supports the income of partially unemployed persons is optional.

Unlike earlier social security conventions, Convention 168 is essentially aimed at transforming the function of national unemployment regimes and not at protecting or guaranteeing a replacement income to the unemployed, specifically for atypical or part-time workers. By lowering the acceptable level of benefits that a national regime can provide and still comply with Convention 168, this instrument departs from traditional ILO social security conventions whose goal is continual improvement of the economic protection provided by social security regimes.

The provisions of Convention 168 find many applications in the more advanced OECD countries.[42] Canadian NGOs echoed them at the most recent review of Canada's periodic report to the Committee on Economic, Social and Cultural Rights in 1998.[43] Although the Committee expressed its deep concern, it would have been helpful to receive more precise guidance from the Committee as to what the realisation of the right to social security means in Canada. Again, this case shows the need for a more in-depth understanding of this human right because even its most essential elements reveal fairly technical aspects. This knowledge cannot remain in the protected realm of the ILO, although ILO expertise is required to facilitate an informed debate on the right to social security as protected by the Covenant. Recent economic transformations as well as the need for a more flexible understanding of the right to social security require a better informed civil society as well as more interested UN treaty bodies.

4.3 Social Security and Discrimination

Discrimination is a process in which personal and socio-economic characteristics operate against the possibility of benefiting equally from the law or from a policy, programme or measure. Often, dis-

---

42 See Lamarche "Le régime canadien d'assurance-emploi: l'emploi au service de l'ajustement structurel" in *Politiques actives d'emploi et mesures d'employabilité, éléments de comparaison Belgique-Canada-France,* Actes des journées d'étude des 27 et 28 octobre 1997, Bruxelles, TEF-SSTC, Point d'appui, Dossier 18, Bruxelles, novembre 1998, pp. 57-73. Centre d'économie et de sociologie régionales de l'Université libre de Bruxelles, Université libre de Bruxelles.

43 See supra, note 49.

crimination is indirect because, although neutral in appearance, conditions of access will in fact exclude certain groups from benefiting from a law or programme.

In matters related to social security, indirect discrimination may occur in various contexts. These can be summarised as occurring when access to and benefits from a statutory social security scheme are restricted to full-time workers and subjected to the existence of an employer-employee relationship, either because a statute makes employers' and employees' contributions compulsory or because access to a certain scheme, such as pensions, requires an attachment to work for a set period of time or occupation of a specific job. In these cases, occasional, part-time and short-term workers, and female workers who have interrupted their work for reasons related to family responsibilities will be excluded from the regime or receive lower benefits. These situations express the classic problem of statutory and occupational social security schemes linked to long-term attachment to work, as has been the case in most developed and industrialised countries.

Social security schemes may also produce discriminatory effects by openly excluding certain persons or providing them with reduced benefits. These forms of discrimination are often based on age or gender. Communications with the U.N. Human Rights Committee in the 1980s describe some cases in which such discrimination was criticized on the basis of the equality guarantee in Article 26 of the International Covenant Civil and Political Rights.[44] For example, an unemployment scheme providing lower benefits for a married woman than for a married man was deemed to be discriminatory.[45]

Social security schemes that provide coverage for certain categories of workers, such as civil servants or workers in specific industries, can also produce discriminatory results, either because some social or ethnic groups do not have access to these categories of employment or because they belong to classes of workers that are not included. Although in these cases, the law itself cannot be deemed to produce discriminatory results, a high percentage of the population is nevertheless deprived of the benefit of social security, including a large proportion of women.

---

[44] International Covenant on Civil and Political Rights, *opened for signature* 16 December 1966, *entered into force* 23 March 1976, 99 UNTS 171 (hereinafter ICCPR).
[45] See UN Human Rights Committee, *P.H. Zwaan-de-vries vs Netherlands*, Communication no 182/1984 and *L.G. Danning vs Netherlands*, Communication no 180/1984.

Newer forms of social security patterns, such as privatised pensions or health care plans, can indirectly exclude large groups of the population, because the benefits depend solely on personal and individualised contributions made during the duration of different jobs. In certain cases, the contributions will be largely insufficient to provide a decent benefit, while in others, the interrupted relationship with work will itself contribute to the inadequacy. In this case, the law providing for the implementation of such privatised plans, as well as the absence of basic universal coverage, will contribute to the impoverishment of social and ethnic groups unable to maintain an attachment to work or to economic activities that facilitate contributions to a social fund.

At the other end of the spectrum, the consequences of being deprived of access to formal work clearly lead to exclusion and deprivation if the social security regime links the income replacement measures to contributions withheld from salary and/or shared between the employer and employee. More and more people are facing the problem of what is called social exclusion.

Schematic representation of the possible discriminatory effects of social security mechanisms leads to recognition of the need for a more inclusive approach to social security than one deriving from formal employment. The ILO's more recent normative work provides interesting examples of such an approach.

In 1958 the ILO adopted Convention 111 on discrimination (employment and occupation). This Convention guarantees the fundamental right to be protected from workplace discrimination and engages the ratifying states to promote equal opportunity and treatment with respect to employment and occupation, with a view to eliminating workplace discrimination.[46] One hundred and thirty eight Member States of the ILO have ratified this Convention. Convention 111 does not expressly refer to the issue of discrimination in matters related to social security. Only Recommendation 111 does so by providing that equality of treatment is to be promoted, in particular, in relation to statutory social security protection.[47] In 1996, a General Survey of Convention 111 led the ILO Experts to conclude that:

> Under Article 5 of the Convention, distinctions in respect of employment-related social security, to the extent that they do not constitute a special measure of protection or assistance

---

46 See Article 2 of Convention 111.
47 See Article 2 of Recommendation 111.

provided for in other international labor Conventions or are generally recognized as necessary, constitute unlawful forms of discrimination. Any discriminatory treatment in respect of benefits or of conditions of entitlement to social security, the application of compulsory or voluntary statutory or occupational schemes, contributions and the calculation of benefits should be eliminated.[48]

Although clear progress was made in various national contexts in eliminating the discriminatory effects of statutory and occupational social security schemes related to work, the international scene had to wait for the adoption of ILO Convention 175 on Part time Work and of Convention 177 on Home Work to see an acknowledgment of the need for solutions adapted to new forms of work. Although Article 6 of Convention 175 on Part Time Work promotes the principle of proportionality of access to statutory social security benefits for part-time workers, the more concrete option concerning inclusiveness is found in Article 6 of Recommendation 182 on the same topic:

> The adaptations to be made in accordance with Article 6 of the Convention to statutory social security schemes which are based on occupational activity should aim at:
> (a) if appropriate, progressively reducing threshold requirements based on earnings or hours of work as a condition for coverage by these schemes;
> (b) as appropriate, granting to part-time workers minimum or flat-rate benefits, in particular old-age, sickness, invalidity and maternity benefits, as well as family allowances.

A clear tendency to universalise a basic or "flat-rate" protection for part-time workers with regard to certain social risks is hereby expressed.

This Recommendation, adopted in 1994, emphasises the original possibility provided for by Convention 102, authorizing a ratifying state to implement all parts of the Convention by providing the equivalent of minimal coverage to all persons by means of

---

[48] See 1996, ILO, Equality in Employment and Occupation: Fields covered by the Convention: Access to training, occupation and employment, terms and conditions of employment, General Survey, Convention 111, Report III Part 4B), 83rd Session, 1996, para 113.

a system that can be partially or totally based on general taxation. Recommendation 182 marks an important shift in the original philosophy of social security conventions by considering universal and minimal social security regimes as other than a "second class" solution to social risks. In fact, Recommendation 182 departs from a vision of social security solely connected to the partial replacement of wages in order to partially correct discriminatory practices in the field of social security. The "flat-rate" benefits approach is not altogether good news, though, as no percentage of average or previous wages to which the replacement of working income can be compared is provided, and no new benchmarks are suggested to assess the sufficiency of the "flat-rate benefit technique".

Recommendation 184 on Home Work, adopted with Convention 177 on the same topic, addresses not so much the issue of "second class" workers as the need to develop appropriate and accessible social security devices:

> s. 25. Homeworkers should benefit from social security protection. This could be done by:
> (a) extending existing social security provisions to homeworkers;
> (b) adapting social security schemes to cover homeworkers; or
> (c) developing special schemes or funds for homeworkers.

In matters related to social security, discrimination must not be confused with exclusion. There are cases where the law, or the relevant social security scheme, directly or indirectly produces prejudicial effects. There are other cases in which the historical limits of social security patterns must be explored in order to produce more inclusive social security devices. Recent initiatives show this tendency to eradicate discrimination and extend protection to classes of citizens who have been historically excluded from different social security regimes. In all cases, the technical requirements will be useful in aiming at the ultimate goal of the right to social security: the maintenance or protection of a decent standard of living in all cases where personal or economic conditions make it impossible to rely on individual initiatives.

The examples used in the preceding section all show the need to reconsider the right to social security in a globalised and more uncertain context. These examples provide useful guidelines for conceptualising the need for social protection as a human right to which social security can contribute. The emphasis placed on the technical dimensions of the right to social security is not an expression of nostalgia. It is more an attempt to avoid legitimising all anti-poverty strategies as promoting human rights. In this last regard, market ideology plays an increasing role and can be counterbalanced by a human rights perspective that maintains at the centre of the debate the need to respect three basic principles: equality, dignity and the need for the state to guarantee decent living conditions by all available means.

5 CONCLUSION

The proposals in this paper show the need for a more in-depth analysis of appropriate ways of implementing and monitoring Articles 9 and 11 of the Covenant, as well as the need for increased concern amongst human rights activists for social security to be seen as a significant contribution to the right of all people to an adequate standard of living. If social security is not a universal answer to all problems of social exclusion, it can also be said that no one is to be deprived of his or her right to social security in the name of a vague policy objective based on the need to fight social exclusion. The right to social security suggests a methodology to assess the content of such a policy and to monitor human rights violations.

It is important to recall that the market has never been prevented from protecting everyone against loss of the ability to earn his or her own living, as well as the family's. But many new individualised "products" against social exclusion, now offered by many different markets (local or international), do not all pass the test of conformity to human rights standards.

It is well known that human rights monitoring relies heavily on NGOs' capacity to highlight violations and participate in identifying proper solutions. In this regard, NGOs need a signal from UN treaty bodies, for example a revised list of guidelines addressed to states parties to the ICESCR, based on which they can work at the national level by entering into a national dialogue with the state, and, often, with international financial institutions as well. A General Comment on the right to social security, adopted by the Committee, would also be very useful. To this end, the Committee might consider engaging in a dialogue with the ILO, which will soon revisit the issue of social security.

Finally, it must be stressed that in the context of globalised trade and international trade agreements, social security must be seen as highly susceptible to commodification. Social security schemes are now offering huge investment possibilities, and social security products (for example, health benefits) are vulnerable to the new institutionalised trade rules. It would be a paradox to see corporations claiming in the near future a right to invest and operate in the field of social security that the most vulnerable cannot even dream of: the right to benefit from the protection that social security schemes are supposed to guarantee.

THE RIGHT TO SOCIAL SECURITY: RESPONSE FROM A SOUTH AFRICAN PERSPECTIVE

Sandra Liebenberg

1 THE SOUTH AFRICAN CONTEXT

The South African Constitution[1] has taken the bold step of recognising social security as a fundamental human right in its Bill of Rights. Moreover, it has taken this recognition a step further by providing that this right, like the other rights in the Bill of Rights, may be enforced in the courts.

Section 27(1)(c) provides that "Everyone has the right to have access to ... social security, including, if they are unable to support themselves and their dependants, appropriate social assistance."

The recognition of this right must be seen against the profound poverty and inequality that exists in this country. Among comparable middle-income developing countries, South Africa has one of the worst records in terms of social indicators (health, education, safe water, fertility), and among the worst records in terms of income inequality. The White Paper for Social Welfare (1997) records that the poorest 40% of households in South Africa

---

1   Constitution of the Republic of South Africa, 1996.

earn less than 6% of total national income while the richest 10% earn more than 50% of the total national income.[2] It is estimated that 53% of the population live in the poorest 40% of households and are thus classified as poor.[3] Poverty in South Africa has strong racial (nearly 95% of South Africa's poor are African), gender (female-headed households have a 50% higher poverty rate than male-headed households), rural (some 75% of SA's poor live in rural areas, concentrated in the former homelands and TBVC states) and age dimensions (over 45% of the poor are children below 16 years).[4] Poverty also has a strong employment dimension, if one takes into account estimates of the unemployment rate in the formal sector, varying between 30 and 50%. The White Paper records that the formal sector of the economy is becoming less labour-intensive and can only provide employment for half of the labour force. Unemployment, the lack of access to productive resources such as land and to social services such as water has increased the vulnerability of many households.

2 THE SOCIAL SECURITY SYSTEM IN SOUTH AFRICA

Compared to other countries in Africa, South Africa has a relatively well-developed social security system. However, the system has had to overcome a deep legacy of racial discrimination and administrative fragmentation.

In the field of social assistance, the level of benefits and the conditions for accessing the various grants were all racially differentiated. The system was highly susceptible to corruption and administrative inefficiency. The Committee for the Restructuring of Social Security (CRSS) has described the situation as follows:

> The segregation of the social security system of the past put into place 14 separate systems each with its own management and information systems, rules and procedures, leading to loopholes which could easily be exploited by unscrupulous officials and members of the public.[5]

---

2 White Paper for Social Welfare, February 1997, at 1.
3 *Key indicators of poverty in South Africa*, an analysis prepared for the Office of the Reconstruction and Development Programme (RDP) by the World Bank, based on the South African Living Standards and Development Survey, coordinated by the Southern Africa Labour and Development Research Unit (SALDRU) at the University of Cape Town, October 1995 (hereinafter *Key indicators of poverty in South Africa*), at 8.
4 *Key Indicators of Poverty in South Africa*, at 3–4.
5 CRSS Report, December 1996, p. 5.

Racial parity in the grant system was achieved in the early 1990's. Although discriminatory legislative provisions were abolished, racial and inter-provincial inequities in the distribution of social assistance grants remain. Poor administrative capacity in areas comprising the former TBVC states and self-governing territories impedes equal access to social grants.

The various mechanisms of social insurance were also characterised by direct and indirect racial discrimination. For example, unemployment insurance legislation initially excluded all black workers in the agricultural, domestic and mining sectors, and African workers earning less than a defined minimum income.[6] The 1946 Act removed the minimum income restriction, but still excluded all black agricultural, domestic and mining workers. Until the late 1970's UIF usually did not cover Black workers. Racial discrimination in payments under the Unemployment Insurance Act was eventually abandoned in 1977. In the field of occupational retirement insurance, a form of indirect racial discrimination took place in terms of which lower-skilled workers were generally excluded from coverage. In the context of apartheid this had the effect of excluding most Black workers. Occupational insurance only widened to include less skilled workers in the late 1960's and early 1970's when increasing industrialisation drew black workers into industry.

Today the social security system in South Africa is constructed on two main pillars. In the first place there are different schemes of social assistance consisting of a variety of non-contributory grants funded from general revenue. Eligibility for these grants is determined through a means test. The main grants are:

- The Grant for the aged (women are eligible at the age of 60 years, and men at 65 years)
- War veterans' grant
- Grant for the disabled
- Care dependency grant
- Foster child grant
- Grant-in-aid
- Child support grant.

These grants are paid in terms of the Social Assistance Act 59 of 1992.

In addition, the Special Pensions Act 69 of 1996 provides for special pensions to be paid to persons over the age of 60 years

---

6 The Unemployment Benefit Act of 1937.

who made sacrifices or served the public interest in the establishment of democracy as well as the dependants of those persons.

In the second place there are various social insurance schemes. These include:
- Unemployment insurance;[7]
- Compensation for Occupational Injuries and Diseases;[8]
- Occupational retirement insurance; and
- Health insurance (currently under investigation).

3 SOCIAL SECURITY AND THE REDRESS OF POVERTY AND INEQUALITY IN SA: STRENGTHS AND WEAKNESSES OF THE SYSTEM

The right to social security and the values of human dignity, equality and freedom that are central to our new Constitution are inextricably related. Only a very formalistic concept of human rights would deny that hunger, destitution and homelessness undermine a person's capacity to live a life of human dignity, freedom and equality. Access to social security protects people from the worst ravages of poverty and inequality, and enables them maintain an adequate standard of living. To what extent does the current social security system in South Africa contribute to the realisation of these values?

Social assistance in South Africa represents one of the most significant mechanisms of poverty alleviation and income redistribution. Grants for aged and disabled and remittances are the main sources of income for over 40% of the poor (the poorest 40% of the population), and nearly 50% of the ultra poor (the poorest 20% of the population).[9] These social transfers reach communities who have otherwise been poorly provided with social services such as education and health.[10] With the high level of unemployment in the formal sector, occupational social insurance (whether public or private) can at best reach only half the labour force, leaving the most vulnerable dependent upon various forms of social assistance. In its Medium Term Budget Policy Statement for 1997,

---

7   Unemployment Insurance Act 30 of 1996.
8   Compensation for Occupational Injuries and Diseases Act 130 of 1993.
9   *Key indicators of poverty in South Africa*, at 15, para 7.
10 Ardington and Lund *How the social security system can complement programmes of reconstruction and development* (1995) Development Bank of South Africa; Case and Deaton *Large cash transfers to the elderly in South Africa* (1996) Discussion Paper No 176, Princeton: Research Program in Development Studies.

the Ministry of Finance observes that "household survey data indicate that social grants are a crucial source of income to poor households." Even Government's macro-economic policy document, GEAR, recognises that social transfers in the form of social grants reaching three million elderly, disabled or needy children play "a vital role in poverty alleviation."[11]

This is particularly the case with regard to the social grant for the aged, which comprises the largest portion of the social security budget (62,4% of social security), and is received by approximately 1.8 million beneficiaries mostly in rural areas. Research has shown that it has the following advantages as a poverty alleviation measure:
- it is well targeted for rural areas;
- it has a positive impact on the welfare of other household members (including children) as the pension is used as a source of "pooled" income to support other household members;
- it is well targeted for poverty;
- it has achieved an excellent take-up rate (around 80%);
- it contributes 29% of income to the poorest 20% of the population;
- it contributes to household security;
- it performs well in gender terms; and
- performs well in terms of inter-provincial equity.[12]

However, these positive indicators do not apply to the grant for the disabled or the child support grant, which have a number of shortcomings. For example, the system of disability grants does not have a good correlation with poverty, nor with respect to the achievement of racial equity. The child support grant also does not target all poor children in need in the relevant age cohort of 0–7 years, it has not achieved a good take-up rate due to the administrative complexity of the regulations governing access to the grant, and the initial amount of R100 per primary care-giver when the grant was first introduced in April 1998 has not been increased (unlike the other social grants). Its value is thus continuing to decline in real terms.

The disadvantages of the main forms of social insurance available in South Africa (unemployment insurance, compensation for

---

11 At 15.
12 Ardington and Lund *Report of the Lund Committee on Child and Family Support* (1996) at 6 – 8; Financial and Fiscal Commission *Public expenditure on basic social services in South Africa*, FFC Report for UNICEF and UNDP, at 91–92.

occupational injuries and diseases, and occupational retirement insurance) is their exclusion of a number of vulnerable groups such as the long-term unemployed, domestic workers, casual workers, seasonal workers and independent contractors. By their very nature, they are tied to those in formal, mostly permanent, employment. Women are most disadvantaged by the nature of these schemes due to a range of reasons: gender discrimination in the labour market, and the interrupted nature of women's employment due to the disproportionate burden of family and caring responsibilities still falling on their shoulders. The exclusion of domestic workers from legislation like the Compensation for Occupational Injuries and Diseases Act, 1993, indirectly discriminates against the 860 000 black women in domestic employment in South Africa. Although legislative proposals are on the table to extend coverage of unemployment insurance to categories of workers currently excluded such as casual, seasonal and domestic workers, these have yet to become legally and administratively enforceable.[13]

Occupational retirement insurance has expanded its coverage to most industries, and it is usually mandatory for employees in such industries to join their pension or provident fund.[14]

Servaas van der Berg notes that:

> Coverage is still low in agriculture, trade, catering and accommodation (mainly employees of small traders and shopkeepers), and domestic service. Coverage amongst men is probably much higher than among women, who are disproportionately present in services, including both trade and domestic service.[15]

Although coverage of those in formal employment is high (about 73%), the large extent of unemployment means that only some 40% of the labour force is covered.[16]

There is a host of underlying policy issues that need urgent attention and that are currently being debated. The National Retirement Consultative Forum (NRCF) which was recommended

---

13 The Unemployment Insurance Bill.
14 Workers and employers typically contribute 7.5% of the monthly wage to a retirement fund, and workers can then claim benefits upon retirement. The 16 000 retirement funds are regulated through The Pensions Funds Act of 1956 with the aim of safeguarding members' interests.
15 Van der Berg "South African social security under apartheid and beyond" (1997) 14 *Development Southern Africa* at 489.
16 *Ibid.* Discrimination is also present in certain schemes.

by the Mouton Commission (1992) is currently investigating many policy issues related to retirement provision.

It is also acknowledged that the social security system is fraught with administrative problems. For example, many beneficiaries have been adversely affected by the manner in which the process of re-registering for social grants was conducted during the course of the last two years. This process was embarked on in order to eliminate fraudulent ("ghost") beneficiaries from the system. Many beneficiaries found themselves in desperate straits when their grants were simply suspended (often without notice) in the re-registration process. Rent, electricity, burial policy payments, school fees and food needs could not be met. The debt burden of these families increased as they struggled for survival.[17] At the National "Speak Out on Poverty" Hearings organised by the SA National NGO Coalition (SANGOCO), the South African Human Rights Commission and the Commission for Gender Equality in 1998, common complaints about the social grants voiced by beneficiaries included:

- long delays in the processing of grants; administrative bungling (such as sending the money to the wrong address or depositing it in the incorrect bank account);
- computer malfunctioning;
- the unexplained stoppage of payments for a certain period of time;
- and the obstructionist and unresponsive attitude of certain welfare officials.[18]

These administrative problems have led to a flood of litigation on behalf of grant recipients against welfare departments.[19] The Department of Welfare has also faced severe criticism from its inability to spend poverty relief funds, including funds allocated to the implementation of the new child support grant, in the 1998/99 fiscal year.

The social security system is based on an archaic and rigid distinction between social insurance and social assistance. It lets

---

17 Liebenberg and Pillay *Poverty and human rights* Report of the National Speak Out on Poverty Hearings, March to June 1998 (Johannesburg: South African National NGO Coalition, 1998), at 23.
18 *Ibid.*
19 In *Bacela v MEC for Welfare (Eastern Cape Provincial Government)* 1998 (1) All SA 525 (E), the decision of the MEC to suspend payment of arrear pensions, payable in terms of the Social Assistance Act 59 of 1992, due to budgetary constraints, was successfully challenged. Also see recent press report by Paul Kirk "Court demands Mhlongo explain KZN pension chaos" *Mail & Guardian*, August 25 to 31 2000, p. 14.

those who are or have been in formal employment benefit from relatively well-developed social insurance coverage, while social assistance grants reach only limited categories of persons in need and do not provide a level of benefit that can sustain an adequate standard of living. There is therefore insufficient social solidarity in the system with a widening gap between those privileged enough to be in formal employment and those who eke out a living through the informal economy, subsistence agriculture, and other forms of a-typical work, not to mention those who are unable to engage in any income-generating activities at all (those with caring responsibilities towards children and ill relatives, people living with severe disabilities, and people living with full-blown AIDS). The Department of Welfare has acknowledged the need to develop "a comprehensive social security system that links contributory and non-contributory schemes and prioritises the most vulnerable households." Unfortunately, the vital role of the social assistance grants in poverty alleviation is under-emphasised when the Minister for Welfare and Development refers to the need to "reduce dependency on non-contributory cash payments and give consideration to food security."[20]

It is also evident that the social security system as a whole faces severe pressures from the AIDS pandemic. Health insurance, adequate social security and services for people living with HIV or AIDS, and provision for the increasing numbers of AIDS orphans are just some of the challenges that face the social security system.

It is against this background that we turn to consider the scope and the nature of the duties imposed by the right of access to social security in section 27(1)(c). In doing so, I will use as points of reference some of the suggested elements of the minimum core content of the right to social security as well as the duty of progressive realisation discussed by Ms. Lamarche in her paper.

4 THE SCOPE OF THE RIGHT TO SOCIAL SECURITY

It is clear from the drafting of section 27(1)(c) that social security includes both contributory forms of social insurance, and needs-based assistance received from public funds (social assistance).

---

20 Minister Skweyiya *Launch of the 10-Point Programme of Action for Welfare and Development*, 14 January 2000.

The White Paper for Social Welfare in South Africa (February 1997) defines the scope of social security to cover –

> a wide range of public and private measures that provide cash or in-kind benefits or both, first, in the event of an individual's earning power permanently ceasing, being interrupted, never developing, or being exercised only at unacceptable social cost and such person being unable to avoid poverty. And secondly, in order to maintain children.[21]

In essence, social security is understood as those measures that aim at guaranteeing a certain minimum subsistence level, as well as protecting the income of people in situations where it is imperilled owing to various contingencies.

The right of access to social assistance (non-contributory forms of support provided from public funds) is restricted to those who are "*unable* to support themselves and their dependants" in section 27(1)(c). This raises the question whether the right is restricted to those who because of their physical or mental situation are unable to provide for their own or their dependants' basic needs (because of old age, illness, disability etc). Alternatively, it has a broader interpretation, referring also to those who are unable to support themselves due to an inability to find employment or generate sufficient income through other activities. It may even extend to the working poor whose incomes are too low to provide a minimally decent standard of living. In light of the high levels of structural unemployment and poverty in South Africa, the scope of the right to social assistance is particularly significant. It is suggested that a broad interpretation of the right is appropriate as the vital interest that this right protects is an adequate standard of living for everyone.[22] If the economy cannot generate enough jobs to enable people to support themselves and their dependants, social assistance becomes an important means of poverty alleviation and social compensation. The broad scope of the right is, however, subject to the latitude expressly afforded the state to achieve access to social assistance progressively (gradually) and within its available resources. A minimum core obligation can also be identified to ensure that at least particularly vulnerable and disadvantaged groups enjoy basic forms of social assistance (see below).

---

21 Chapter 7, para 1.
22 See Article 11 of the ICESCR.

It is suggested that a rights-based approach to social security should consist of the following key elements:
- The system and its different elements should be publicly administered or regulated, and promote participation by beneficiaries and organisations of civil society to give effect to the principle of solidarity. In this regard, I would question the inclusion of private savings in the White Paper's conception of social security.
- Comprehensiveness: The social security system as a whole should provide comprehensive coverage against all contingencies and life circumstances that threaten their income-earning ability and ability to support themselves and their dependants – unemployment, ill health, disability, maternity, old age; child support for impoverished care-givers; death benefits etc.
- Universality: all those in need of social security should be able to gain access to it.
- Adequacy and appropriateness: the level of benefits provided under the various schemes should meet a defined minimum standard. The benefit provided will depend on the type of social security scheme and its rules (e.g. contributory occupational retirement insurance). However, with regard to needs-based social assistance the benefit provided should at least be sufficient to ensure that the recipient does not fall below an accepted poverty line/minimum subsistence level in South Africa.[23] The kind of benefits provided should also be appropriate to the kind of risk or contingency faced (e.g. maternity benefits should be paid for a period appropriate to the demands of child-birth and infant-care).
- Equality: The social security system must not discriminate directly or indirectly against any person or group on grounds such as race, sex, gender, sexual orientation, ethnic or social

---

23 In terms of Article 13(1) of the European Social Charter, Contracting Parties undertake –
"to ensure that any person who is without adequate resources and who is unable to secure such resources either by his own efforts or from other sources, in particular under a social security scheme, be granted adequate assistance, and, in the case of sickness, the care necessitated by his condition."
The Committee of Independent Experts, which supervises these obligations, has held that the assistance to which a person is entitled may be in cash or in kind and must be adequate. The term "adequate" is not defined in the Charter but it appears that the Committee regards assistance as adequate if it is sufficient to allow the person concerned to provide for the necessaries of life in accordance with the prevailing cost and standard of living in the State concerned. In this regard, adequate information must be supplied on the amount of benefits under the social assistance system (basic and maximum amounts, percentage of minimum legal wage etc). The Committee retains the right to determine whether this is appropriate. (Samuel *Fundamental Social Rights* (1997) Council of Europe Publishing at 316.)

origin or the other grounds in terms of section 9(3) and (4) of the Constitution.
- Administrative justice: The system must be in accordance with the administrative justice rights set out in section 33 of the Constitution.[24] If social security is to be regarded as a right as opposed to mere charity subject to the discretion of government officials, it is imperative that the rules governing eligibility for, and the termination of, benefits are reasonable and procedurally fair.[25] The system as a whole should also be efficient, integrated, and accessible to users.

5 THE STATE'S DUTIES IN RELATION TO THE RIGHT

What are the Ministry and Department of Welfare and Population Development's specific duties in relation to the right as defined above?

5.1 Progressive realisation

It is clear that the full realisation of the right cannot be achieved overnight. The Bill of Rights expressly allows the state to realise the right "progressively" (gradually) and "within its available resources." In order to give effect to the right the state must adopt reasonable legislation and other measures (e.g. financial, administrative and educational measures) that clearly and directly advance and improve access to social security.

If progress is to be measured, the Ministry should put in place a transparent plan of action for realising the right. This plan of action should include benchmarks (targets) tied to specific time-frames.[26] Without this plan of action, there is a real risk that policy commitments will simply remain noble sentiments on paper.

---

24 This aspect of the right is strongly protected in international and comparative jurisprudence relating to the right to social security: see, for example, the case of *Goldberg v Kelly* (1970) 397 US 254); and *Salesi v Italy*, judgment of 26 Feb. 1993, Publications of the European Court of Human Rights, Ser A, No 257-E; *Schuler-Zraggen v. Switzerland*, judgement of 24 June 1993, Publications of the European Court of Human Rights, Ser A, No 263.

25 The Committee of Independent Experts supervising the European Social Charter have emphasised the importance of a right of appeal under Article 13(1) of the Charter. See Samuel *Fundamental Social Rights* (1997) Council of Europe Publishing at 314.

26 The plan of action provides the SA Human Rights Commission with a tangible tool to evaluate progress in the realisation of the relevant rights (section 184(3) read with section 184(1)(c) of the Constitution).

Progressive realisation also implies that the state should in general avoid retrogressive measures which reduce the coverage, universality (the number of people who have access to social security) or level of benefits provided under the social security system.[27]

5.2 Minimum core duty

The UN Committee on Economic, Social and Cultural Rights has emphasised that there is a "minimum core obligation" on states parties to the International Covenant on Economic, Social and Cultural Rights (ICESCR)[28] "to ensure the satisfaction of, at the very least, minimum essential levels of each of the rights". This minimum core obligation has a priority claim on the state's resources.[29]

In relation to the right to social security in South Africa this should include at least that the most disadvantaged and vulnerable groups are provided with basic levels of social security. These groups include the elderly, people living with disabilities and HIV/AIDS, and the primary care-givers of poor children, and more generally those who are destitute and have no other means of supporting themselves and their dependants. The White Paper for Social Welfare acknowledges that: "Every South African should have a minimum income, sufficient to meet basic subsistence needs, and should not have to live below minimum acceptable standards."[30] This basic minimum duty of the state is the foundation for the progressive improvement in the social security system until the right is fully realised.

A current policy proposal that may address this minimum duty is the basic income grant. It forms part of the mandate of a Committee of Enquiry into Social Security established by the Minister of Welfare and Population Development. This committee is charged with developing recommendations on the establishment of a comprehensive social security system.

---

27 *General Comment 3: The nature of States parties obligations* (1990) CESCR UN Doc E/1991/23, para 9.
28 International Covenant on Economic, Social, and Cultural Rights, *opened for signature* 16 Dec 1966, *entered into force* 3 Jan 1976, 993 UNTS 3 (hereinafter the ICESCR).
29 *Ibid*, para 10.
30 At 33, para 27.

IN SEARCH OF THE CORE CONTENT OF THE RIGHT TO EDUCATION

Fons Coomans

1 INTRODUCTION

Although the right to education is little known as a human right, it has a solid basis in the international law on human rights. It has been laid down in several universal and regional human rights documents. Examples include the Universal Declaration on Human Rights[1] (Article 26), the European Convention on Human Rights[2] (Article 2 of the First Protocol), the UNESCO Convention against Discrimination in Education,[3] and the International Covenant on Economic, Social and Cultural Rights[4] (ICESCR) (Articles 13 and 14).[5] Over the years, a lot of research has been done regarding the

---

1 Universal Declaration of Human Rights, UN GA resolution 217 A (III) of 10 December 1948 (hereinafter UDHR).
2 Convention for the Protection of Human Rights and Fundamental Freedoms, *opened for signature* 4 November 1950, *entered into force* 3 September 1953, ETS No 5 (hereinafter European Convention).
3 Convention against Discrimination in Education, *opened for signature* 14 December 1960, *entered into force* 22 May 1962, 429 UNTS 93.
4 International Covenant on Economic, Social, and Cultural Rights, *opened for signature* 16 Dec 1966, *entered into force* 3 Jan 1976, 993 UNTS 3 (hereinafter ICESCR).
5 See also, the International Convention on the Elimination of All Forms of Racial Discrimination, *opened for signature* 7 March 1966, *entered into force* 4 January 1969, 60 UNTS 195 (hereinafter ICERD) (Article 5(e)(v)), the Convention on the Elimination of All Forms of Discrimination against Women, *opened for signature* 18 December 1979, *entered*

important question: what does realisation of the right to education entail?[6] This paper aims to clarify the normative content of the right to education and of the corresponding obligations of states. It focuses on the nature, meaning and scope of Articles 13 and 14 of the ICESCR. Occasionally there will be references to other relevant treaty provisions. Sections 2 and 3 deal with the nature of the right to education as a human right and its special characteristics, in particular with regard to the ICESCR. In Section 4 other relevant universal instruments will be discussed briefly. Section 5 deals with the concept of a core content of human rights, with particular attention to the core content of the right to education. Section 6 discusses the feasibility of using a typology of state obligations ("to respect", "to protect", "to fulfil") in order to specify the nature of (minimum) state obligations resulting from treaty provisions and as a mechanism to determine whether a state is complying with its obligations in relation to the implementation of the right to education. Finally, in a short addendum, I will make a few observations on the topic of a core content of the right to education in the light of the discussions of the Pretoria conference of 28-29 August 2000.

2 THE RIGHT TO EDUCATION AS AN "EMPOWERMENT" RIGHT

The right to education may be characterised as an "empowerment" right. Such a right provides "the individual with control over the course of his or her life, and in particular, control over (…) the state".[7] In other words, exercising an empowerment right enables a person to experience the benefit of other rights.

---

    into force 3 September 1981, 1249 UNTS 13 (hereinafter CEDAW) (Article 10), the Convention on the Rights of the Child, *opened for signature* 20 November 1989, *entered into force* 2 September 1990, 28 ILM 1456 (hereinafter CRC) (Articles 28 and 29), the African Charter on Human Rights and Peoples' Rights, *opened for signature* 26 June 1981, *entered into force* 21 October 1986, 21 ILM 59 (hereinafter African Charter) (Article 17) and the Additional Protocol to the American Convention on Human Rights in the Area of Economic, Social and Cultural Rights (Protocol of San Salvador), *opened for signature* 17 November 1988, *not yet in force*, OAS Treaty Series No 69 (hereinafter Protocol of San Salvador) (Article 13).

6   To mention just a few old and recent studies within the framework of the United Nations: Ammoun *Study of discrimination in education* (1957) United Nations; Tomasevski *Preliminary report on the right to education* UN Doc E/CN.4/1999/49, and *Progress report* UN Doc E/CN.4/2000/6, as well as a report on a mission to Uganda, UN Doc E/CN.4/2000/6/Add.1.

7   Donnelly and Howard "Assessing national human rights performance: a theoretical framework" (1998) 10 *Hum Rts Q* 214 at 215.

Education is an empowerment right because of its links with other rights: "the key to social action in defence of rights . . . is an educated citizenry, able to spread its ideas and to organise in defense of its rights".[8] Civil and political rights such as freedom of expression, freedom of association or the right to political participation, obtain substance and meaning only when a person is educated. The same holds true for the right to take part in cultural life. For ethnic and linguistic minorities, the right to education is an essential means to preserve and strengthen their cultural identity. Education enhances social mobility and helps to facilitate escape from discrimination based on social status. Furthermore, education promotes the realisation of other social and economic rights such as the right to work, the right to food or the right to health: an educated person will have a greater chance of finding a job, will be better equipped to secure his or her own food supply and will be more aware of public health dangers. In general, the right to education promotes the fulfilment of the right to an adequate standard of living; it guarantees people access to the skills and knowledge needed for full membership in society. In short, the right to education contributes in an important way to the essence of promoting human rights, that is, living in dignity, which is the basic value underlying the idea of human rights.[9] In addition, the right to education has a clear overlap with other human rights, for example with the freedom of religion and the right to privacy. The freedom of parents to determine the (religious) education of their children is part of the freedom of religion, as well as of the freedom of education, and it is a matter belonging to the private life of people, protected by law. In other words, through its links with other rights, the right to education accentuates the unity and interdependence of all human rights.

3 THE SCOPE AND MEANING OF ARTICLE 13 OF THE ICESCR

The scope and meaning of Article 13 ICESCR will be analysed here from the angle of the text of the Article itself, and, in addition, from the text of General Comment No. 13 on the Right to

---

8   Donnelly and Howard "Assessing national human rights performance: a theoretical framework" (1998) 10 *Hum Rts Q* 214 at 234, 235.
9   See Schachter "Human dignity as a normative concept" (1983) 77 *American Journal of International Law* 848.

Education, adopted by the United Nations Committee on Economic, Social and Cultural Rights (CESCR or the Committee) in December 1999.[10]

With respect to the right to education as laid down in international documents, two aspects can be distinguished. On the one hand, realisation of the right to education demands an effort on the part of the state to make education available and accessible. It implies positive state obligations. This is the social aspect. The social dimension is the dimension that concerns state involvement, and it usually entails positive state obligations. On the other hand, there is the personal freedom of individuals to choose between state-organised and private education. This can be translated, for example, into parents' freedom to ensure their children's moral and religious education according to their own beliefs. From this stems the freedom of natural persons or legal entities to establish their own educational institutions. This is the freedom dimension of the right to education. It requires the state to follow a policy of non-interference in private matters, and it implies negative state obligations. Both aspects can be found in Articles 13 and 14 of the ICESCR. Article 13(2) and Article 14 cover the social aspect, while Article 13(3 and 4) embodies the freedom dimension.

In terms of individual rights, the right to education has been defined in the European context as a right of access to educational institutions as they "exist ... at a given time" and the right to draw benefit from the education received, which means the right to obtain official recognition of the studies completed.[11] When Article 13 was drafted, the UNESCO representative suggested the following definition of the right to education: "The right of access to the knowledge and training which are necessary to full development as an individual and as a citizen",[12] which is a rather broad and general definition. Both definitions refer to the social aspect of the right to education.

The elements of the freedom of education are well expressed in paragraphs 3 and 4 of Article 13: the freedom to choose and the freedom to establish. This aspect of freedom is typical for a democratic, pluralistic society. Its origin lies in ideas about respect for individual liberty.

---

10 See *General Comment 13: The Right to Education* (1999) CESCR UN Doc E/C.12/1999/10.
11 *Belgian Linguistic Case*, Case relating to certain aspects of the laws on the use of languages in education in Belgium, Judgment of the European Court on Human Rights, 23 July 1968, Publications of the Court, Series A, vol 6, 31.
12 UN Doc E/CN.4/SR.226, at 14 (4 May 1951).

The right to education laid down in Article 13 is a universal right, granted to every person, regardless of age, language, social or ethnic origin or other status. Articles 13 and 14 are rather comprehensive in comparison to other rights in the ICESCR. They set out the steps to be taken by states in realising the right to education. This applies particularly to paragraph 2 of Article 13, which enumerates the separate steps in achieving the full realisation of this right.[13] At issue here is the specific obligation of the state to make education available and accessible in a non-discriminatory way. In performing this duty, states have a degree of discretion within the limits of the norms set in Article 13 and the key provisions of Article 2(1) of the ICESCR.

It should be stressed, however, that one should differentiate between sub-paragraphs 2(a) (primary education), 2(b) (secondary education) and 2(c) (higher education) of Article 13. The obligation contained in sub-paragraph 2(a) ("Primary education shall be compulsory and available free to all") is unconditional, plainly defined, without a reference to progressiveness. Subparagraphs (b) and (c) contain conjugations of the verb "to make" and this strengthens their character of progressive realisation. That the legal obligation contained in sub-paragraph 2(a) is stronger than the others can also be inferred from Article 14, which is devoted to the implementation of compulsory and free primary education for all for states parties that have not yet reached that goal. The Committee on Economic, Social and Cultural Rights attaches great value to the guarantee of compulsory and free primary education. When discussing, for example, the report of Zaire (as it was known then), the Committee made it clear that charging fees for primary education is contrary to Article 13, para 2(a). A state party cannot justify such a measure by referring to severe economic circumstances: "The provision of such education was an obligation which remained incumbent upon a State Party whatever economic system it had adopted".[14]

The structure of the general comment on Article 13, adopted by the CESCR in December 1999, is as follows: After a brief introductory section, General Comment 13 contains a section on the normative content of Article 13, with subdivisions relating to separate aspects of the right to education: a section on obligations of states parties, divided into general and specific legal obligations; then a brief section on violations of the right to education; and

---

13 This paper does not deal with the aims of education laid down in Article 13(1).
14 UN Doc E/C.12/1988/SR.19, para 10; see also E/C.12/1988/SR.17, para 27, 40, 41 and 48.

finally, a section on obligations of actors other than states parties. In this general comment, the CESCR defines Article 13(2) as the right to receive an education. It distinguishes between four inter-related and essential features of education, namely:[15]
- availability: functioning educational institutions and programmes have to be available in sufficient quantity in a state;
- accessibility: educational institutions and programmes have to be accessible to everyone, without discrimination; this implies both physical and economic accessiblity;
- acceptability: the form and substance of education, including curricula and teaching methods, have to be relevant, culturally appropriate and of good quality; and
- adaptability: education has to be flexible, so it can adapt to the needs of changing societies and communities, and respond to the needs of students within their specific social and cultural context.

This four "A" scheme is a useful device to analyse the content of the right to receive an education, as well as the general obligations for a state party that result from it.[16]

4 OTHER RELEVANT INTERNATIONAL INSTRUMENTS

In this paragraph I want to highlight briefly two universal treaties containing extensive provisions on the right to education. The first instrument to be discussed is the Convention on the Elimination of All Forms of Discrimination Against Women (CEDAW), adopted in 1979. The first sentence of Article 10 mentions the purpose of this provision: namely, an obligation for states parties to eliminate discrimination against women in order to ensure them equal educational rights with men. In order to realise that goal states parties must ensure, inter alia, on a basis of equality of men and women, access to the same curricula, the same examinations, teaching staff with qualifications of the same standard, and school premises and equipment of the same quality. In addition, states parties are under an obligation to take specific measures to meet the special educational needs of girls and

---

15 *General Comment 13: The Right to Education* (1999) CESCR UN Doc E/C.12/1999/10 para 6.
16 This scheme has also been used by the Special Rapporteur on the right to education in her preliminary report. See UN Doc E/CN.4/1999/49, chapter II.

women, for example, reducing the dropout rates of female students, organising programmes for girls and women who have left school prematurely, and providing access to specific educational information relating to women's health and family planning. It is obvious from this Article that states parties have positive obligations which may have drastic effects in those states in which discrimination against girls and women is a structural characteristic of society and everyday life.

The second instrument to be discussed is the Convention on the Rights of the Child (CRC), adopted in 1989. The characteristic feature of obligations of states parties under this treaty is the idea that the best interests of the child must be the guiding principle for measures taken for the care and protection of children (Article 3(1)). Articles 28 and 29 deal with educational rights of children. These provisions link up with the corresponding article of the Universal Declaration of Human Rights and the ICESCR. However, compared to to these provisions the CRC contains a number of special characteristics which deserve a brief discussion here. First, Article 28(1a) puts more emphasis on the progressive realisation of the right to primary education (use of the verb "to make"), while Article 13(2a) and 14 of the ICESCR are mandatory and more strict. Furthermore, Article 28(2) stipulates that "states parties shall take all appropriate measures to ensure that school discipline is administered in a manner consistent with the child's human dignity and in conformity with the present Convention". Such a provision is lacking in other instruments. Article 28(2) would imply, in my view, that corporal punishment in school is contrary to the rights of the child. Article 28(1e) emphasises the importance of regular school attendance and the reduction of dropout rates, aspects that are also lacking in other instruments. Article 29(1) is more extensive and specific with regard to the aims of education in relation to the development of a child's personality. Finally, Article 32(1) provides for protective measures by the state against economic exploitation of children (child labour), which might impede their education. The Convention on the Rights of the Child adds a number of important elements for the protection and education of children, making it a step forward on the way to securing their rights.[17]

---

17 A comparative analysis of international provisions concerning the right to education may be found in a paper prepared by Mr. José L. Gomez del Prado, UN Doc E/C.12/1998/23.

5 THE CONCEPT OF A CORE CONTENT OF ECONOMIC, SOCIAL AND ULTURAL RIGHTS

5.1 The term "core content"

In this section, I intend to make some general observations on the concept of the core content of economic, social and cultural rights, and illustrate these observations by identifying some elements of the core content of the right to education.

It is well known that economic, social and cultural rights have long been neglected in the human rights debate. This is partly due to the fact that, in the words of Philip Alston, their promotion and realisation require skills and expertise that are alien to lawyers, diplomatic representatives, national policymakers, officials of international organisations and representatives of nongovernmental organisations, who have focused mainly on civil and political rights.[18] Generally speaking, proper discussion of the core content of individual rights has just started.[19] The term "core content" is to be regarded as a useful means of helping to analyse the normative content of economic, social and cultural rights, which are often described as vague and open-ended, with a view to assessing the conduct of states in this field in general, and to identifying violations in particular. Thus, analysis of this concept should not be regarded as an end in itself.

Article 4 of the ICESCR can be of use in rendering the term "core content" more specific and workable in practice. This Article provides for limitations to the enjoyment of the rights conferred, but imposes criteria for such limitations. They may not, for example, conflict with the nature of a right. In my view, the nature of a right must be understood as meaning its core or essence, that is, the essential element without which a right loses its substantive significance as a human right.[20] This idea is also implicit in Article

---

18 Philip Alston "The importance of the inter-play between economic, social and cultural rights, and civil and political rights" in *Human rights at the dawn of the 21st century*, proceedings of the interregional meeting organised by the Council of Europe in advance of the World Conference on Human Rights, Strasbourg, 1993, pp. 59-74, at p. 65. See for an overview of recent developments regarding legal character, implementation, standard-setting and supervision, Fons Coomans "Economic, social and cultural rights" in (1995) SIM Special No. 16, Netherlands Institute of Human Rights, 3.
19 See, for example, Toebes *The right to health as a human right in international law* (1998) Intersentia-Hart, chapter V.
20 See Coomans *De internationale bescherming van het recht op onderwijs (The international protection of the right to education)* (1992) Thesis, Maastricht University at 38, 39. See also The Limburg Principles on the Implementation of the International Covenant on Economic, Social and Cultural Rights (1986), UN Doc E/CN.4/1987/17, Principle No. 56.

5(1) of the ICESCR, which provides, inter alia, that limitations of rights to a greater extent than is provided for in the ICESCR are not allowed. In fact, therefore, the core content embodies the intrinsic value of each human right. The elements of a right which cannot be regarded as part of its core content (the peripheral part) are not less important, but constitute, as it were, a derivative or consequence of the core content. The character of these elements is such that they can often be realised only gradually; for example, they impose on governments considerable (financial) obligations, which for many states are not currently achievable. In addition, these peripheral elements are mostly less essential for the very existence of that right as a human right.

The core content of a right should be universal. A country-dependent core would undermine the concept of the universality of human rights. In cases where the core of a right has been realised in a rich state without much difficulty, this would not mean that the state could lean back and argue that it is complying with its treaty obligations. On the contrary, the task would then be to implement the peripheral part of the scope of a right. The point of departure for a core content approach would be, in my view, the concept of human dignity. The core of a right is to be considered as a floor, or a bottom from which governments should endeavour to go up, trying to reach higher levels of realisation. Complying with obligations that relate to the core of a right should not be dependent upon the availability of resources. In other words, when a government is facing policy dilemmas as a result of limited or insufficient financial resources, priority should be given to the realisation of the core of a right. In conclusion, human rights gives rise to state obligations, not the other way around. Indeed, the individual right (the norm) should be central. The right, including its core, gives rise to state obligations, some of which relate to the core (core obligations). Core obligations may be negative as well as positive.

5.2 Elements of the core content of the right to education

Some of the elements constituting the core content of the right to education are stated directly, while others may be inferred from Article 13 and 14 ICESCR.

(a) *Access to education on a nondiscriminatory basis*
The essence of the right to education means that no one shall be denied an education. In practice, this means an individual right of

access to the education available, or in more concrete terms, a right of access to the existing public educational institutions on a nondiscriminatory basis.[21] An example of a violation of this right is restricting access to the existing public educational institutions to people belonging to a specific ethnic, linguistic or religious group. In addition, education provided by the state should be of the same quality for all groups in society. Girls, for example, should not receive an inferior quality education compared to boys.[22] Another (extreme) example is the situation in Afghanistan where the Taliban regime banned girls and women from all types of educational institutions.[23]

(b) *The right to enjoy free and compulsory primary education*
A second element of the core content of the right to education is the right to enjoy primary education in one form or another, although not necessarily in the form of traditional classroom teaching. Primary education is so fundamental for the development of a person's abilities that it can be rightfully defined as a minimum claim. International law on human rights does not define the term "primary education", but guidelines for using this concept and others have been developed within the framework of international organisations, such as UNESCO.[24] Primary education relates to the first layer of a formal school system. It usually begins between the ages of 5 and 7 and lasts approximately six years, but in any case no fewer than four years.[25] Primary education includes the teaching of basic learning skills or basic education. The term "basic education" is nowadays often used within the framework of international conferences on education, such as the World Conference on Education for All, held in Jomtien, Thailand in 1990. Basic education relates to the content of education, not to the form (formal or non-formal schooling) in which it is presented. As stated in the Jomtien Declaration: "the focus of basic education must, therefore, be on actual learning acquisition

---

21 Compare Article 2(2) ICESCR and Limburg Principles at 35 and 37.
22 See Article 1(1) UNESCO Convention Against Discrimination in Education (1960) for a definition of the term "discrimination in education". In 1996, the Kuwaiti Parliament adopted a bill that provided for the segregation of male and female students in higher educational institutions. In my view, this segregation will lead to discrimination of women, given the influence of Muslim fundamentalist groups in that country. See the Dutch daily newspaper *NRC Handelsblad*, 3 July 1996.
23 See for example, Human Rights Watch 1999 World Report, http://www.hrw.org/worldreport99/women/women3.html.
24 See, for example, UNESCO *Statistical Yearbook* (1996) and the *Revised Recommendation concerning the Standardisation of Educational Statistics* (1978).
25 UNESCO *Statistical Yearbook* (1996) at 3.

and outcome, rather than exclusively upon enrolment, continued participation in organised programmes and completion of certification requirements" (Article 4). Apart from a school and classroom system, basic education may be given in less traditional forms, such as village- or community-based or open air schooling. This may be necessary due to shortcomings of the formal school system (lack of adequate buildings, teaching materials or teachers), or because parents are unable to pay for formal schooling. Basic education, as an element of the core content of the right to education, would, in my view, include literacy, numeracy, skills relating to one's health, hygiene and personal care, and social skills such as oral expression and problem-solving.[26] In addition, basic education must also include some teaching of the concepts and values laid down in Article 26(2) of the Universal Declaration of Human Rights, Article 13(1) of the ICESCR and Article 29(1) of the Convention on the Rights of the Child, including respect for human rights. One very important core element of the right to education is that it should respect the rights of minorities and indigenous populations, in the sense that it should recognise their cultural identity, plight and heritage. An example is teaching reading and writing in the students' mother tongue.[27]

Basic education is usually aimed at children within the framework of primary schooling. However, basic education is also relevant for other persons lacking basic knowledge and skills. This dimension is referred to as "fundamental education" in Article 13(2)(d). This type of education is rather broad and would include, *inter alia*, basic literacy and numeracy skills, as well as basic professional skills enabling people to function as members of society, to take part in social and cultural life, to generate income, to

---

26 An example may illustrate the practice of basic education: in India, the Social Work and Research Centre (SWRC), an Indian NGO, has been working with the poorest of India's rural population. This NGO has set up a number of schools in which:
    children are made aware of their rights through songs, puppets and classroom theatre. The curriculum gives them an idea about language and reading and writing in Hindi, as well as the basics of mathematics. Then they make links between letters and words, and between words and phrases. Over the following years, they are taught about social and rural behaviour, how to be self-sufficient, and about the caste system. Then come the theories of social and political thinkers and national heroes, as well as lectures on agriculture and cattle-breeding. The focus of the lessons is the environment they live in. The children are taught to make arid land cultivable, and the destructive effect of chopping down trees for firewood. Powerful links are established between the school and everyday working life.
    (Klotz "India: the children's republic" *UNESCO Sources*, No 116 (Oct 1999), 6)
27 For more information, see Dall "Children's right to education: Reaching the unreached" in Himes (ed) *Implementing the Convention on the Rights of the Child – Resource mobilization in low-income countries* (1995) Martinus Nijhoff/UNICEF 143 at 153, 158-163.

participate in projects aimed at community development, and to have access to and utilise information from a variety of sources (for example, the new computer technologies). The enjoyment of this right is not limited by age or gender; it extends to children, youth and adults, including older persons, and it is an integral component of adult education and life-long learning.[28]

A core element of primary education is that no one, including parents or employers, can withhold primary education from a child.[29] A state has an obligation to protect this right from encroachments by third persons. The obligation of the state to provide for primary education may be characterised both as an obligation of conduct and an obligation of result. When seen from the perspective of Article 14 of the ICESCR, it is an obligation of conduct, because it requires a state to set up and work out a plan of action, within two years of becoming a party to the ICESCR, for the progressive implementation of compulsory primary education free of charge for all within a reasonable period of time. On the other hand, primary education is also an obligation of result in terms of meeting basic learning needs. This obligation may be met by means of a variety of delivery systems (for example, formal or non-formal education), provided that specific levels of knowledge and skills are acquired. In my view, providing secondary and other forms of education would not belong to the core of the right. These levels of education have a lower priority than basic education.

According to Article 13(2a), primary education shall be compulsory. Usually the starting age for compulsory primary education is six or seven years old, but the duration of compulsory schooling varies considerably among countries. Worldwide there is a trend to lengthen compulsory schooling beyond the primary level. The rationale for a minimum duration of compulsory schooling beyond eleven years of age is that it should last at least to the minimum age of employment.[30] Obviously it is not sufficient that primary education be compulsory by law. An official state inspection service to supervise this duty with respect to parents, schools, employers and the pupils themselves is also necessary.

---

28 *General Comment 13: The Right to Education* (1999) CESCR UN Doc E/C.12/1999/10 para 23, 24.
29 See also *General Comment 11: Plans of Action for Primary Education* (1999) CESCR UN Doc E/C.12/1999/4 para 6.
30 See the progress report submitted by Katarina Tomasevski, Special Rapporteur on the Right to Education, UN Doc E/CN.4/2000/6, para. 46 and Table 3.

There are a number of factors which may influence children's actual school attendance.[31] These factors include inadequate school services, such as lack of transportation between a student's home and the school, or lack of running water and sanitation facilities at school. Other factors relate to the socio-economic and cultural status of parents. These factors could include inability to pay for their children's school attendance; traditional attitudes that downgrade the education of girls; loss of the family income that a child attending classes would otherwise earn; other constraints arising from religion, class, occupation or custom; and the inability of parents to help their children in the learning process. Particularly relevant is the physical and mental health condition of children, which may influence school attendance. Other factors which may negatively influence school attendance include instruction in a language other than the child's native tongue; a school timetable that is incompatible with the requirements of seasonal work, particularly in rural areas; and the incompatibility of teaching materials and methods with the cultural background of children and their parents.

Article 13(2a) also stipulates that primary education shall be free. The degree to which primary education is really free is determined by a number of direct and indirect costs,[32] such as school fees,[33] expenses for textbooks and supplies, costs for extra lessons, expenses for meals at school canteens, expenses for school transport, school uniforms or other items of clothing and footwear, medical expenses, and boarding fees where applicable. In some countries it is the practice that the village community or parents provide labour for constructing, running or maintaining the school. This may be seen as a form of indirect costs for those involved. Another form of indirect costs for parents is taxation. Through the fiscal policy of the state, families contribute to the costs of education. The effects of taxation on the accessibility of education will depend upon the progressiveness of the tax system: do low-income groups

---

31 These factors are largely drawn from UNESCO's *Questionnaire for the consultation of Member States on the implementation of the Convention against Discrimination in Education* (1985) UNESCO Doc 23 C/72, Annex A.
32 *Ibid.*
33 According to the UN Special Rapporteur on the Right to Education:
   school fees represent a form of regressive taxation. Their justification routinely points to the inability (or unwillingness) of a Government to generate sufficient revenue through general taxation. Payment for primary schooling ruptures the key principle of taxation whereby people who cannot contribute to public services that are meant for all are not required to do so.
   UN Doc E/CN.4/2000/6, para. 52. See also *General Comment 11: Plans of Action for Primary Education* (1999) CESCR UN Doc E/C.12/1999/4 at para 7.

pay less, in absolute and relative terms, compared to high-income groups?³⁴ One should also consider the effects of IMF Structural Adjustment Programmes upon the accessibility of education, if an increase in school fees is part of the package of measures agreed on by the concerned government and the IMF. It is then important to know whether financial or other forms of assistance or compensatory measures are available for underprivileged persons and groups, to safeguard continued access to education.³⁵

Primary education must have priority in resource allocation, because it deals with the fundamental basis for a person's development and the development of society as a whole.³⁶ This is consistent with the idea of a core content of rights, which should be seen as a bottom or floor from which states should endeavour to go up. It is the responsibility of the state to provide primary education and to maintain educational services. A government cannot waive that responsibility by giving more room to the private sector, or stimulating public-private partnerships for financing educational infrastructure.³⁷

(c) *Special facilities for persons with an educational deficit*
Related to the aspects discussed above is another element of the social dimension of the right to education which, in my view, belongs to its core content. This concerns the obligation of the state to take special measures or provide special facilities for those persons who are faced with an educational deficit, or who would otherwise have no access to education at all. One can think of girls in rural areas, street children and working children, children and adults displaced by war or internal strife, and persons with disabilities.³⁸ The type of education offered to these students

---

34 See the background paper prepared by Ms. Katarina Tomasevski, Special Rapporteur on the right to education of the Commission on Human Rights, UN Doc E/C.12/1998/18, para 12.
35 See the report on the mission to Uganda by the UN Special Rapporteur on the Right to Education, UN Doc E/CN.4/2000/6/Add.1, para 29-34.
36 See also in this respect, *General Comment 13: The Right to Education* (1999) CESCR UN Doc E/C.12/1999/10, para 51: "States parties are obliged to prioritise the introduction of compulsory, free education".
37 In a number of African countries, the state monopoly on education is coming to an end. In addition, there is a tendency to involve the private (business) sector in the funding and building of schools. The privatisation of education is supported, and sometimes even imposed, by the IMF and the World Bank within the framework of structural adjustment programmes. For more information about this development, see *UNESCO Sources*, No. 102, June 1998, p. 12, 13.
38 Compare Article 3 of the World Declaration on Education for All (1990) (Jomtien Declaration). See also the *Statement to the World Conference on Human Rights on behalf of the Committee on Economic, Social and Cultural Rights* UN Doc A/CONF.157/PC/62/Add.5, Annex I.

should be geared to their specific educational needs, and it will often require specially trained teachers.

(d) *Quality of education*

Another core element of the right to education which is less concrete and consequently more difficult to assess is the quality of education at each educational level. A state party is under an obligation to provide and maintain this quality; otherwise attending classes would be meaningless. When assessing educational quality, a state should take into account various factors, such as the results of students' tests, the efforts and training level of teachers, the availability and quality of teaching materials, and the condition of school buildings. The quality dimension of education should also encompass standards regarding the purposes of education as defined in Article 13(1) ICESCR and Article 29(1) CRC. Quality of education should be determined by the national educational authorities and supervised by an independent educational inspection unit.

(e) *Free choice of education*

Still another core element of the right to education is free choice of education without interference from the state or a third person, particularly, but not exclusively, in terms of the family's religious or philosophical convictions. This element would be violated if a state failed to respect the free choice of parents with regard to the religious instruction of their children.[39] This means, in practice, that a state must ensure an objective and pluralist curriculum and avoid indoctrinating students.[40] This is important, because public education entails the danger of political goals, that is, that the most influential "philosophy of life" will correspond to the political goals promoted by the state.[41] However, one should realise that in many countries there is limited or no opportunity for educational choice: either the only option available is state-controlled

---

39 See Coomans *De internationale bescherming van het recht op onderwijs (The international protection of the right to education)* (1992) Thesis, Maastricht University at 39, 238.
40 Case of *Kjeldsen, Busk Madsen and Pedersen*, (1976), Judgment of the European Court of Human Rights, Series A, Vol. 23, at 26, 27. The Court emphasised that Article 2 of the First Protocol should be interpreted in the light of Article 8 (right to privacy), Article 9 (freedom of conscience and religion) and Article 10 (freedom to receive information) of the European Convention.
41 Compare Article 17(3) of the African Charter, which states: "The promotion and protection of morals and traditional values recognized by the community shall be the duty of the State".

education, or, in a mixed system, private education is too expensive for parents.[42]

These core elements constitute the essence of the right to education as a human right. Violation of one or more of these elements by the state means that the right would lose its material and intrinsic value as a human right. Realisation of the right would not be possible if the state violated the core elements embodying the material and intrinsic value of the right as a human right.

(f) *The right to be educated in the language of one's own choice*
A more controversial question is whether the right to be educated in the language of one's own choice is part of the core content of the right to education. In the *Belgian Linguistic Case*, the European Court for Human Rights stated that "the right to education would be meaningless if it did not imply, in favour of its beneficiaries, the right to be educated in the national language or in one of the national languages, as the case may be".[43] This means that the state determines whether a specific language is a national or official language and therefore qualifies as a medium of instruction. In addition, the Court stressed that an individual cannot claim a right to state-funded education in the language of his or her own choice. The Court rejected the claim that the state has positive obligations in this situation.[44]

On the other hand, it is submitted that a state must respect the freedom of individuals to teach, for instance, a minority language in schools established and directed by members of that minority. This does not imply, however, that a state must allow the use of this language as the only medium of instruction; that decision would depend upon the educational policy of the state. At a minimum, however, states must not frustrate the right of members of national, ethnic or linguistic minorities to be taught in their own language at institutions outside the official system of public education. However, there is no state obligation to fund these institutions.

---

42 Private education refers to educational institutions established and run by private individuals or organisations. These private institutions may be partially or fully funded by the state, or alternatively, receive no financial contributions at all from local, regional or national public authorities. According to Article 13(4) of the ICESCR, states may establish minimum educational standards for private schools.
43 *Belgian Linguistic Case* (1968), Judgment of the European Court of Human Rights, Series A, Vol. 6, at 31.
44 Compare the critical observations of the Committee on Economic, Social and Cultural Rights when it discussed the periodic report of Mauritius on the implementation of the ICESCR. The Committee noted with concern that Kreol and Bhojpuri, the only languages spoken by the large majority of the population, are not used in the Mauritian educational system. See UN Doc E/C.12/1994/8, para 16.

5.3 Peripheral elements

Other elements within the scope of Article 13 ICESCR would, in my view, not belong to the core content, but should be characterised as peripheral elements. General availability of different forms of secondary education, including vocational guidance and training, and higher education, would belong to the periphery of the right to education. The same classification would apply to the progressive introduction of free secondary and higher education (compare Article 13(2b and c) ICESCR, and Article 28(2b and c) CRC). Other examples of elements outside the core of the right include access to specific educational information to help ensure the health and well-being of families, including information on family planning (Article 10(h) CEDAW); the promotion of education for refugees (Article 22(2) Convention Relating to the Status of Refugees); and promoting the instruction of indigenous children in their own language (Article 28(1) ILO Convention No. 169). Although these elements are important for the full realisation and enjoyment of the right to education, they are less essential from the perspective of the fundamental values that the right to education embodies. In a way, these elements derive from the core claim and guarantee of the right to education.

6 A TYPOLOGY OF OBLIGATIONS RELATING TO THE IMPLEMENTATION OF THE RIGHT TO EDUCATION

In order to further analyse and specify the normative content of the right to education and the nature and content of the corresponding obligations of the state, I propose to follow Asbjörn Eide's obligations approach. He identified three levels of obligations with respect to the implementation of the right to food.[45] He distinguished among the obligations "to respect", "to protect" and "to fulfil", which states parties to the ICESCR owe to individuals under their jurisdiction. This typology of state obligations has also been applied in recent general comments of the Committee on Economic, Social and Cultural Rights, including General Comment No. 12 on the Right to Adequate Food and General Comment No. 13 on the Right to Education.[46] The first type of obligation is the "obligation to

---

45 Eide *The right to adequate food as a human right* UN Doc E/CN.4/Sub.2/1987/23, para 66-71.
46 See *General Comment 12: The Right to Adequate Food* (1999) CESCR UN Doc E/C.12/1999/5 para 15 and *General Comment 13: The Right to Education* (1999) CESCR UN Doc E/C.12/1999/10 para 46-50.

respect". This obligation prohibits the state itself from acting to contravene recognised rights and freedoms. This means that the state must refrain from interfering with or constraining the exercise of these rights and freedoms. The second type of obligation is the "obligation to protect". The obligation to protect requires the state to take steps - through legislation or by other means - to prevent and prohibit the violation of individual rights and freedoms by third persons. The third is the "obligation to fulfil". This obligation can be characterised as a programme obligation and it implies a longer-term view. This obligation often requires a financial component which cannot be contributed by individuals alone. This obligation also includes establishing and maintaining a supportive legal and policy framework, whose costs are generally borne by the state. This typology of obligations is applicable to economic, social and cultural rights as well as to civil and political rights. It demonstrates that the realisation of a particular right may require either abstention or intervention on the part of governments. On the basis of Eide's proposal for a "food security matrix",[47] it is possible, in my view, to devise a comparable matrix to identify the nature and levels of obligations relating to the implementation of the right to education. The matrix is presented as an appendix to this paper (see p. 172). The matrix distinguishes between the "social" dimension and the "freedom" dimension of the right to education, discussed above. Within each dimension, a further categorisation is proposed. The "social" dimension includes the elements of accessibility and availability of education, whereas the "freedom" dimension refers to the liberty to choose and the liberty to establish. The proposed matrix does not offer an exhaustive list of concrete state action, but merely serves as an illustration of possible options for states. Other measures can be substituted, depending on the educational situation in a particular country. The matrix is applicable to developing countries with an inadequate educational system, as well as to countries with a highly developed system of education. It is a device for the elaboration of obligations, which can help to determine whether a state's legislation, policy and practice are in conformity with its obligations under the ICESCR. The nature of the obligations remains the same; only the measures taken to implement them differ. In rich countries, for example, it is necessary to maintain the existing level of education in a quantitative and qualitative sense, because a drop in services would endanger the accessibility and availability of education.

---

47 Eide *The right to adequate food as a human right* UN Doc E/CN.4/Sub.2/1987/23 at 29.

The following examples illustrate how the matrix can be applied.[48] The obligation "to respect" the right to education requires the state to abstain from interfering; the state must respect the exercise of individual freedoms without interference. In addition, it prohibits the state from discriminating on the basis of sex or ethnic origin, with respect to admission to public schools. Detailed standards of nondiscrimination and equal treatment of individuals in education are laid down in the UNESCO Convention against Discrimination in Education (1960), particularly in Articles 1 and 3. The obligation "to respect" can be characterised as an obligation of conduct: it requires the state to follow the course of action specified in the treaty provision.[49]

The obligation "to protect" requires the state to guarantee the exercise of the right to education in horizontal relations, between private groups or individuals. For example, it must protect against discrimination in admitting students to private schools. Another example of the obligation to protect would be the adoption of legislation to combat bonded labour or exploitative forms of child labour in private labour relations.

The nature of the right to education is such that positive state action is needed to achieve its full realisation. In the opinion of the CESCR, "it is clear that Article 13 regards states as having principal responsibilty for the direct provision in most circumstances",[50] which can be seen as an elaboration of the obligation to fulfil. The obligation "to fulfil" requires states to make the various types of education available and accessible to all and to maintain that level of realisation. In order to achieve this goal, states must take a variety of measures. Although legislation may be necessary to provide a legal framework, it is primarily policy measures and financial and material support that are needed to realise this right.[51] The obligation "to fulfil" implies that states have a substantial degree of latitude in complying, depending also upon the specific level of education and the wording of the treaty obliga-

---

48 For other examples, see *General Comment 13: The Right to Education* (1999) CESCR UN Doc E/C.12/1999/10 para 50.
49 See Coomans *De internationale bescherming van het recht op onderwijs (The international protection of the right to education)* (1992) Thesis, Maastricht University, at 231, 232 and Nowak "The right to education – Its meaning, significance and limitations" (1991) 9 *Netherlands Quarterly of Human Rights* 418 at 421 – 422.
50 See *General Comment 13: The Right to Education* (1999) CESCR UN Doc E/C.12/1999/10 para 48.
51 See the "The Limburg Principles on the Implementation of the International Covenant on Economic, Social, and Cultural Rights" (1987) 9 *Hum Rts Q* 122 at no 17. Legislative measures would be imperative if existing legislation is contrary to the obligations under the ICESCR; see "Limburg Principles" no 18.

tion.[52] Therefore, this obligation should be characterised as an obligation of result, leaving the choice of means to the state, provided the result conforms to international standards.

(a) *Minimum core obligations*
It can also be seen from the matrix that specific elements of the core content of the right to education give rise to concrete obligations. These obligations may be characterised as minimum core obligations, as defined by the Committee on Economic, Social and Cultural Rights in its General Comment No. 3, on the Nature of States Obligations.[53] Such obligations are not limited to the cost-free (negative) obligations to respect, but also include positive obligations to protect and to fulfil. Minimum core obligations resulting from the core content of the right to education apply irrespective of the availability of resources.[54] The CESCR also briefly refers to the core content concept in its general comment on Article 13, echoing General Comment No. 3 by framing its treatment of the concept in terms of states' core obligations. According to the Committee, the minimum core obligation with respect to the right to education includes an obligation:

> to ensure the right of access to public educational institutions and programmes on a nondiscriminatory basis; to ensure education conforms to the objectives set out in Article 13(1) [including "full development of the human personality and the sense of its dignity" and "strengthen[ing] the respect for human rights and fundamental freedoms."]; to provide primary education for all in accordance with Article 13(2)a; to adopt and implement a national educational strategy which includes provision for secondary, higher and fundamental education; and to ensure free choice of education without interference from the state or third parties, subject to conformity with "minimum educational standards" (Article 13(3) and (4)).[55]

---

52 *General Comment 13: The Right to Education* (1999) CESCR UN Doc E/C.12/1999/10 para 48. For example, according to Article 13, primary education should be free, while secondary education may be introduced progressively.
53 *General Comment 3: The nature of States parties obligations* (1990) UN Doc E/1991/23 para 10.
54 Van Boven, Flinterman, and Westendorp (eds) *The Maastricht Guidelines on Violations of Economic, Social, and Cultural Rights* (1989) Netherlands Institute for Human Rights para 9. See also Dankwa, Flinterman and Leckie "Commentary to the Maastricht Guidelines on Economic, Social and Cultural Rights" (1998) 20 *Hum Rts Q* 705 at 717.
55 *General Comment 13: The Right to Education* (1999) CESCR UN Doc E/C.12/1999/10 para 57.

The CESCR clearly decided to retain the "obligations" language used in General Comment No. 3. In practical terms, however, there seems to be little difference between a core content approach on the one hand, and a core obligations approach on the other, because core elements of the human rights of individuals give rise to equivalent obligations for the state.

7 CONCLUDING REMARKS

This paper contains a tentative effort, from a legal perspective, to shed more light on the normative content of the right to education. Contributions from disciplines other than law are necessary, because many activities and measures dealing with the implementation of the right to education will be of a policy, financial or pedagogical nature. There is a risk that identifying the core elements of a right and the corresponding minimum obligations could lead to neglect of peripheral elements of the same right and to undermining its universal character. I believe, however, that the search for core elements of economic, social and cultural rights and the corresponding minimum state obligations serves, first of all, analytical purposes. From a human rights perspective, it is of the utmost importance to clarify (vague) treaty norms in order to make clear to governments the precise meaning of the treaty obligations that they have accepted voluntarily, and then to scrutinise the acts and omissions of governments in terms of their observance of these rights and obligations. In addition, it is important to assist monitoring bodies, both at the intergovernmental and non-governmental levels, to identify violations, to seek redress, and to prevent future such violations by ensuring that governments alter their legislation and practice. Finally, clarification of rights and obligations in the field of economic, social and cultural rights may contribute to strengthening the justiciability of these rights at the national and international levels. After all, from the perspective of the equality, interdependence and indivisibility of human rights, the overall aim should be to strengthen the legal basis and the implementation of economic, social and cultural rights which, unfortunately, have been neglected too long.

Addendum

On the basis of the discussions during the Pretoria conference, and reflecting a bit more on the concept of the core content of economic, social and cultural rights, I think it is attractive to read into this concept a progressive or evolving dimension. From this perspective the concept can be seen as an expanding floor from which states should endeavour to move upwards. This concept also creates a link to the idea of progressive realisation contained in Article 2(1) of the ICESCR: this provision embodies a dynamic element, meaning that realisation of a right does not stop when a given level is reached.

In this paper I have suggested that the core content of a right would mean that the minimum essential level for each right has a universal scope, instead of a country-dependent core. This would imply that in general terms the core of a right should be the same everywhere. However, this core should be translated, or operationalised at the national or regional level, taking into account national, regional or local characteristics and circumstances and the specific needs of individuals and groups. In this respect I do not agree with the Judgment of the Constitutional Court of South Africa in the *Grootboom* case,[56] in which the Court stated that one must first identify the needs and opportunities for the enjoyment of a right before determining the minimum core in a given context. This implies that the people's needs and the available opportunities would determine the core of a right, rather than starting with the right itself. In effect this would make implementation of a right dependent on the outcome of a political bargaining process that would entail identifying the needs of the people along with the desirable and feasible opportunities, and abandoning a rights-based approach. Instead, guidance about the core content of a right should come from the international supervisory bodies, for example the UN Committee on Economic, Social and Cultural Rights, which have developed their expertise on the basis of many years of examining state reports. Core elements of the right to education, such as access to education on a nondiscriminatory basis, the right to free and compulsory primary or basic education, and special facilities for persons with an educational deficit, should be translated into carefully targeted policies and programmes in order to pro-

---

56 *The Government of the Republic of South Africa and Others v Grootboom and Others* 2000 (11) BCLR 1169 (CC) para 31-33.

tect, as a matter of priority, the rights of the most vulnerable.[57] For example, adequate schoolbuildings that provide protection against the elements; additional teachers with adequate salaries; a fellowship system; transport facilities for pupils; teaching materials such as pencils, books and blackboards; and water and sanitation facilities are among the elements that should be provided. The question of course remains, where to begin. That question should be answered by the competent authorities, taking into account the overarching guarantee of human dignity in the South African Constitution, which would protect, as a matter of priority, the rights of the most disadvantaged.[58]

I found it interesting to note that during the conference discussions on the core content of the right to education, there was little mention of those elements of the core content related to the freedom dimension of the right to education (for example, free choice of education, and respect by the state for teaching in minority languages). Indeed, one might question the relevance of the freedom to establish educational institutions by a minority in the light of the heritage of apartheid and the need to end the discrimination of the black majority in South Africa and to promote equality, intercultural and bi- and multilingual education, unity and nation-building. I believe that these needs are more pressing at present than funding single medium public educational institutions as provided by section 29 (2) of the Constitution. One of the purposes of guaranteeing minority rights in education under international law is to protect the rights of minorities from discrimination by the majority, which is probably not the situation in South Africa presently. In addition, on the basis of the international law of human rights the South African government does not have an obligation to subsidise the independent educational institutions provided for in section 29 (3) and (4). It has only the obligation not to discriminate among private educational institutions.

This does not mean that protection of the freedom dimension will be less pertinent in other countries as well. When civil and political rights, such as freedom of religion or freedom of association, are being violated in a given country, protecting the right of parents freely to choose their children's education and/or to establish their own schools is clearly of great importance.

---

57 See *General Comment 3: The nature of States parties obligations* (1990) UN Doc E/1991/23 paras 10 and 12.
58 *The Government of the Republic of South Africa and Others v Grootboom and Others* 2000 (11) BCLR 1169 (CC) para 83.

Analysis of state obligations relating to the right to education

NATURE OF STATE OBLIGATIONS	SOCIAL DIMENSION OF THE RIGHT TO EDUCATION		FREEDOM DIMENSION OF THE RIGHT TO EDUCATION	
	ACCESSIBILITY	AVAILABILITY	LIBERTY TO CHOOSE	LIBERTY TO ESTABLISH
TO RESPECT	• Respect free access to public education both in legislation, policy and practice without discrimination [m.c.o.]	• Respect existing public education in minority languages;	• Respect religious and philosophical convictions (granting exemption), Respect freedom of school choice, • Respect human dignity, • Respect teaching in minority languages [m.c.o.]	• Respect free establishment of private schools (subject to legal minimum standards); • Respect (cultural) diversity in education
TO PROTECT	• Apply and uphold equal access to education in legislation policy and practice against violations by third persons (parents, employers); • Adopt and implement legislation against child labour	• Regulate recognition of private educational institutions and diplomas;	• Combat indoctrination or coercion by others; Protect legally freedom to choose [m.c.o.]; • Combat discrimination in the admission of students to private institutions; • Guarantee pluralism in the curriculum	• Apply and uphold the principle of equality of treatment; • Protect legally private teachers' training institutions and diplomas
TO FULFIL	• Provide special educational facilities for persons with an educational back-log (e.g. the disabled, girls, drop-outs, street children) [m.c.o.]; • Eliminate passive discrimination; introduce progressively free secondary and higher education; • Promote scholarship system	• Secure compulsory and free primary education [m.c.o.]; • Make transportation facilities and teaching materials available; Combat illiteracy; • Promote adult education; • Guarantee quality of education [m.c.o.]	• Promote pluralism in the curriculum; • Promote intercultural education	• Provide financial and material support to institutions for private education on a non-discriminatory basis

OF FLOORS AND CEILINGS: MINIMUM CORE OBLIGATIONS AND CHILDREN

Geraldine Van Bueren

1 OF FLOORS AND CEILINGS

As Paul Simon sang, one man's ceiling is another man's floor. There is a risk that governments can perceive the minimum core as the maximum of a State party's duty. This risk is particularly great with children, as Article 10(3) of the International Covenant on Economic, Social and Cultural Rights (ICESCR)[1] is so wide-ranging.

Article 10(3) is almost a mini-convention in its own right, potentially spanning all the economic and social entitlements of the child. The first sentence of the article is broad, calling for "[s]pecial measures of protection and assistance" to be taken "on behalf of all children and young persons".[2] In essence "special

---

1   International Covenant on Economic, Social, and Cultural Rights, *opened for signature* 16 Dec 1966, *entered into force* 3 Jan 1976, 993 UNTS 3.
2   Affirmative action in international law is referred to as "special measures". UN Doc E/CN.4/Sub.2 2000 at para 4. Although the Convention on the Rights of the Child had not yet been drafted, the drafters of the Covenant would have been aware of both the first and second Declarations of the Rights of the Child adopted by the League of Nations in 1924 and by the United Nations in 1959. The phrase "special measures" is closely akin to "special safeguards and care", which occurs in the preamble of the 1959 Declaration: "Whereas the child, by reason of his physical and mental immaturity, needs special safeguards and care". Similar phrasing also occurs in principle 2, "The child shall enjoy special protection ... 'to enable children to develop in conditions of freedom and dignity'". Reproduced in Van Bueren *International documents on children* (1998) Kluwer.

measures" for children is child affirmative action. So there appears to be an inherent tension in finding a minimum core for state policies and action, which narrows the field, and affirmative action, which implies a more expansive approach. It is therefore essential that the minimum core and progressive realisation be seen as integral.

2 WHAT IS THE MINIMUM CORE?

The minimum core is extracted by reference to the language of Article 10(3), to the *travaux préparatoires*, and to the comments of the Committee on Economic, Social and Cultural Rights (CESCR) on States parties' reports. However, this alone would freeze the minimum core in time and undermine the essence of the progressive nature of international human rights law. Reference must also be made, as a matter of international law, to the Convention on the Rights of the Child (CRC)[3] and to subsequent United Nations treaties, resolutions and programmes of action. Indeed the states themselves have sought to expand the minimum core by adopting three more treaties specifically focusing on different aspects of the exploitation of children with which Article 10(3) is expressly concerned.[4]

That the minimum core expands over time must be correct; otherwise, treaty obligations would be rendered ineffective when confronting developments that did not exist at the time of the drafting of the Covenant, such as the impact of HIV/AIDS.

This still leaves a number of questions. Is the minimum core a universal minimum core or does it vary from state to state, depending upon resources? Although at first sight it may appear strange to conclude that the minimum core is the same for Benin as for Canada, there would be no point in having a minimum core of state responsibility if it were not universal.

---

3 Convention on the Rights of the Child, *opened for signature* 20 November 1989, *entered into force* 2 September 1990, 28 ILM 1456 (hereinafter CRC).
4 Optional Protocol to the Convention on the Rights of the Child on the involvement of children in armed conflicts, adopted by General Assembly resolution A/RES/54/263 (May 2000), enters into force 13 February 2002; Optional Protocol to the Convention on the Rights of the Child on the sale of children, child prostitution and child pornography, adopted by General Assembly resolution A/RES/54/263 (May 2000), enters into force 18 January 2002; International Labour Organisation, Convention No. 182 concerning the Prohibition and Immediate Action for the Elimination of the Worst Forms of Child Labour (1999), entered into force 19 November 2000.

The duty of a state is twofold. First it must implement the minimum core, and secondly, it must realise progressively the remaining facets of the right. The minimum core of the obligation is the same for developing and industrial states but the duty on states in implementing the remaining parts of the rights varies from state to state depending upon resources.

The minimum core of each right, however, has not been defined. The advantages of a lack of definition are flexibility – allowing for change and non-limitation. The disadvantages are obvious and outweigh the advantages. Instead of flexibility there is vagueness and lack of clarity leading to a difficulty in implicating government responsibility.

One cannot excavate the minimum core of Article 10(3) in isolation. The minimum core of Article 10(3) is complementary to the other rights to which children are entitled under the ICESCR.

2 THE NATURE OF RESOURCES

The progressive duty is linked to resources, and too often resources have been too narrowly defined, taking into account only direct economic resources. There is no legally binding reason why resources should be so narrowly defined. Indeed, international human rights law offers a more expansive and more inclusive approach to measuring a state's resources.

Also to be included in the equation are human and organisational resources.[5] Human resources include the time, energy, motivation, skills, professionalism, vision and desire of individual adults, children and communities. Organisational resources include both the formal and informal relationships by which actions are taken in society, encompassing political organisations, indigenous peoples' organisations, families and non-governmental organisations. The submission and consideration of such data present a new and challenging approach for both lawyers and courts. However, such resource and impact studies are, in reality, only a conceptually logical extension of the Brandeis brief.

---

5   Parker "Resources and child rights: An economic perspective" in Himes (ed) *Implementing the Convention on the Rights of the Child: Resource mobilisation in low income countries* (1995) UNICEF/Martinus Nijhoff 35-37.

4 READING IN THE PRINCIPLES OF THE CRC TO THE MINIMUM CORE.

Reading in is an interpretative method by which a court will interpose words to a law as a remedy, thereby extending its scope and ensuring compliance with a constitution.[6] There is no principled reason why it cannot also be applied to international law, so that earlier treaty provisions comply with the obligations imposed on a government in later treaties.

The Covenant's travaux préparatoires make clear that states are obligated to protect children and to provide them with "positive assistance".[7] Protection and assistance imply that the minimum core of Article 10(3) focuses on the prevention, protection and provision rights of the child. However, by virtue of the CRC, to which all ICESCR states parties are bound, as well as other states including South Africa, the participation rights of the child are now included in the minimum core.[8] Consequently children, according their age and maturity, have the right to be consulted and to have their opinions considered in relation to any special measures of protection and assistance.[9] Children now have the right to be consulted not only on individual decisions affecting them but also at earlier policy formulation periods such as with child health policies, including HIV/AIDS.[10] The Committee on the Rights of the Child recommended to South Africa the full participation of youth (defined as those below the age of 25) in the development of strategies to respond to HIV/AIDS.[11]

The UN Committee on the Rights of the Child has been concerned about the lack of child-friendly procedures to address complaints from children concerning violations of their economic and social rights.[12] Thus the child's participation is a part of the minimum core of states' obligations with respect to each and every relevant substantive article in the ICESCR.

---

6 See for example *Schachter v Canada* 1992 93 DLR 1.
7 Official Records of the General Assembly, Third Committee para 37, 14 January 1957.
8 For the four Ps of the CRC (protection, provision, prevention and participation) see Van Bueren *The international law on the rights of the child* (1995) Kluwer at 15.
9 Articles 12 and 13 CRC.
10 On the child's right to freedom of expression see Van Bueren *The international law on the rights of the child* (1995) Kluwer at 131.
11 UN Doc CRC/A/55/41.
12 The Committee's comments concerned all the rights in the CRC including economic and social rights. In relation to South Africa see UN Doc CRC/A/55/41 at para 144.

5 TO WHOM DOES THE MINIMUM CORE OF STATES OBLIGATIONS APPLY?

I have deliberately used the words child and children, but Article 10(3) refers to children and young persons. To whom then does this minimum core of special protection and assistance extend?

The phrase "young persons" is not a term of art in international law and has never been defined. An analysis of the *travaux préparatoires* of the ICESCR demonstrates that the words "children and young persons" were proposed by the United Kingdom to replace the word "minors".[13] This implies that the phrase "children and young persons" is limited to all those who have not reached the age of majority in their respective states.[14]

The term "child" is now defined, at least for every state in the world bar two (the USA and Somalia),[15] by reference to Article 1 of the CRC, which sets 18 as the standard, "unless under the law applicable to the child, majority is attained earlier."[16] For States parties to the African Charter on the Rights and Welfare of the Child, 18 is the absolute standard with no exceptions.[17]

The minimum core applies to all those under the age of 18 living in the States parties. This is supported by the fact that Article 10 as a whole refers to the family, and the discussions during the drafting of Article 10 refer to the protection and assistance of children whilst they are still of an age to be dependant on their family.[18]

This raises another facet of the minimum core. How can a government design and plan economic and social polices concerning children if they do not know the number of inhabitants under the age of 18 or in which part of the country the children live?

---

13 UN Doc A/C.3/L.574. Adopted by 43 votes to 7 with 12 abstentions.
14 At first reading it would seem to indicate those who are not children. It also appears linguistically close to the term "youth", which has been defined by the United Nations as below age 25. This raises the question whether Article 10(3) is also applicable to those above the age of 18 who are not children under their domestic legislation. As the trend in domestic legislation has been for states to reduce their age of majority, spurred on, in some cases, by recommendations from regional organisations, the minimum core of Article 10(3) applies to those under the age of 18 unless they have reached their age of majority earlier. For African states, once the African Charter on the Rights and Welfare of the Child comes into effect, the provisions concerning the social and economic exploitation of children apply to all those under the age of 18 without exception, because of the inherently degrading nature of exploitation.
15 Only Somalia and the United States of America are not party to the CRC.
16 See further Van Bueren *The international law on the rights of the child* (1995) Kluwer 36 – 38.
17 Article 2.
18 See Record of the General Assembly, Tenth Session, Agenda Item 31.

Birth registration is a precondition of special protection and assistance for all those under 18. In some states children without a birth certificate are not eligible for education, supplementary feeding and access to health services. Individual impoverished children are invisible partly because they have no birth certificate. If there is little incentive, that is, if the family perceives that they will receive nothing in return, then non-registration is understandable, particularly when compounded by illiteracy and distance to travel for registration. In Bangladesh an experiment is beginning in developing certificates that will withstand water and will also be decorative and attractive to keep. In Angola mobile birth registration units in lorries have been organised because of the country's lack of infrastructure. The Committee on the Rights of the Child has recommended similar mobile clinics to South Africa.

Weak or inadequate birth registration procedures in turn undermine a minimum age for child labour as is required by Article 10(3)'s minimum core.

6 DISCRIMINATION AND SPECIAL PROTECTION AND ASSISTANCE FOR CHILDREN

Article 10(3) links its call for special measures of protection and assistance to the principle of non-discrimination. Thus the ICE-SCR emphasises that states are not only under a duty not to discriminate against specific groups of children, but that the minimum core extends their duty even further and obliges them to provide vulnerable groups with special protection and assistance to ensure equality.[19] The principle of equality and non-discrimination does not undermine the principle of special protection and assistance. Rather it supports it, by seeking to ensure that all children, including those from vulnerable groups, are entitled to equality of opportunity. In particular, there was much concern during the drafting of Article 10(3) that the special measures of protection and assistance should not be denied to children without families or to non-marital children.

The CRC adds ethnic origin and disability and prohibits discrimination and punishment, not only on the basis of the child's parentage but also on the status, activities, expressed opinions or

---

19 On Equality and the rights of children see Van Bueren *The international law on the rights of the child* (1995) Kluwer at 38 – 45.

beliefs of the child's parents, legal guardians or family members. Such grounds also form a part of the minimum core of states' obligations of equality and non-discrimination to children under the ICESCR. This is determined not only by applying the non-binding Limburg Principles in interpreting Article 2(2) of the ICESCR,[20] but also by applying Article 2 of the CRC, to which all the States parties to the ICESCR are also party.

The principle of non-discrimination prohibits unjustifiable advantage being given to groups of children on the basis of their parents' activities or status. The number of vulnerable groups makes it impossible to point to specific approaches that constitute exhaustively the minimum core. These groups include children of other nationalities and children who are born stateless. The special measures of protection and assistance should be aimed at preventing children of ethnic minorities becoming more marginalised.[21] The Committee on Economic, Social and Cultural Rights has expressed concern over the nationality of Haitian children and of children of Haitians born in the Dominican Republic,[22] and concern with Spain over discrimination against aliens, particularly amongst Romani and North African children.[23]

The particular needs of the specific group of vulnerable children dictate the solution. Although the groups of children who are particularly vulnerable and entitled to special measures of protection and assistance may vary from state to state, guidance can be sought from the comments of both the Committee on Economic, Social and Cultural Rights and the Committee on the Rights of the Child. The Committee on Economic, Social and Cultural Rights has, for example, expressed concern over preferences given to certain groups of children, including the children of war victims and the children of decorated families.[24]

The minimum core obligations encompass special protection and assistance to children who are in the care of the state, including:
- those in children's homes;[25]
- children who are also mothers;

---

20 Reproduced in (1987) 9 *Hum Rts Q* 122.
21 See the comments of the Dutch Commission of Jurists on the Netherlands in UN Doc E/C.12/1998/NGO.1.
22 See UN Doc E/C.12/1997/9.
23 UN Doc E/C.12/1/Add.2.
24 See the *Concluding observations of the Committee on Economic, Social and Cultural Rights in relation to Vietnam.* UN Doc E/C.12/1993/8.
25 See the *Concluding observations of the Committee on Economic, Social and Cultural Rights on the United Kingdom* in UN Doc E/C.12/1/Add.19 December 1997.

- non-marital children;
- homeless children;
- children of ethnic minorities;
- children with disabilities;
- children living in rural communities; and
- children living and/or working on the streets.

The Committee on Economic, Social and Cultural Rights has also recommended that all "necessary legislative and economic measures" be taken to protect children living and working on the street, including information programmes in respect of mental and physical health care. The failure to provide protection and assistance to children living and working on the streets is also a common violation amongst states including Kenya.[26]

The twin principles of non-discrimination and special protection can also be used creatively to help combat child labour, an issue upon which Article 10(3) also focuses. Special protection and assistance, when combined with non-discrimination and the right to equality, implies that children should not be paid at a lower rate than adults for the same work when their work rate is equally effective.[27] This principle of fair remuneration has an unappreciated potential in combatting child labour. If children were paid equally to adults would child labour be so widespread?

To ensure that States parties are implementing the minimum core of their obligations under Article 10(3), they must identify in their reports the groups of children who are vulnerable to discrimination.

7 PROTECTION FROM ECONOMIC, SEXUAL AND SOCIAL EXPLOITATION

Article 10(3) places a clear duty on states to protect children from economic and social exploitation and prohibits the employment of children in harmful work. The nature and content of these duties have now been clarified by two optional protocols to the CRC on armed conflict and sexual exploitation[28] and the new ILO

26　UN Doc E/C.12/1993/6.
27　See for example the provision in para 13 of the regional treaty, the European Social Charter, *opened for signature* 18 October 1961, *entered into force* 26 February 1965, ETS 35 (European Social Charter) on fair remuneration and the principle of equal pay for equal work.
28　Optional Protocol to the Convention on the Rights of the Child on the involvement of children in armed conflicts, adopted by General Assembly resolution A/RES/54/263 (May

Convention 182 on the Prohibition and Immediate Elimination of the Worst Forms of Child Labour. The original minimum core has been expanded by obliging states to prevent the forced or compulsory recruitment of those under the age of 18 for use in armed conflicts.[29]

It is also clear that it is the abuse of child labour that is prohibited, and not child labour itself.[30] There is no precise definition of child labour, as it is a portmanteau term covering many diverse situations. Child labour can be divided into six categories: domestic, non-domestic, non-monetary, bonded labour, wage labour and marginal economic activity. It extends to paid employment, piecework at home and unpaid work within the family.

International law does not regard all child labour as constituting exploitation. Economic exploitation occurs when labouring is at the expense of development. Child labour is exploitative when it threatens the physical, mental, emotional or social development of the child. However, many children welcome an opportunity to work, regarding it as a "rite of passage to adulthood".[31] Traditional

---

2000), enters into force 13 February 2002; Optional Protocol to the Convention on the Rights of the Child on the sale of children, child prostitution and child pornography, adopted by General Assembly resolution A/RES/54/263 (May 2000), enters into force 18 January 2002; International Labour Organisation, Convention No. 182 concerning the Prohibition and Immediate Action for the Elimination of the Worst Forms of Child Labour (1999), entered into force 19 November 2000. The Optional Protocol on the sale and exploitation of children covers the same ground as Articles 32 to 36 of the CRC. It also prohibits the sale of children, child prostitution and child pornography but it does make significant improvements in the enforcement of law and in creating child-centred proceedings. The Protocol usefully clarifies that it may be necessary for a state to exercise extraterritorial jurisdiction, thus taking the issue of universal jurisdiction for such violations out of the backwoods realm of state sovereignty. Offences concerning the sale of children, child prostitution and child pornography are deemed extraditable. When a request for extradition is received from a state with no extradition treaty, the requested state may usefully consider the Protocol as the legal basis for such extradition. The Protocol is particularly valuable in focusing government responsibilities on the creation of child-friendly proceedings. Article 8 seeks to protect the rights of child victims and witnesses without prejudicing the rights of the accused to a fair trial. States should inform child victims of their rights, the role, scope, timing and progress of the proceedings, and provide "appropriate support services to child victims", including protection of the children's privacy. Uncertainty as to the actual age of the victim should not prevent the initiation of criminal investigation.

29 Article 3(a) ILO Convention 182.
30 International law distinguishes between child labour and the exploitation of children. This fact is made clear by the title of the Report of the Special Rapporteur, who did not study all child labour, but only the "exploitation" of child labour. Similarly the CRC recognises "the right of the child to be protected from economic exploitation and from performing any work that is likely to be hazardous or to interfere with the child's education or to be harmful to the child's health or physical, mental, spiritual, moral or social development". The use of the word "and" confirms that economic exploitation and work are not identical. These legislative approaches underline the fundamental difference between the right to work and being obliged to work.
31 Fyfe *Child labour* at 9.

family agricultural work is regarded as a productive social function, although increasingly the family is no longer able to act as a protective barrier between the child and the employer.

Work is exploitative when it is undertaken at too young an age and is detrimental to the well-being of the child, who as a consequence of working too young is also deprived of educational entitlements, vocational training and personal progress for the future. Exploitation of children at work also occurs when the financial remuneration or services in kind are less than what would be paid to adults for undertaking the same work. Factors signalling exploitation include:
- beginning full time work at too early an age;
- working for too many hours a day;
- inadequate remuneration;
- work that causes excessive physical, psychological and social strain;
- work and life on the streets;
- excessive responsibility at too young an age;
- work that hampers the psychological and social development of the child; and
- work that inhibits the child's self-esteem.[32]

To this one can add situations in which children are working in breach of international standards.

The minimum core obligations of states include taking all the necessary measures – legislative, educational, social and financial – to prevent the economic exploitation of children.

The state's duties in relation to social exploitation are slightly less clear than in relation to economic exploitation because of the lack of clarity surrounding the term "social exploitation". During the drafting of the CRC the term "social exploitation" was said to cause confusion and needed greater specificity. Instead of repeating the term, specific forms of exploitation were highlighted. Hence, the CRC assists in identifying key elements of the minimum core including:
- the prevention of child abduction, sale and trafficking;
- the protection of children from the illicit use of narcotic drugs and psychotropic substances and the use of children in the production and trafficking of these substances; and
- the protection of children from all forms of sexual exploitation and abuse including prostitution and pornography.

---

32   UNICEF *Exploitation of working and street children* (1986) Executive Board Paper.

The CRC also incorporates a catchall provision. Article 36 obliges states to "protect the child against all other forms of exploitation prejudicial to any aspects of the child's welfare"; this would include protecting children living and working on the street.[33] All these situations are considered forms of social exploitation.

8 EMPLOYMENT IN HARMFUL WORK

In addition to prohibiting sexual exploitation, Article 10(3) prohibits the employment of children in all work that is harmful to their morals, life-threatening or likely to hamper their development. Employers who subject children to such "work" should be punished by law. All such work is inherently exploitative and therefore is prohibited by the second sentence of Article 10(3).

The inclusion of the prohibition against harmful work is to provide guidance for states concerning the type of work that amounts to exploitation. The parameters of the minimum core of states' obligations are clear and have been made even clearer by IL0 Convention No. 138 (Minimum Age Convention) and by the recent ILO Convention No. 182 on the worst forms of child labour. All those under the age of 18 are prohibited from performing any form of hazardous or exploitative "work".

The duty is placed on States parties to determine, after consultation with organisations of employers and workers, which types of work are harmful.[34] To do this states should take full account of any relevant treaties to which they are party, including those concerning dangerous substances, the lifting of heavy weights, and underground work. Also as part of the minimum core, States parties should periodically revise these definitions to take account of advancing scientific knowledge and epidemiological research. They should also take particular account of the dangers to girls.

The duty in the minimum core of states' obligations is to protect children against both overt and covert exploitation. Children are overtly exploited when they work in an environment that would be hazardous or unsafe for adults. They may be covertly exploited when performing tasks that are considered safe for adults, but that are not necessarily safe for children because children are still in a

---

33 See the *Concluding observations of the Committee on Economic, Social and Cultural Rights in relation to Vietnam*. UN Doc E/C.12/1993/8.
34 Article 3(2).

period of growth and development. Children's toxicological reactions cannot be regarded as the same as adults', nor can it be assumed that their working capacities can be calculated in direct proportion to those of adults.[35]

Children may react differently from adults to certain psychosocial factors. In addition there are forms of employment that are not in themselves hazardous but that may become hazardous in certain circumstances because of the length of the hours worked. The CRC provides for the appropriate "regulation of the hours and conditions of employment."[36] Specifically, in Article 31 of the Convention, children are entitled to the right to rest and leisure; this includes working children. Hence, another facet of states' minimum obligations toward children includes the regulation by law of the number of working hours and the creation of the mechanisms for child labour supervision.

9 THE ESTABLISHMENT OF MINIMUM AGES AND FAIR REMUNERATION FOR CHILD LABOUR

The ICESCR itself does not incorporate a specific minimum age for entry into child labour. The minimum age is found in two later instruments: ILO Convention No. 138 and Recommendation No. 146 concerning the Minimum Age for Admission to Employment. The minimum age coincides with the ending of basic education. The ILO Convention 138 sets 15 as the minimum age although it allows states "whose economy and educational facilities are insufficiently developed" to specify a minimum age of 14 years. States parties, however, may set the lower minimum age only after consultation with organisations of concerned employers and workers if they exist. Article 10(3) obliges States parties to prohibit employment below the minimum age and to punish those responsible for violations.[37] This obligation underlines the importance of registering births and requiring the employer to keep documents on employees' names and ages or dates of birth.[38]

Article 10(3) is also intrinsically linked with the minimum core of the child's right to education. Fifteen, the age of eligibility for

---

35 World Health Organisation *Children at work: Special health risks. Report of WHO Study Group Technical Report* (1987) Series 756, at 7.
36 Article 32(2)(b).
37 Article 9 of the ILO Convention 138 provides that "[a]ll necessary measures including the provision of appropriate penalties" should be taken.
38 Article 9(3) Convention 138.

most labour, is not an arbitrary age; it coincides with the minimum age for the completion of basic education. It is grossly inadequate for a state to prohibit children from performing labour without providing alternatives for the child and the child's family. Hence, in relation to South Africa the Committee on the Rights of the Child recommended that South Africa expand its Child Support Grant or develop alternative programmes to support children who are still in school, up to the age of 18. Such an approach reinforces the core goal of preventing economic and social exploitation.

In addition to the increasing but still comparatively small number of States parties to Convention 138, the age of 15 is reinforced by the duty in the CRC to establish a minimum age of employment.[39] However, it is difficult to argue that the minimum ages of 14 and 15 can automatically be read into Article 10(3) of the ICESCR because there is insufficient state practice, as evidenced by the small number of States parties to ILO Convention 138. Because of this lack of clear universal acceptance it is difficult to conclude that the age of 15 represents the standard in international or regional customary law. However, because of the repeated references to the ILO standard,[40] any state that adopts an age lower than 14 or 15 has the onus of justifying the lower age. Therefore, paradoxically, although the precise age is not part of the minimum core, the requirement that states set a minimum age is a part of the minimum core of states' obligations.

When a State party to the ILO Convention has set 14 as the minimum age for child labour, then it is a part of the minimum core to keep this age under review, and to ensure that the reasons for the lower age continue to exist.

10 RECOVERY AND REINTEGRATION SERVICES FOR CHILDREN

The minimum core of states' obligations extends from preventing problems from arising to preventing problems from recurring. This can only be achieved through recovery and reintegration services provided under conditions that foster the health, self-respect and dignity of the child. Whenever possible, recovery and

---

39 Article 32(2) CRC.
40 See, for example, article 15 African Charter on the Rights and Welfare of the Child 1990 reproduced in Van Bueren *International documents on children* (2d ed 1998) Kluwer.

reintegration should occur within families and communities, with effective action taken to prevent the social stigmatisation of children. In addition, non-exploitative alternative means of livelihood for child victims and their families should be promoted to prevent further exploitation.[41] This is part of the minimum core of states' obligations protecting children against both social and economic exploitation. It is read into the ICESCR because all the States parties to Article 10(3) are also bound by Article 39 of the CRC.

The Programme of Action for the Prevention of Sale of Children, Child Prostitution and Child Pornography adopted by the Commission on Human Rights proposes that recovery and reintegration services adopt interdisciplinary approaches[42] and that this principle be applied to all recovery services. It is also essential that medical personnel, teachers, social workers and NGOs helping child victims receive gender-sensitive training.

11 THE INTERDEPENDENCE OF ARTICLE 10(3) WITH CIVIL AND POLITICAL RIGHTS

Children's rights are holistic. Combatting child poverty is a way out of the unnecessary quagmire of the generations of rights debate.[43] There was a deliberate attempt by the drafters of the Convention on the Rights of the Child to break free from the generational chains and integrate civil and political rights with economic, social and cultural rights. The CRC instituted a different approach to classification, based on the assumption that protecting children's rights requires a more positive approach than the prevailing generational wisdom, which owed its origins more to the negative diplomatic strategies of the Cold War than to a deep understanding of the nature of human rights.

This approach is the four Ps: participation, prevention,[44] provision and protection. The breakdown of the Convention in this

---

41 Agenda for Action of the World Congress Against Commercial Sexual Exploitation of Children, reproduced in Van Bueren *International documents on children* (2d ed 1998) Kluwer.
42 Commission on Human Rights, Res 1992/74 5 March 1992, annex.
43 Referring to the notion that civil and political rights are "first generation" rights and economic, social and cultural rights are "second generation" rights. See also de Vos "The economic and social rights of children and South Africa's constitution" (1995) *SA Public Law* 233.
44 See Van Bueren *International documents on children* (2d ed 1998) Kluwer at 13, 381-83. The author was one of the drafters of the CRC.

way is useful, as it moves away from the old generations of rights approach in favour of a more dynamic one. It also reflects the truer legal reality: In terms of the CRC, children's economic, social and cultural rights are so fundamental that no derogations are allowed to their implementation, even in times of emergency that threaten the life of the nation.[45] In addition, some rights that may have been conceptualised historically as economic and social rights in reality mask violations of children's civil rights, amounting to violations of their right to freedom from torture, and cruel, inhuman and degrading treatment.

According to General Comment No. 3, Article 10(3) "would seem to be capable of immediate application by judicial and other organs in many national legal systems".[46] According to the Committee on Economic, Social and Cultural Rights any suggestion that Article 10(3) is inherently non-self executing "would seem difficult to sustain".[47] The argument that Article 10(3) enshrines an immediately binding minimum core of states' obligations is strengthened by the prohibition on exploitation, which is inherently degrading and often cruel, and so falls within the immediate prohibition on states of torture, and cruel, inhuman and degrading treatment.[48] Such a prohibition is found in numerous treaties, including Article 37(a) of the CRC, and arguably amounts to *ius cogens*. Specific forms of economic exploitation such as debt bondage and commercial sexual exploitation[49] are also regarded as contemporary forms of slavery and so are similarly prohibited. It is beyond doubt that all the necessary measures that need to be taken to prevent all forms of exploitation must form a part of the minimum core of Article 10(3).

Article 10(3) must also include within its immediately binding minimum core the obligation of states to establish an accessible register of birth, as without a verifiable record of ages it is not possible to ascertain with certainty who is a child entitled to special protection and assistance. In addition, a lack of verifiable birth

---

45 The CRC deliberately omits a derogation clause so that no derogations are permitted. There is, however, under section 37 of the South African Constitution the possibility of derogation in relation to section 28(l)(c), children's rights "to basic nutrition, shelter, basic health care services and social services". Should this ever occur, it could be problematic in light of South Africa's international obligations under the CRC.
46 UN Doc E/1991/23.
47 *Ibid.*
48 See further Van Bueren (ed) *Childhood abused – Protecting children against torture, cruel, inhuman and degrading treatment and punishment* (1998) Dartmouth, Programme on International Rights of the Child Series.
49 Article 3 Declaration and Agenda for Action Against the Commercial Sexual Exploitation of Children 1996.

records makes minimum age legislation impossible to enforce effectively. In this way Article 10(3) reinforces the duty on states under the International Covenant on Civil and Political Rights[50] and the CRC for immediate registration of births.

According to the General Comment any assessment as to whether a State party has discharged its minimum core obligations must also take account of resource constraints applying within the state. In assessing the availability of resources in, for example, drafting legislation on child labour or advising on the necessary special measures of protection and assistance for children without families, account has to be taken of the facilitation of technical advice and assistance under the CRC and in the detailed programmes of action found in other relevant instruments concerning children. As General Comment 3 notes, the obligation to monitor and devise strategies for the promotion of the rights is not "in any way eliminated as a result of resource constraints."

General Comment No. 3 also underlines the fact that even in times of economic recession and restructuring, "the vulnerable members of society" (and although this is not specified, it must by implication include children), "must be protected by the adoption of relatively low cost targeted programmes." Indeed it is arguable that in such times the duty on the state is higher, as it is precisely during periods of economic recession that children are most at risk from economic and social exploitation.

12 SANCTIONS AND THE MINIMUM STATES OBLIGATIONS UNDER ARTICLE 10(3)

During the 1990s the Security Council imposed sanctions upon a number of states including Somalia, Iraq, parts of the former Republic of Yugoslavia, Libyan Arab Jamahariya, Rwanda and the Sudan. The Secretary-General has stated that there is a need to assess the impact of sanctions on vulnerable groups. This approach was taken up in the Graça Machel study on children and armed conflict.[51]

The imposition of sanctions does not reduce the minimum obligations of States parties. The duty, for example, to prevent

---

50 International Covenant on Civil and Political Rights, *opened for signature* 16 December 1966, *entered into force* 23 March 1976, 99 UNTS 171 (hereinafter ICCPR).
51 UN Doc A/51/306 Annex 1996 para 128.

economic and social exploitation becomes even more important in times of hardship and consequential increased vulnerability. The majority of the permanent members of the Security Council are party to the ICESCR, and minimum core obligations ought to be taken into account when designing sanctions regimes. As Minear observes, the decisions to reduce "the suffering of children or to minimise other adverse consequences can be taken without jeopardising the policy aim of sanctions."[52] It is in this way that the minimum core duties of one state can be used to expand the responsibilities of one state to another.

13 COMMON VIOLATIONS OF ARTICLE 10(3)

Based on the preceding analysis it can be stated that common violations of Article 10(3) include:
- The lack of adequate inspection services for both the informal and the formal sectors to supervise the prohibition on child exploitation.
- The lack of special protection and assistance for children working as domestic servants, in rural areas, and in the informal and traditional sectors.[53]
- The trafficking of children for the purposes of adoption and sexual exploitation. States are required as a part of the minimum core to have in place an effective legal regime for controlling inter-country adoption. In the absence of such a regime, children may be subject to sexual abuse and exploitation.[54]
- The lack of minimum age legislation and legislation prohibiting and preventing child sexual exploitation.

14 IMMEDIATE STATE OBLIGATIONS UNDER ARTICLE 10(3)

States must immediately identify the groups of children who are most vulnerable and who need special assistance and protection. Included in this task is the immediate effective prohibition of dis-

---

52 Minear *Towards more humane and effective sanctions management: Enhancing the capacity of the UN system* (1997).
53 See for example Morocco UN Doc E/C.12/1994/5.
54 See the concern expressed by the Committee on the Rights of the Child to Azerbaijan UN Doc/E/C.12/1. Add 20.

crimination based on parentage or other grounds such as ethnicity, religion and disability.

A state must eliminate immediately all forms of exploitative and hazardous child labour. It must immediately establish a minimum age, consistent with international principles, for admission into employment and the regulation of children's working hours. Mechanisms for inspection and supervision should be established for both the formal and informal sectors.

States must immediately identify and ameliorate the factors contributing to the sexual exploitation of children, and states must have in place effective legislation to prevent it. They must immediately criminalise the sale of and trafficking in children, making the penalties consistent with the principles of international human rights law.

15 CONCLUSION

The importance of children's enjoyment of their economic and social rights is so fundamental that all imaginative and constructive approaches need to be fully explored. A minimum core approach is one approach, which, because of its promise of a degree of certainty, may appeal to governments and to the courts.[55] It is, however, not the first or the last word and there also may be other approaches that ought not to be discounted.

As further explorations of the minimum core are undertaken one thing is certain. The minimum core must never be used as a reason for inertia or retrenchment. Its only justification is as a springboard for further action.

---

55 Although see the Constitutional Court of South Africa's ambivalence to a minimum core approach inherent in their judgement in *Government of the Republic of South Africa and Others v Grootboom and Others* 2000 (11) BCLR 1169 (CC).

CHILDREN'S RIGHTS: A RESPONSE FROM A SOUTH AFRICAN PERSPECTIVE

Frans Viljoen

As Geraldine Van Bueren indicated, children's rights at the global level are protected in "general" human rights treaties, and in "child-specific" human rights treaties. This distinction reminds us that children are part of the "everyone" (in for example the International Covenants on Civil and Political Rights[1] (ICCPR) and on Economic, Social and Cultural Rights[2] (ICESCR)), but are also targeted in a particular protective framework, peculiar to children (the Convention on the Rights of the Child).[3] For example, children are included in the phrase "every human being" who has the right to life (Article 6 of the ICCPR) and in the "no one" who "shall be subjected to torture" (Article 7 of the ICCPR). In the Convention on the Rights of the Child, on the other hand, the bearers of rights are children: "a" or "the" child.[4] One may add that the same duality also exists in respect of regional human rights instruments in Africa. The African Charter on Human and

---

1   International Covenant on Civil and Political Rights, *opened for signature* 16 December 1966, *entered into force* 23 March 1976, 99 UNTS 171 (hereinafter ICCPR).
2   International Covenant on Economic, Social, and Cultural Rights, *opened for signature* 16 Dec 1966, *entered into force* 3 Jan 1976, 993 UNTS 3 (hereinafter ICESCR).
3   Convention on the Rights of the Child, *opened for signature* 20 November 1989, *entered into force* 2 September 1990, 28 ILM 1456
4   See eg Articles 13 and 20.

Peoples' Rights[5] provides for the rights of "every individual" (including children). The OAU adopted a regional pendant to the Convention on the Rights of the Child, the African Charter on the Rights and Welfare of the Child in 1990. This charter, which entered into force at the end of 2000, guarantees the rights of "every child" in state parties.

The same distinction exists also at the domestic level, under South African law. On the one hand, children are part of "everyone" in South Africa, and consequently qualify for all the rights under the Constitution,[6] unless they are explicitly excluded as bearers of rights. An example of a right from which children are excluded is the right to vote, which is guaranteed only to "adult citizens".[7] On the other hand, in section 28, a number of rights are listed in respect of which children alone are the bearers.

Section 28 reads as follows:
(1) Every child has the right-
    (a) to a name and a nationality from birth;
    (b) to family care or parental care, or to appropriate alternative care when removed from the family environment;
    (c) to basic nutrition, shelter, basic health care services and social services;
    (d) to be protected from maltreatment, neglect, abuse or degradation;
    (e) to be protected from exploitative labour practices;
    (f) not to be required or permitted to perform work or provide services that-
        (i) are inappropriate for a person of that child's age; or
        (ii) place at risk the child's well-being, education, physical health, mental health, or spiritual, moral or social development;
    (g) not to be detained except as a measure of last resort in which case, in addition to the rights a child enjoys under sections 12 and 35, the child may be detained only for the shortest appropriate period of time, and has the right to be –
        (i) kept separately from detained persons over the age of 18 years; and
        (ii) treated in a manner, and kept in conditions, that take account of the child's age.

---

5   Arican Charter on Human Rights and Peoples' Rights, *opened for signature* 26 June 1981, *entered into force* 21 October 1986, 21 ILM 59.
6   Constitution of the Republic of South Africa, 1996.
7   Section 19(2).

(h) to have a legal practitioner assigned to the child by the state, and at state expense, in civil proceedings affecting the child, if substantial injustice would otherwise result; and

(i) not to be used directly in armed conflict, and to be protected in times of armed conflict.

(2) A child's best interests are of paramount importance in every matter concerning the child.

(3) In this section "child" means a person under the age of 18 years.

As far as socio-economic rights are concerned, both the provisions on the rights of "everyone" (sections 26 and 27), and section 28, on children specifically, are of relevance. It is argued here that the minimum obligation of the state differs in relation to the two categories of rights.

"Everyone", for example, has the right to have access to adequate housing and sufficient food.[8] These rights are to be realised progressively over time, within the state's available resources. Insofar as it is appropriate to seek benchmarks in this process, the position of children (as part of "everyone") has to be kept in mind. Children are some of the most vulnerable members of society, and can be exploited easily, for instance in a working environment. Children cannot fend for themselves, especially because they do not have a political voice that counts in formal democratic processes. Children are perceived as weak and exploitable. For these reasons, their needs have to be prioritised in the allocation of resources.

The rights in section 28 are not qualified in the same way. Using the concept of minimum obligations or core content in respect of section 28 rights allows the danger of a "floor" (a minimum) becoming a "ceiling" (a maximum). These rights are already qualified, or defined as core rights. Children have the right to basic nutrition, and to "shelter". Is it possible, or feasible, to define a core of "basic" nutrition, distinct from a periphery of what is "less than basic", but still more than "not basic"? Clearly, such an approach may undermine the essence of the protection granted in the first place.

The "access" rights in sections 26 and 27 are qualified in three ways: "reasonable" measures have to be taken to "progressively" realise these rights within the state's "available" resources. If these

---

8   Section 26(2) and 27(2) of the Constitution.

rights have a "core content", it follows that these three qualifiers are not infinitely open-ended, but also have a minimum meaning and imply minimum obligations on the state. Measures providing for the core content will always be *reasonable*; the core content will be the point at which *progress* starts to be measured; resources will have to be *available* to ensure the realisation of the core content of a right.

Section 28 does not provide for similar qualifications, but rather sets out rights that are unqualified or "directly enforceable". In the absence of the need to set benchmarks along a flexible continuum, the usefulness of the "core content" concept in respect of section 28 is obviated.

An argument in favour of identifying the core content of these rights is the need to clarify vague norms. "Exploitative labour practices" is such a vague term. Children need to be protected against these practices. But what are they?

The phrase may be given concrete content by referring to South Africa's international law obligations, as is required by section 39 of the Constitution. South Africa ratified the Convention on the Rights of the Child on 16 June 1995, and the African Charter on the Rights and Welfare of the Child on 7 January 2000. These treaties give some indication about the scope and content of "exploitative labour practices". The African Charter on the Rights and Welfare of the Child, in particular, requires the following:[9]

- States should adopt legislation to provide for a minimum wage.
- States should regulate the hours and conditions of employment.
- States must ensure that there are penalties and sanctions in place to ensure the effective enforcement of the prohibition on exploitative labour practices.
- States must disseminate information about the hazards of exploitative child labour.

The International Labour Organisation (ILO)'s Convention 182 of 1999 (on the worst forms of child labour) provides the best guidance in this respect. It lists practices such as debt bondage, the use of children for producing or trafficking in drugs, and forced recruitment in an armed conflict as examples of the "worst forms"

---

9   Article 5 of the African Charter on the Rights and Welfare of the Child.

of child labour. South Africa ratified ILO Convention 182 of 1999 on 30 March 2000, but the Convention has not yet entered into force.

In addition to the provisions of the various international treaties, the general comments of treaty bodies and concluding observations issued by these bodies after considering state reports may inform the interpretation of these rights by our courts.

But many of the other rights in the South African Bill of Rights are also vague. Examples are the right to dignity and to privacy. Despite the inherent need for precision, it has not been suggested that the terms "dignity" or "privacy" be given a "core" and "peripheral" content.

In a recent judgement[10] Davis J (in the court a quo) had to interpret the concept "shelter" (in section 28(1)(c) of the Constitution). Finding in favour of the applicants, he left it to the responsible state agency to choose the means of compliance. He emphasised that he would not be prescriptive about solutions which the state is called upon to implement in order to discharge its constitutional obligations. But, "in order to contain future debate", Davis J identified the "bare minimum" of "shelter" as constituting "tents, portable latrines and a regular supply of water (albeit transported).[11] He then added: "Perhaps something better can be offered".[12] This last remark, in particular, suggests that the state agencies may provide more than is constitutionally required, as a bonus, exceeding a predetermined minimum.

However, Davis J's remarks need not be understood to imply that the notion of core content should be applied to section 28. Rather, his remarks remind us of the difficulties of interpretation, particularly in the constitutional sphere.

Rather than making use of the notion of minimum core content of obligations, every right should be interpreted in its context within the Constitution. Every right should be interpreted to give effect to its purpose by *advancing one of the core values* of the Constitution rather than to *establish some core or minimum content* of a right. This would be in line with the main approach adopted by the Constitutional Court on numerous occasions. This approach is referred to as "contextual" and "value-based" (or "teleological") and has indeed been reiterated in the Constitutional Court's judgment in the *Grootboom* case.[13]

---

10 *Grootboom v Oostenberg Municipality* 2999(3) BCLR 277(C).
11 At 293 A.
12 At 293 B.
13 *Government of the Republic of South Africa v Grootboom* 2000 (11) BCLR 1169 (CC) eg par 25.

In this process of interpretation, the interrelationship between sections 26 and 27 (on the one hand) and 28 (on the other) should be kept in mind. As far as the right of "access to housing" is concerned, "shelter" serves as the basic understanding of the right in respect of children. As far as the right of "access to sufficient food" is concerned, "basic nutrition" serves as the core of the right in respect of children. In this way, the demarcated rights in section 28 become the threshold which the state has to meet in respect of children, in order to realise its obligations under section 26 and 27 in respect of "everyone".

This approach is not very different from that of Scott and Alston,[14] who propose that section 28 should be treated as spelling out, in the case of children, the core content of section 26. They continue: "While such core content would exist by necessary implication within s26 were s28 not there, s28 makes certain that there is no chance of the core entitlements of children being lost in the interpretative evolution of the Bill of Rights".[15] They then suggest that the qualified or limited obligation inherent the notion of "progressive realisation" (in section 26) should be clarified: which obligations must be achieved within the shortest possible time? To determine the answer to this question, the "core content" provided for in section 28 should be taken into account.

My approach yields the same result but does not incorporate the notion of "core entitlements" into our jurisprudence. In my view the emphasis should fall on a contextual interpretation of the provisions of our Constitution, in which an interpretation of section 26 has to take cognisance of the provisions of section 28.

---

14 "Adjudicating constitutional priorities in a transnational context: A comment on *Soobramoney's* legacy and *Grootboom's* promise" (2000) 16 *SAJHR* 206 at 260.
15 At 260.

THE RIGHT TO WORK: SOUTH AFRICA'S CORE MINIMUM OBLIGATIONS

Richard L Siegel

1 INTRODUCTION

The August 28-29, 2000, conference in Pretoria entitled "Exploring the Minimum Core Content of Economic and Social Rights" raised issues concerning the scope of the right to work and the core minimum obligations of states relating to that human right. It also included discussion of the appropriateness of "core minimum obligations" as a standard for compliance with the International Covenant on Economic, Social and Cultural Rights (ICESCR)[1] and other relevant global and regional instruments.

Further, questions were raised concerning the applicability of such provisions as Article 6, the major right to work provision of the ICESCR, given the absence of a South African ratification of that instrument and the lack of a direct reference to a right to work or employment in South Africa's new constitution. Conference participants also questioned the binding status of certain relevant instruments and actions concerning the right to work that have been initiated by the United Nations, the International Labour Organisation, and other intergovernmental organisations.

---

1 International Covenant on Economic, Social, and Cultural Rights, *opened for signature* 16 Dec 1966, *entered into force* 3 Jan 1976, 993 UNTS 3 (hereinafter ICESCR).

South Africa must be concerned about its core minimum obligations relating to the right to work insofar as its government is preparing to ratify the ICESCR, a step that would imply that it judges the core minimum obligations to be met and/or in the process of "progressive realisation."

In addition, South Africa is bound by ratifications of such other global and regional human rights instruments as those concerning the rights of women and children, civil and political rights, and racial discrimination. It is also bound by the conventions of the International Labour Organisation that it has ratified. The ILO has made all of its member states subject to various obligations relating to the right to work as a result of its adoption of the 1998 Declaration on Fundamental Principles and Rights at Work, and it expects broad compliance with its official recommendations on that subject.

The obligations undertaken by South Africa under its new constitution include essential elements of the right to work. Although the right is not stated in those words in that progressive document, the constitution that took effect on 4 February 1997 includes critical aspects of the right to work as that concept is defined in the ICESCR and by committees that supervise the implementation of UN, ILO and other intergovernmental instruments on that subject. Aspects of the right to work in South Africa's constitution include equal pay and treatment, free choice of occupation, freedom of association, fair labour practices, the prohibition of exploitative child labour, the right to a healthy environment, freedom of movement, remedies for past educational discrimination, and the rejection of slavery and forced labour. Furthermore, it has been pointed out by South African courts that the enjoyment of other rights guaranteed by that country's constitution, particularly access to housing, is complicated by widespread unemployment and poverty.[2]

South Africa's duties regarding work will necessarily be influenced by interpretations of core minimum obligations offered by a variety of courts, commissions, committees and governing bodies at the national, regional and global levels. The UN Committee on Economic, Social and Cultural Rights (CESCR or the Committee) and other bodies reviewing state compliance apply formulations that derive from nonbinding as well as binding instruments. This Committee is necessarily strongly influenced

---

2 Government *of the Republic of South Africa and Others v Grootboom and Others* 2000 (11) BCLR 1169 (CC) para 59.

by interpretations made by ILO supervising bodies and by determinations offered by committees responsible for monitoring related human rights conventions.

Beyond the purely legal considerations noted above, the right to work involves political imperatives that match or exceed those derived from other economic and social rights. Exploitative child labour, forced labour, slavery and apartheid constitute crimes in existing domestic and international criminal law, and their prevention and elimination are human rights obligations of states as well. In such cases as pre-1994 South Africa and present-day Myanmar and Sudan, among others, these violations of the right to ensure that work is freely chosen can result in serious international sanctions as well as global ostracism. Domestically, prolonged neglect of obligations to create and secure work can shift political support from one party or leader to another and bring down national governments and political orders. With unemployment and underemployment rates in South Africa persisting at extremely high levels, political accountability for mass unemployment does not appear to be avoidable.[3]

The conference also directly addressed the adequacy of the concept of core minimum obligations as a standard for approaching the implementation of economic, social and cultural rights. In relation to the right to work, such concepts as minimum core content must be reviewed as possible standards for global efforts to implement the right to work and other economic, social and cultural rights. The conception of minimum core obligations developed by the UN committees monitoring each of the several covenants and conventions is actually not altogether minimal. It includes responsibility of states for policy development (i.e., consultation), data collection, legislative and other forms of policy, implementation, evaluation and reporting. In addition, committees monitoring economic and social rights, civil and political rights that bear on economic, social and cultural rights, and the rights of women and children have often taken expansive positions on the substance and scope of such rights even as they label these perspectives "core minimum obligations." As such, the concern of some participants in the August 2000 Pretoria conference that core minimum obligations is too restrictive an approach is probably not altogether warranted. Further, it makes sense to

---

3   See also the discussion of the relationship between jobs and crime in Grundy "South Africa: Transition to majority rule, transformation to stable democracy" in Bradshaw and Ndegwa (eds) The *uncertain promise of South Africa* (2000) Indiana University Press 49-51.

label as "minimum" those obligations that need to gain a measure of acceptance from governments and employers on a global basis.

2 CORE LABOUR/WORKERS' RIGHTS AND THE RIGHT TO WORK

Some confusion has resulted from the simultaneous efforts of intellectuals and official bodies to define core labour rights and the right to work. These efforts have overlapped to a substantial extent but also reflect differing focuses. Core labour or workers' rights center on the rights to associate freely through a trade union, pursue collective bargaining, and seek acceptable conditions of work with respect to minimum wages, hours of labour, and occupational safety and health. A consensus on such rights or standards was largely achieved by the 1990s, enunciated by the 1995 World Social Summit and in the 1998 ILO Declaration of Fundamental Principles and Rights of Work.[4] As summarised in an important 1996 study prepared by the Organisation for Economic Cooperation and Development (OECD),[5] the core labour standards accepted by the international community at the beginning of the twenty-first century are:
- Freedom of association and collective bargaining, i.e., the right of workers to form organisations of their own choice and to negotiate freely their working conditions with their employers.
- Elimination of exploitative forms of child labour, such as bonded labour, that put the health and safety of children at serious risk.
- Prohibition of forced labour, in the form of slavery and compulsory labour.
- Non-discrimination in employment, i.e., the right to equal respect and treatment for all workers.[6]

The OECD selected these from other possible standards because "they embody basic human rights as exemplified in the Declaration of the World Social Summit," they "are widely recognized

---

4   See International Labour Conference 86th Session, Record of Proceedings, Vol 1, (1998) International Labour Office 20A/2-3.
5   OECD *Trade, employment and labour standards* (1998) Organisation for Economic Cooperation and Development.
6   Ibid at 26.

to be of particular importance," they derive from the Universal Declaration of Human Rights, they are embodied in major global human rights covenants with large numbers of ratifications, and there exist "relatively detailed provisions" concerning these standards.[7] It is basic to the idea of core labour standards that they provide "framework conditions" that make other labour standards possible, this relating primarily to the rights of free association and collective bargaining.[8] Yet it is not automatic that the acceptance of other labour or work standards, including an expectation that governments will work against unemployment and for at least minimal standards of health, safety, and human dignity, will result from the widespread enjoyment of these framework conditions. It is necessary to maintain a critical approach to consensus core standards that omit fundamental aspects of the right to work. It is the position of this author that the core rights associated with the right to work include each of the rights stated in the OECD's Trade, Employment and Labour Standards, but also include rights to insist that governments promote full employment, constrain arbitrary termination of available employment, and assure that employment meets minimum standards concerning health, safety, and human dignity. The core elements of the right to work do not include every individual's right to demand a job but do include the right to demand that each state carry out policies, strategies, and programmes that advance full employment.[9] Such obligations do not require a hopeless diversion of resources to the maintenance of useless jobs or the rejection of reasonable flexibility in labour markets. What they entail in terms of core minimum obligations is taken up in the following section.

3 CORE MINIMUM OBLIGATIONS WITH RESPECT TO THE RIGHT TO WORK

Having identified the needed "core rights" in this complex arena, the next step is to specify "core minimum obligations" of states and others in relation to such rights. The concept of minimum core obligations is articulated in the Maastricht Guidelines on Violations of Economic, Social and Cultural Rights and in General

---

7   *Ibid* at 10, 26.
8   *Ibid* at 28.
9   As stated in the Protocol of San Salvador (Additional Protocol to the American Convention on Human Rights in the Area of Economic, Social and Cultural Rights

Comment No. 3 of the UN Committee on Economic, Social and Cultural Rights.[10] The CESCR and the ILO's Committee of Experts on the Application of Conventions and Recommendations and Governing Body Committee on Freedom of Association can be viewed as the paramount global authorities on the right to work and core labour rights. However, many other global and regional intergovernmental organisations, periodic global conferences on human rights and social affairs, treaty monitoring committees and commissions, nongovernmental organisations (NGOs), and independent experts have also made important contributions to the formulation of minimum core obligations relating to the right to work.[11] These contributions have influenced the evolution of international law in relation to rights and duties in this area.

(Protocol of San Salvador), *opened for signature* 17 November 1988, *not yet in force*, OAS Treaty Series No 69), each State party to that Inter-American instrument need "undertake to adopt measures that will make the right to work fully effective, especially with regard to the achievement of full employment" (Article 6 (2)). As framed in the Revised European Social Charter of 1996 each government signatory must "accept as one of their primary aims and responsibilities the achievement and maintenance of as high and stable a level of employment as possible, with a view to the attainment of full employment." (Article 1(1)).

10 The text of the Maastricht Guidelines appears in (1998) 20 Hum Rts Q 691-704. General Comment No 3: *The nature of States parties obligations* (1990) is contained in UN Doc E/1991/23, Annex III.

11 A recent authoritative textbook identifies as international legal authorities relevant to "the right to work and other employment-related rights," Articles 23-25 of the Universal Declaration of Human Rights UN GA resolution 217 A (III) of 10 December 1948 (hereinafter UDHR); Articles XIV-XXXVII of the American Declaration on the Rights and Duties of Man *adopted* 2 May 1948 OAS Doc OEA/Ser.L/V/II.65, Doc 6, 19 (hereinafter American Declaration); Articles 15 and 29 of the African Charter on Human and Peoples' Rights *opened for signature* 26 June 1981, *entered into force* 21 October 1986, 21 ILM 59 (hereinafter African Charter); Article 5 (e) of the International Conventions on All Forms of Racial Discrimination *opened for signature* 7 March 1966, *entered into force* 4 January 1969, 60 UNTS 195 (hereinafter ICERD); Article II (I) of the Convention on the Elimination of All Forms of Discrimination Against Women *opened for signature* 18 December 1979, *entered into force* 3 September 1981, 1249 UNTS 13 (hereinafter CEDAW); Article 17-19 and 24 of the Convention Relating to the Status of Refugees, *opened for signature* 28 July 1951, *entered into force* 22 April 1954, 189 UNTS 150; Articles 23 and 32 of the Convention on the Rights of the Child *opened for signature* 20 November 1989, *entered into force* 2 September 1990, 28 ILM 1456 (hereinafter CRC); and Articles 3 and 6-8 of the ICESCR (Martin et al International human rights law and practice: cases, treaties and materials (1997) 1010). Such a list is far from exhaustive and should also include pertinent sections of the International Covenant on Civil and Political Rights, *opened for signature* 16 December 1966, *entered into force* 23 March 1976, 999 UNTS 171; the 1996 Revised European Social Charter; the Additional Protocol to the American Convention on Human Rights in the Area of Economic, Social and Cultural Rights (Protocol of San Salvador), *opened for signature* 17 November 1988, *not yet in force*, OAS Treaty Series No 69; the European Union's Treaty of Rome, the ILO conventions and recommendations cited above (especially Convention No. 122 (1964) and Recommendation No. 169 (1984)), and other documents.

Our starting point is the Committee's formulation in its General Comment No. 3 (1990) of a minimum core obligation required of every state party "to ensure the satisfaction of, at the very least, minimum essential levels of each of the rights."[12] In this and other general comments the Committee asserts that each state under review need demonstrate that it has made every effort to use all resources at its disposal to meet those minimum obligations, to ensure that there is the widest possible enjoyment of the relevant rights under the prevailing circumstances, to monitor progress in relation to unachieved goals, and to devise appropriate strategies and programmes to achieve the necessary ends. No State party should act arbitrarily or from omission to deprive its people of such rights. Minimum core obligations as well as all other duties covered by the ICESCR are to be judged in relation to the Committee's expectations of results as well as conduct. This obligation of result is stated as the assurance of "minimal essential levels of each of the rights." The state's duties include but are not limited to making sure that no "significant number of individuals" is deprived of basic forms of each right.[13] Such requirements are deemed universal obligations regardless of level of development, although "special difficulties" faced by a given state at a particular stage of its development are to receive due consideration. The Committee also asserts that although certain rights may be met "progressively," steps toward the full meeting of obligations are required of every State party beginning soon after its ratification of the ICESCR. Finally, General Comment No. 3 declares that various sections of the ICESCR, including those pertaining to equal rights for men and women, free association, and the right of children to special protection, "would seem to be capable of immediate application by judicial and other organs in many national legal systems."

Four aspects of the right to work are addressed in this section in relation to core minimum obligations and the nature of violations of those rights and obligations. These areas involve full employment, nondiscrimination and equal treatment, the assurance of work that is freely chosen, and the prohibition of exploitative child labour. Such obligations also exist, as argued above, in relation to free association and other employment-related issues. Space limitations and the need to emphasise the selected areas of obligation are the basis for the choices made here.

---

12   UN Doc E/1991/23, Annex III, §10.
13   "Maastricht Guidelines on Violations of Economic, Social and Cultural Rights" (1998) 20 *Hum Rts Q* 691 at 695.

4 CORE MINIMUM OBLIGATIONS: FULL EMPLOYMENT

The Committee has not yet adopted a general comment specifically on the right to work. This omission may relate to several factors, including the enormity and complexity of the legal, administrative, political, and other dimensions of efforts to assure labour and employment rights at the subnational, national, regional and global levels. It may also reflect the problems of establishing even minimal state obligations in an era in which a policy model based on active labour market policy and at least limited state responsibility for social protection and employment security has been challenged and at least partly superseded.

In recent decades leading intergovernmental organisations have endorsed approaches to the labour market and various other aspects of national economic policies that reflect neoclassical ideological preferences to a large extent. Various organisations have also responded to significant evidence, some of which the present writer finds persuasive, indicating that in various industrialised states some measures designed to assure social protection and employment security have proven counterproductive in relation to such concerns as employment promotion, budgetary imbalance and competitiveness.[14] Further, state duties regarding the fostering of full employment are stated notably less forthrightly in the ICESCR than in the Universal Declaration of Human Rights, in various significant regional documents, and in relevant ILO conventions. These factors make it difficult for the Committee to relate core minimum obligations to such a central aspect of the right to work as duties to foster full employment. Nevertheless, there would be no core minimum obligations equivalent to those cited for other economic and social rights if obligations of states to undertake duties and achieve results relating to full employment and employment security were not included. These duties must start with state obligations to (1) refrain from taking steps calculated to create or sustain high levels of unemployment for the society generally and vulnerable groups and sectors in the society in particular; and (2) create and implement strategies and programmes to maximise employment and reduce comparatively high levels of unemployment and underemployment.

---

14 See Commission of the European Communities Growth, Competitiveness, Employment: The Challenges and Ways Forward into the 20th Century (1993) White Paper, Bulletin of the European Communities, Supplement 6/93.

The typology that demands that States parties to the ICESCR and other conventions respect, protect and fulfil their obligations facilitates the present effort to delineate core minimum obligations regarding employment opportunity.[15] The obligation to respect – to refrain from interfering with a set of rights – involves the duty to take overall employment opportunity and security into account when an array of social and economic policies are implemented. The ILO Committee of Experts has observed, "When a country is faced with changing circumstances which result in rising unemployment . . . it is the Committee's task to seek to ascertain that the protection and promotion of employment are among the central goals of national policy."[16] The state interferes with the right to work when it develops policies that ignore or seek to create or perpetuate high levels of unemployment and underemployment.[17] The International Covenant on Economic, Social and Cultural Rights and other instruments grant substantial latitude to all states to choose a mix of policies designed to promote employment opportunity and security. Yet minimum core obligations of conduct and result apply to overall efforts to promote full employment.

For nearly forty years the international community has provided advice and technical assistance concerning issues, solutions and programmes that can promote full employment and not conflict with other important economic objectives. Most of these initiatives tend to be compatible with neoclassical, social democratic, and social market views on social protection. They include support for state responsibilities for basic and vocational education, employment training and retraining, regional development, transition from school to work, and assistance for workers and families displaced by structural adjustment programmes and foreign trade. Such programmes relating to employment opportunity

---

15 This typology, originally developed by UN Special Rapporteur Asbjörn Eide, appears as Maastricht Guidelines 6 and is discussed in Dankwa et al "Commentary to the Maastricht Guidelines on Violations of Economic, Social and Cultural Rights" (1998) 20 Hum Rts Q 713.
16 ILO *Report of the Committee of Experts on the Application of Conventions and Recommendations: General Report and Observations Concerning Particular Countries* (1981) International Labour Conference, Annual, para 39, as cited by Mayer "The concept of the right to work in international standards and the legislation of ILO member states" (1985) 124 *International Labour Review* 225.
17 It may well be asked why a state or political regime would set such a course. Reasons may include the goal of weakening the trade union sector or some of its components as well as the aim of creating and maintaining downward pressure on compensation. A desperate labour force may also help to attract domestic and foreign investment that may offer direct financial benefits to the regime in power through corruption.

and security are critical components of needed state conduct to protect and fulfil the right to work even as variations in state policies are tolerated or encouraged.

Fulfilment involves the effective facilitation, promotion or provision of such programmes in relation to state capacities and circumstances. Protection is central to obligations to respect the right to work when employment opportunity and security are brought into question in the context of structural adjustment programmes. Core minimum obligations in relation to structural adjustment programmes involve the following:
- the chosen strategies, policies and programmes must not disproportionately affect women, minorities, or other disadvantaged groups in negative ways;
- the state must have a national strategy to assure social protection and employment opportunity to such groups; and
- the particular measures taken to increase the flexibility of labour markets must not reflect policies to weaken the political power of labour and other groups or shatter systems for social protection.[18]

How have the authors of the Maastricht Guidelines and the international bodies supervising economic and social rights defined violations of such core minimum obligations? The Maastricht Guidelines offer as examples of violations of economic and social rights, state actions that are "deliberately retrogressive," that intentionally contravene or ignore ICESCR obligations, or involve "the adoption of legislation or policies which are manifestly incompatible with pre-existing legal obligations relating to these rights."[19] In 1983 the ILO Committee of Experts on Conventions and Recommendations addressed perceived violations of these obligations based on its reading of ILO Convention No. 122 (Employment Policy) when it found that in Thatcherite Britain, "it is not apparent that employment considerations as defined by the Conventions are the subject of an active policy on the part of the Government".[20] In 1998 this ILO Committee addressed concerns about Peru's policies under Convention No. 122, perceiving seri-

---

18 On this point see comments of Workers' members of the International Labour Conference in International Labour Conference Record of Proceedings (1990) International Labour Office 14/23.
19 "Maastricht Guidelines on Violations of Economic, Social and Cultural Rights" (1998) 20 *Hum Rts Q* 691 at 695-96.
20 ILO *Report of the Committee of Experts* (1983) International Labour Conference, Annual at 254.

ous deterioration in the results of that country's approach to employment. A Peruvian labour spokesman argued during the ILO Committee's review that his country's 1991 Promotion of Employment Act had resulted in massively decreased employment opportunities and had legalised arbitrary dismissals.[21] Such steps would, if confirmed, constitute the kind of act of commission by the state contemplated in the Maastricht Guidelines, namely "the formal removal or suspension of legislation necessary for the continued enjoyment of an economic, social or cultural right that is currently enjoyed".[22] This could also be deemed an act of omission: "the failure to reform or repeal legislation which is manifestly inconsistent with an obligation of the Covenant".[23]

Both the ILO Committee of Experts and the UN Committee on Economic, Social and Cultural Rights have moved cautiously in identifying state violations in this area. These entities have focused their criticism on the inadequacy of state reporting of data and other information as well as inadequate consultation with representatives of both employers and employees in relation to employment policy. Nonetheless, the ILO Committee of Experts noted in two recent reviews of Bolivia's policies that such procedural obligations are "an essential stage for the formulation and execution of an active employment policy, in the meaning of Articles 1 and 2 of the Convention (No. 122)."[24] This ILO Committee has focused on such procedural issues while exhibiting obvious frustration with various countries' approaches to structural adjustment. In one instance it referred to a report that Zambia's structural adjustment programme had led to "a deterioration in the potential of human resources."[25]

Both committees have tended to direct criticisms such as those cited above to states with high rates of unemployment and/or underemployment. The existence of obligations of result as well as conduct bears heavily on core minimum obligations regarding full employment. High rates of unemployment and underemployment

---

21 See International Labour Conference 86th Session Record of Proceedings Vol 1 (1998) International Labour Office 18/128.
22 "Maastricht Guidelines on Violations of Economic, Social and Cultural Rights" (1998) 20 *Hum Rts Q* 691 at 696-697.
23 *Ibid* at 697. On unjustified dismissal see ILO Protection Against Unjustified Dismissal, Report III (Part 4B) (1995) International Labour Conference, 82nd Session. This report reviews the implementation of the 1982 Termination of Employment Convention (No. 158) and Recommendation (No. 166).
24 ILO *Report of the Committee of Experts, Report III, Parts 1A* (1997) at 345.
25 ILO *Report of the Committee of Experts* (1999) at 504.

should trigger increasing efforts by states and, in particular, greater emphasis on the promotion of employment in relation to other economic objectives. Because its unemployment rate has been the highest in the European Union for much of the past two decades, Spain has faced close scrutiny from the ILO and the CESCR despite its relatively strong record of taking expected measures to promote employment.[26] Given the tendency after 1973 for unemployment in Europe and elsewhere to climb to levels not seen since the Great Depression, the ILO gradually reduced its emphasis on defining a particular unemployment rate as a full employment rate. It did, however, continue to work to retain the focus of the international community on the goal of full employment.

The October 1998 South African Presidential Jobs Summit was a step toward meeting the country's obligations concerning employment creation within the context of a tight fiscal policy.[27] It incorporated needed consultation with "social partners" and others, and underscored the theme that the primary objective of economic policy is to create jobs and sustain employment. Yet this summit, together with earlier and subsequent economic policy steps taken by the national government, reflected the increasing divisions between government and the trade unions concerning economic policies and their effects on employment. These divisions reflect such government policy initiatives as the inauguration of the Growth, Employment and Redistribution (GEAR) Programme. It incorporates fiscal and monetary discipline as well as measures to increase labour market flexibility. Further, recent levels of net foreign investment and GDP growth have not generated enough jobs to improve the overall unemployment rate of "perhaps a third of the workforce."[28]

5 EQUAL TREATMENT AND NONDISCRIMINATION

Because equal treatment and nondiscrimination are critical components of the right to work as well as other socioeconomic rights, such authoritative statements on this subject as General Com-

---

26 Committee on Economic, Social and Cultural Rights *Report on the 14th and 15th Sessions* (1996) Economic and Social Council Official Records, 1997, Supplement No 2 UN Doc E/1997/22; E/C. 12/1996/6 at 27-29.
27 Sue Kell and Troy Dyer refer to South Africa's current macro-economic policy framework as in many ways a voluntary structural adjustment programme. Kell and Dyer "Economic Integration in Southern Africa" in Bradshaw and Ndegwa (eds) The *uncertain promise of South Africa* (2000) Indiana University Press at 378.
28 "Thabo Mbeki, Micro-Manager" The Economist 15 July 2000 at 46.

ments 4 (1981), 15 (1986), and 18 (1989) of the UN Human Rights Committee, the UN body monitoring state party compliance with the International Covenant on Civil and Political Rights, are of obvious relevance to the determination of minimum core obligations for the right to work.[29] The Maastricht Guidelines and the Committee on Economic, Social and Cultural Rights agree that "any discrimination" tolerated or imposed by the state "with the purpose or effect of nullifying or impairing the equal enjoyment or exercise of economic, social or cultural rights" protected in the Covenant violates the ICESCR.[30] Other major global and regional conventions and other authoritative statements of rights and obligations concerning discrimination against women, racial and religious groups, aliens, and other targets of discrimination or protected classes amplify these documents.

The Committee on Economic, Social and Cultural Rights has consistently considered discrimination as a central concern that extends even beyond the categories specified for protection in Articles 2 and 26 of the ICCPR and Article 2 of the ICESCR. Not every group subject to discrimination (i.e., gay and lesbian people, foreign workers, migrant workers, the disabled, and older persons) is expressly protected in these covenants. Yet some of the first General Comments of the Committee on Economic, Social and Cultural Rights extended protection to persons with disabilities[31] and to older persons.[32]

What is the meaning of the term "discrimination" in relation to employment-related rights? The International Convention on the Elimination of All Forms of Racial Discrimination (ICERD) (1965) refers to "any distinction, exclusion, restriction or preference based on race, colour, descent, or national or ethnic origin which has the purpose or effect of nullifying or impairing the recognition, enjoyment or exercise, on an equal footing, of human rights and fundamental freedoms in the political, economic, social, cultural or any other field of public life".[33] The Convention on the Elimination of All Forms of Discrimination Against Women (CEDAW) addresses "any distinction, exclusion or restriction made

---

29 See 36 ANGER, Supplement No 40 (A/36/40), annex VII; 41 ANGER, Supplement No 40 (A/41/40), annex VI; and 45 ANGER, Supplement No 40 (A/45/40), annex VI.
30 Maastricht Guidelines of Violations of Economic, Social and Cultural Rights, para 11, (1998) 20 *Hum Rts Q* 691 at 695.
31 CESCR *General Comment No. 5, Persons with disabilities* (Eleventh Session, 1994), UN Doc. E/C.12/1994/13 (1994).
32 CESCR *General Comment No. 6, The economic, social and cultural rights of older persons* (Thirteenth Session, 1995), UN Doc. E/C.12/1995/16/Rev.1 (1995).
33 ICERD, Article 1.

on the basis of sex which has the effect or purpose of impairing or nullifying the recognition, enjoyment or exercise by women, irrespective of their marital status, on a basis of equality of men and women, of human rights and fundamental freedoms in the political, economic, social, cultural, civil or any other field".[34] The ILO Discrimination (Employment and Occupation) Convention No. 111 defines discrimination as "any distinction, exclusion or preference made on the basis of race, colour, sex, religion, political opinion, national extraction or social origin which has the effect of nullifying or impairing equality of opportunity or treatment in employment or occupation."[35]

As such, not all "distinctions" mandated or tolerated by states and private actors are considered discriminatory. ILO Convention No. 111 declares that, "Any distinction, exclusion or preference in respect of a particular job based on the inherent requirements thereof shall not be deemed to be discrimination."[36] The several supervisory committees' support for affirmative action indicates one kind of distinction that each encourages.

Any discrimination or inability or unwillingness to provide equal opportunity and equal protection relating to employment is at least potentially violative of states' core minimum obligations concerning the right to work. Such obligations extend to public and private action as well as actions and inaction regarding such diverse areas of employment-related rights as equal compensation for men and women, officially mandated segregation in employment (defined by the UN in relation to racial apartheid), and discrimination that involves employment recruitment, access to self-employment, retention, termination, promotion, training, benefits, health and safety issues, social security, and patriarchal constraints on women's opportunities and working conditions. Minimum state duties are invoked in relation to both state conduct and results in cases of discrimination and denial of equal treatment with respect to each of these areas of policy and rights.[37]

Are there distinct patterns of obligation and violation in relation to discrimination that are imposed by the state itself? National and other governments discriminate when the governing elite or party reflects particular criteria relating to nationality, tribe, language, religion and other such group considerations.

---

34 CEDAW, Article 1.
35 Article 1(1).
36 Article 1(2).
37 Klerk "Working paper on article 2(2) and article 3 of the International Covenant on Economic, Social and Cultural Rights" (1987) 9 *Hum Rts Q* 250 at 261.

States are also prone to utilise tests of political loyalty or risk, the latter commonly involving discrimination based on citizenship, partisan affiliation, and sexual orientation. Although states are likely to apply affirmative action to themselves before mandating it for the private sector, they often have long histories of preserving managerial and professional positions for males and socioeconomic or ethnic elites and using discriminatory tests for entrance and promotion toward this end.[38] Finally, states tend to be more successful than most private actors in gaining judicial consent for discrimination on at least some bases, including national security. Although few if any such justifications deserve great respect from human rights advocates, the existing core minimum obligations concerning state employment need necessarily reflect authoritative decisions to allow states to invoke national security, and in some cases, "national tradition."[39]

The Committee on Economic, Social and Cultural Rights has spoken directly of "violations" in regard to discrimination by state actors against indigenous people, foreign workers, racial and national minorities, and other targets. In 1997 it found Libya's rationale and action regarding the expulsion of foreign workers to be "a clear violation of the Covenant."[40] Ukraine's policy of excluding such national minorities as the Crimean Tartars from its social indicators, such as those relating to employment and poverty, is also viewed as possibly violative of the ICESCR.[41] The ILO Committee of Experts has focused attention on the abuse of vague eligibility criteria and discriminatory testing methods for state appointments, placing particular emphasis on security criteria that are applied too broadly and without due process.[42]

Core minimum obligations concerning equal treatment in the private sector are weighted towards duties to protect even as they inevitably also involve the Maastricht Guidelines' obligations to fulfil. Scrutiny of state violations concerning equal employment oppor-

---

38 ILO *Equality in Employment and Occupation: General Survey by the Committee of Experts on the Application of Conventions and Recommendations* Geneva (1988) International Labour Office, 75th Session at 111-12.
39 Concurring opinion of the European Court of Human Rights in Kosiek v Germany, Judgement of 28 August 1986 No 105, 9 EHRR 328, as cited in Janis et al European Human Rights Law: Texts and Materials (1995) Clarendon Press at 215-16.
40 Committee on Economic, Social and Cultural Rights *Consideration of Reports Submitted by State Parties Under Articles 16 and 17 of the Covenant* 26 May 1997 at 3.
41 Committee on Economic, Social and Cultural Rights *Consideration of Reports* 28 December 1995, UN Doc. E/C. 12/1995/15, at 3.
42 ILO *Equality in Employment and Occupation: General Survey by the Committee of Experts on the Application of Conventions and Recommendations* (1988) International Labour Office at 114-116.

tunity must focus on results more than on the evidence of state conduct reflected in legislative, administrative, budgetary, and other programmatic steps. This perspective was reflected in 1995 when the CESCR expressed "particular concern" about South Korea's non-enforcement of its legislation concerning equal pay for men and women and "other discriminatory practices in the workplace."[43]

Core minimum obligations involving discrimination and denial of equal treatment in employment cannot be fitted into a narrow range of responsibilities and violations. Employment discrimination involves a continuum of issues relating to every phase of life from early education to retirement. Discrimination at any phase can have severe impacts on the employment situation of individuals, groups and classes. Obligations to respect, protect and fulfil all have to be invoked in a result-oriented context, and it is likely that redistributive policies need be implemented.

Obvious core minimum obligations involving nondiscrimination and equal protection in employment include:
- the avoidance of acts by the state, particularly arbitrary ones, intended to intensify discrimination and unequal treatment in the public and private sectors or to weaken preexisting mechanisms for the protection of vulnerable groups;
- the promulgation and implementation by governments of increasingly effective protective laws and other policies, these including the establishment of rigorous enforcement and judicial or quasi-judicial remedies for individuals claiming violation of their rights;
- demonstration by states of respect for the rights involved by carefully monitoring patterns of unequal treatment, mounting educational campaigns and remedial programs, and cooperating fully with international supervisory bodies;
- meeting tests of result as well as conduct by providing objective evidence of significant ongoing improvement in equality of outcomes relating to employment for all groups protected by international human rights law; and
- ensuring fair and equal treatment for all groups and strata in the face of structural adjustment programmes and economic crises. Each state must demonstrate increasing effectiveness in meeting standards of due diligence in relation to prevention, investigation, prosecution or equivalent recourse to law,

---

43 Committee on Economic, Social and Cultural Rights *Report on the Twelfth and Thirteenth Sessions* May 1995 and December 1995, Economic and Social Council, Official Records, 1996, Supplement No. 2. UN Doc. E/1996/22; E/C.12/1995/18 at 26.

adjudication, and the imposition of just and effective remedies.[44]

It is evident that South Africa has an exceptional burden and legacy in relation to work-related discrimination as well as profound moral and political obligations to the individuals and groups victimised by apartheid. One South African authority cites data indicating that earnings by whites are "70 percent more than their African and coloured counterparts."[45]

The South African government is in a position to present an impressive body of equal protection legislation to its own courts or to the committees supervising international human rights instruments. This includes the Qualifications Authority Act,[46] the Labour Relations Act,[47] the Basic Conditions of Employment Act,[48] the Employment Equity Act[49] and the Skills Development Act.[50] South Africa's legislation appears responsive to disabled peoples' needs and it incorporates affirmative action. South Africa has also taken initial steps to create administrative entities able to pursue equal employment goals. South Africa's constitution and statutes are particularly impressive in terms of the diverse set of groups afforded explicit protection.[51] Clearly, acceleration of progress in education at all levels as well as the enforcement of laws mandating equity and preferences will be crucial when the effectiveness of these governmental measures is assessed.

It was also clear even before the National Conference on Racism, held in Johannesburg from 30 August–2 September 2000, that considerable evidence exists concerning continuing patterns of racial and other forms of discrimination in work-related matters in South Africa. The June 2000 issue of South Africa's Human Rights Committee's *HRC Quarterly Review*, entitled "Labour Rights Are Human Rights," focused in part on the situation of agricultural workers in the Western Cape. The HRC found pervasive and blatant continuing racism on the part of the employers surveyed, patterns that suggested "the entrenched barriers that

---

44 ILO *Equality in Employment and Occupation: General Survey by the Committee of Experts on the Application of Conventions and Recommendations* (1996) International Labour Office, 83rd Session at 79–93.
45 Bhorat "How to reduce SA's wage gaps" *Mail and Guardian* 11–17 August 2000, 39.
46 South African Qualifications Authority Act 58 of 1995.
47 Labour Relations Act 66 of 1995.
48 Basic Conditions of Employment Act 75 of 1997.
49 Employment Equity Act 55 of 1998.
50 Skills Development Act 97 of 1998.
51 Constitution of the Republic of South Africa, 1996, section 9(3).

apartheid's legacy has placed between white and black labourers or farmers."[52] The inadequacy of governmental labour inspection is emphasised. In relation to domestic workers, major gaps in legislation were noted, including the failure to provide unemployment benefits. Clearly, South Africa's minimum core obligations regarding equal protection remain to be "progressively realised" in coming decades despite international and constitutional mandates for immediate implementation.

6 WORK NOT FREELY CHOSEN: SLAVERY, FORCED LABOUR, AND EXPLOITATIVE CHILD LABOUR

Cumulative evidence of contemporary forms of slavery, forced labour, and exploitation of children has helped consolidate a growing global consensus emphasising values of liberty and human dignity. Before 1985, opposition to forced labour derived primarily from anti-colonialism as well as from Cold War considerations. Since the 1980s such opposition has also been stimulated by intensified economic globalisation and ethnic conflict. There is increasing interest in the exposure and eradication of various forms of contemporary slavery as well as exploitation of children, this reflecting broadened awareness of such ongoing and longstanding human rights violations.

Slavery and forced labour constitute violations of the right to work that are very difficult for states to defend as matters of principle or sovereignty. Concern about such violations of liberty interests is supported by classical liberal and contemporary neoliberal ideology, as well as by doctrines generally supportive of social protection. Nonetheless, confirmed findings of abuse in these areas require significant investigatory efforts.

Major international statements of rights and obligations relating to the prohibition of slavery appear in the UDHR[53] and the ICCPR.[54] Multilateral anti-slavery law dates back to 1819, and the movement to abolish the slave trade was of great significance for the history of human rights.[55] Among the most important politi-

---

52 The Human Rights Committee *HRC Quarterly Review – Labour rights are human rights* (2000) at 49.
53 Article 4.
54 Article 8(1, 2).
55 Lauren *The Evolution of International Human Rights: Visions Seen* (1988) University of Pennsylvania Press at 38-45; Eide "The Sub-Commission on Prevention of Discrimination and Protection of Minorities" in Alston (ed) *The United Nations and Human Rights: A Critical Appraisal* (1995) Clarendon Press 211 at 232-35.

cal and legal steps taken internationally against slavery and the slave trade were the 1841 Treaty of London, the 1885 General Act of Berlin, and the General Act and Declaration of the Brussels Conference of 1889-90. The Slavery Convention of 1926 sponsored by the League of Nations defined slavery as "the status or condition of a person over whom any or all of the powers attaching to the right of ownership are attached."[56] The 1956 UN Supplementary Convention on the Abolition of Slavery, the Slave Trade, and Institutions and Practices Similar to Slavery established far-reaching provisions for the criminalisation of such conduct as debt bondage, serfdom, and exploitation of minors delivered by parents or guardians for such purposes.[57] The 1956 Convention called for the complete abolition of debt bondage and serfdom.

Since 1945 forced or compulsory labour has been the central concern of the international community in relation to "work freely chosen." This emphasis flowed from the UDHR[58] and the highly qualified statement on this subject in Article 3 of the ICCPR. The ICESCR speaks generally and without qualification to the right of everyone to work "which he freely chooses or accepts."[59] Leary contends that the prohibition of forced labour and violations of freedom of association are the only aspects of workers' rights arguably part of customary international law.[60]

The most explicit statements on the scope and limitations concerning prohibitions of forced labour appear in ILO Conventions Nos. 29 (1930) and 105 (1957). The ILO considers its conventions on forced labour to embody fundamental principles of human rights, and the older of the two conventions on forced labour was the most widely ratified of all ILO conventions when core labour standards were reviewed by the OECD in 1996.[61]

Determining the definition and scope of prohibited forced and compulsory labour has been a singularly complex issue for the international community. The ILO Protection of Wages Convention of 1949 (No. 95) provides that all workers should have a genuine possibility of terminating their employment. Article 2 of

---

56 See LNTS, 1927, Vol LX, No 1414, Article 1(1).
57 Reproduced in UNTS, 1957, vol CCLXVI, No 3822, Article 1 at 3 – 4.
58 Article 23(1).
59 Article 6(1).
60 Leary "The paradox of workers' rights as human rights" in Compa and Diamond (eds) *Human rights, labor rights, and international trade* (1996) University of Pennsylvania Press 22 at 38.
61 OECD *Trade, employment and labour standards* (1996) Organisation for Economic Cooperation and Development at 34.

Convention No. 29 defines forced labour as "work exacted from any person under menace of any penalty, and for which the said person has not offered himself voluntarily."

Given the ILO's focus on freedom of association and equal treatment, that organisation has declared forced labour relating to labour discipline, punishment strikes, and discrimination against various groups to be unacceptable. ILO Convention No. 105 expressly prohibits work that relates to political coercion, mobilisation for economic development, labour discipline, and discrimination based on racial, social, national or religious grounds.[62] Military and emergency conscription of labour has tended to remain outside definitions of forced labour, and convict labour has been only partially limited – these being the strongest areas of state interest in maintaining access to coerced labour. The International Covenant on Civil and Political Rights specifically exempts from its prohibitions of forced or compulsory labour the sentence of "hard labour" by a competent court, other work in detention, service of a military or emergency character, and "service which forms part of normal civil obligations."[63]

Although child labour is frequently considered separately from forced labour, the two issues overlap in important ways. Children are often not free to choose whether to work or to determine the form of their employment. Further, exploitation is central to both issues. The ILO adopted in 1999 its Convention No. 182 (and accompanying Recommendation) concerning "the prohibition and immediate elimination of the worst forms of child labour," focusing attention on the most serious violations.[64] This Convention is designed to fill gaps that existed in ILO Convention No. 138 concerning minimum age for admission to employment (adopted 1973). The 1999 ILO Convention defines "the worst forms of child labour" as comprising:

> (a) all forms of slavery or practices similar to slavery, such as the sale and trafficking of children, forced or compulsory labour, debt bondage and serfdom; (b) the use, procuring or offering of a child for prostitution, for the production of pornography or for pornographic performances; (c) the use, procuring or offering of a child for illicit activities, in particular

---

62 Article 1.
63 Article 8(3).
64 The relevant ILO and other conventions on slavery, forced labour, and child labour overlap to a considerable extent. Child labour is also addressed in the 1930 ILO Forced Labour Convention and the 1956 UN Supplementary Convention on the Abolition of Slavery.

for the production and trafficking of drugs as defined in the relevant international treaties; [and] (d) work which by its nature or the circumstances in which it is carried out, is likely to jeopardize the health, safety or morals of children.[65]

ILO Convention No. 182 on the Worst Forms of Child Labour increased the emphasis placed by the international community on issues of morality, drugs, and sexual exploitation, while retaining concern about hazardous work. As with forced labour, the international community's positions on child labour are clearly conflicted. It seeks to give rhetorical support to the total abolition of child labour even as it accepts limited work by children well under the stated minimum age of eighteen. The focus of Convention No. 182 on "the worst forms of child labour" was widely accepted as a practical compromise that could secure additional ratifications, more focused supervision, and better compliance.

The UN Convention on the Rights of the Child (adopted 1989) recognises "the right of the child to be protected from economic exploitation and from performing any work that is likely to be hazardous or to interfere with the child's education, or to be harmful to the child's health or physical, mental, spiritual, moral or social development."[66] As such, it offers a conception of unacceptable child labour that is somewhat broader than the "worst forms" approach of the 1999 ILO convention. However, the core minimum obligation of states and other actors is most authoritatively defined by the ILO Convention No. 182 because of its broad support and recent adoption.

Having carved out certain areas in which work not freely chosen is proscribed, the international community then sought to clarify each State party's obligations. One such duty is to ensure that forced labour is not maintained for the profit of private persons and firms. Another is the obligation to assure that workers do not require the consent of their employer to terminate employment.[67] States also have a core minimum obligation to ensure that work is imposed on prisoners only after legitimate conviction in a court of law and that forced labour is not imposed

---

65 ILO *Child labour, Report IV (2B)* (1999) at 7; http://www.ilo.org/public/english ... text/conventions/ lo_conv/conv.htm.
66 Article 32.
67 ILO *Abolition of forced labour: General survey by the Committee of Experts on the Application of Conventions and Recommendations* (1979) International Labour Conference, 65th Session at 34.

on civilians or prisoners of war in the context of armed conflict. The 1957 ILO Forced Labour Convention specifies core minimum obligations of respect and protection concerning labour coerced in order to punish oppositional political views, as a means of labour discipline, as a punishment for having participated in strikes, and as a means of discrimination.

The status of core obligations regarding forced labour was discussed in the July 1998 report of the ILO Commission of Inquiry charged with reviewing Myanmar's (Burma's) "observance" of the ILO's 1930 Forced Labour Convention. The Commission of Inquiry found that forced labour should be defined in terms set out in the relevant ILO conventions, and that perceived violations of the prohibition of forced labour are closely tied to rights and duties to be free from torture as well as the right to life. It contended that states and individuals bear potential criminal responsibilities for breach of the relevant international obligation concerning slavery and forced labour.[68]

Despite the inclusion of various exceptions to prohibitions against forced labour in the conventions cited above, a review of the interpretation and supervision of these documents indicates that those conventions are flexible enough to allow investigation and exposure of at least the most serious cases of forced labour and slavery by states and other actors. Exceptions relating to incarceration, military service, emergencies and other limiting conditions have been interpreted narrowly by the ILO Committee of Experts and other committees supervising pertinent conventions.[69]

What is the time frame for the implementation of state obligations? The 1930 ILO Forced Labour Convention calls on states "to suppress the use of forced labour in all forms within the shortest possible period."[70] Article 2 of the 1957 ILO Convention requires States parties "to take effective measures to secure the immediate and complete abolition of forced or compulsory labour." The new child labour convention demands that ratifying states "shall take immediate and effective measures to secure the prohibition and elimination of the worst forms of child labour as a matter of

---

68 ILO *Report of the Commission of Inquiry appointed under Article 26 of the Constitution of the International Labour Organization to examine the observance by Myanmar of the Forced Labour Convention, 1930 (No. 29)* (1998) International Labour Office, Part IV, Section 9A, paragraph 203, 204; http:www.ilo.org/public/english/20gb/docs/gb273/myanmar3.htm.
69 Ziskind "Forced labor in the law of nations" (1980) 3 *Comparative Labor Law* 253; ILO *Abolition of forced labour: General survey by the Committee of Experts on the Application of Conventions and Recommendations* (1979) International Labour Conference, 65th Session at 77-81.
70 Article 1(1).

urgency."[71] These descriptions of overall state duties appear to be in line with views of the Committee on Economic, Social and Cultural Rights on minimum state obligations. The concept of progressive realisation is not fully applicable to these issues insofar as obligations concerning slavery and forced labour appear in the ICCPR as well as the ICESCR, and the leeway granted by the latter covenant concerning progressive realisation is not appropriate for such rights and obligations that are civil-political as well as socio-economic. The ILO Myanmar Commission takes a hard line on the issue of timing, stating that, "a number of forms of forced or compulsory labour were to be suppressed immediately, regardless of any period of transition."[72] The International Labour Office interprets Convention No. 182 to mean that the worst forms of abuse of child workers must be combated immediately.[73]

Minimum state obligations to respect the right to work in relation to "work freely chosen" include duties of governments not to exact forced or compulsory labour as defined above. Governments must also repeal any constitutional, statutory or administrative instruments that provide for or allow such practices to be conducted by nonstate actors. Each state party has further core minimum obligations to take preventative measures, apply adequate standards of labour inspection, legislate, investigate, prosecute, adjudicate, exact appropriate penalties, and ensure justified compensation concerning violations in the public and private sectors. States parties must also develop data on the prevalence of these violations of rights and cooperate fully with international treaty monitoring committees, domestic social partners, and other states.

Obligations to respect and to protect in relation to the most serious violations of the right to work freely chosen appropriately require states to invoke applicable criminal law as well as labour standards. As noted by the International Labour Office, "Child prostitution, child pornography and the sale and trafficking of children are crimes of violence against children. They must be treated as crimes and attacked as the most serious crimes are attacked."[74] The same can be said for slavery and slavery-like

---

71 Article 1.
72 ILO *Report of the Commission of Inquiry appointed under Article 26 of the Constitution of the International Labour Organization to examine the observance by Myanmar of the Forced Labour Convention, 1930 (No. 29)* (1998) International Labour Office, Part IV, Section 9A, para 216.
73 ILO *Child labour. Report IV (2A), International Labour Conference, 97th Session, 1999* (1999) International Labour Office at 34.
74 ILO *Child labour. Report IV (2A), International Labour Conference, 97th Session, 1999* (1999) International Labour Office at 52.

practices imposed on adults, trafficking in women and children, and various other kinds of forced labour.

The nature of discovered violations of core minimum standards regarding work freely chosen has changed continually in response to patterns of authoritarian and totalitarian rule, military regimes, colonisation and decolonisation, and both international and civil wars. As is evident in ILO Convention No. 182 on the worst forms of child labour, increasing attention to globalisation, drugs, prostitution and pornography underlies more recent concerns. Additionally, the long struggle to gain international awareness of the persistence of slavery in the late twentieth and early twenty-first centuries is succeeding as additional actors investigate and publicise such abuses.[75] Further, apartheid was ruled by the ILO's Mudaliar Commission to be a form of indirect forced labour.[76]

Recent ILO reviews of serious violations of core minimum obligations regarding forced labour have centered on such countries as Brazil, Mauritania, Sudan and Myanmar. Sudan has been repeatedly accused by nongovernmental organisations, and found by ILO organs, of being directly responsible for slavery, slave trading, forced labour and related practices.[77] The ILO Commission of Inquiry concerning Myanmar concluded in July 1998 that "the Myanmar authorities, including the local and regional administration, the military and various militias, forced the population of Myanmar to carry out a wide range of tasks that

---

[75] Ziskind lists studies of state conduct regarding forced labour by the ILO, UNESCO, the Inter-American Commission on Human Rights, the UN Commission on Human Rights, the International Commission of Jurists, Amnesty International, and many other groups through 1980. (Ziskind "Forced labor in the law of nations" (1980) 3 *Comparative Labor Law* 256.) Additional interested NGOs and IGOs are noted in the ILO *Report of the Commission of Inquiry appointed under Article 26 of the Constitution of the International Labour Organization to examine the observance by Myanmar of the Forced Labour Convention, 1930 (No. 29)* (1998) International Labour Office, particularly Anti-Slavery International. Eide stresses the UN Sub-Commission on Prevention of Discrimination and Protection of Minorities (now the Subcommission on the Promotion and Protection of Human Rights) and its Working Group on Contemporary Forms of Slavery's important investigatory work and reports on slavery, slavery-like practices, and child labour. Eide "The Sub-Commission on Prevention of Discrimination and Protection of Minorities" in Alston (ed) The United Nations and human *rights: A critical approach* (1995) Clarendon Press 234. Child labour and related issues of exploitation of children are now major issues for mainstream global and regional NGOs, and this is altering the long-term pattern of neglect of socioeconomic rights by many of these organisations.

[76] See Alcock History of the International Labor Organization (1971) Octagon Books at 270-72, as cited in Ziskind "Forced labor in the law of nations" (1980) 3 *Comparative Labor Law* 253 at 273.

[77] ILO *Report of the Committee of Experts on the Application of Conventions and Recommendations: General Report and Observations Concerning Particular Countries.* (1998) International Labour Conference, Annual at 100-07.

involve forced and uncompensated labour by millions of civilians accompanied by physical abuse (including rape, torture and killing)."[78]

Violations relating to child labour and the need for further standard-setting and supervision in this area have been a central concern of advocates of core labour standards since the mid-1990s. The ILO Committee of Experts has devoted increasing attention to large-scale bonded child labour throughout South Asia as well as to widespread trafficking of women and children for prostitution and other purposes.[79]

While the violations cited by the ILO concerning slavery and forced labour often reflected failure of governments to respect the rights involved, those concerning child labour have been strongly weighted to violations of duties to adequately protect and fulfil. The Committee of Experts noted in regard to India's record on children in bondage that the situation had not improved in the course of the previous decade, and asked that government "to step up actions" and to improve its monitoring.[80] Russia was chastised for lowering its minimum age of employment in 1995 from 16 to 15.[81]

The application of core minimum standards with regard to work not freely chosen poses an array of problems for South Africa. The international community expects South Africa to uncover and to work more effectively to eliminate exploitative child labour, slavery and forced labour in its own domain. It is significant that the South African press, government agencies, and NGOs are currently addressing such difficult issues.[82]

7 CONCLUSIONS

Full employment duties necessarily focus on overall approaches to economic and social policy and require that appropriate attention be given to the "best practices" for development of human

---

78 ILO *Report of the Commission of Inquiry appointed under Article 26 of the Constitution of the International Labour Organization to examine the observance by Myanmar of the Forced Labour Convention, 1930 (No. 29)* (1998) International Labour Office para 274.
79 ILO *Report of the Committee of Experts on the Application of Conventions and Recommendations: General Report and Observations Concerning Particular Countries.* (1998) International Labour Conference, Annual at 98-100.
80 International Labour Conference *Record of Proceedings* (1990) Vol 1, 18/74.
81 International Labour Conference *Report of the Committee of Experts* (1997) Report III (Part 1A) at 384-85.
82 "Working world" (2000) 33 *World of Work* 25; The Human Rights Committee *HRC Quarterly Review – Labour rights are human rights* (2000) at 82-84.

resources and social protection. The essential state duty is to give the promotion and protection of employment prominence in the mix of government policies necessary to maintain social stability, growth and competitiveness. Some governments reject such duties by encouraging or ignoring unconscionably high levels of unemployment and underemployment. State duties center on obligations to respect the right of all persons to maximal opportunity to find work that is consistent with subsistence needs, human dignity, and fundamental standards of health and safety.

Core minimum duties of states relating to nondiscrimination and equal treatment apply to both public and private employment. As the influence of state sectors recedes in many countries, this issue increasingly centers on violations in the private sphere. Minimum duties in this area require each state to set an appropriate example by respecting these principles in the public sector. They also require effective systems of protection of individuals and groups in the private sector, as well as redistributive measures designed to increase the opportunities of minorities, women, and others who have long faced discrimination and require some form of affirmative action.

Slavery, forced labour, and exploitative child labour often involve some of the worst discrimination and unequal treatment encountered by designated groups and social strata. In relation to work not freely chosen, the state must avoid such patterns of exploitation and immediately establish effective systems of protection for affected individuals and groups.

The latter two areas of the right to work involve principles and rights that are fundamentally civil-political as well as socioeconomic. Equal protection and the struggle against coerced labour invoke immediate state duties to create effective legislation and other rules, monitoring, investigation, and administrative and/or judicial recourse. They require just remedies for victims and the elimination of impunity for violators. Justiciability has been authoritatively mandated in both areas,[83] and justifications for neglect (or worse) based on the need for progressive realisation are less acceptable than for most other areas of economic, social and cultural rights.

Indeed, such violations as the toleration of slavery, racial apartheid and certain patterns of forced labour fall within the international community's conception of crimes against humanity and grave violations of human rights. As such, they need to be treated

---

83 Administrative and judicial remedies are discussed in General Comment No. 9: *The domestic application of the Covenant* (1998) CESCR UN Doc E/C.12/1998/24 at C9, 10.

as criminal offences bearing individual and collective responsibility as well as violations of core labour standards and the right to work.

States need to ensure diverse remedies in order to fulfil their core minimum duties to respect, protect, and fulfil the right to work. Such state-level remedies are addressed in the General Comments of the Committee on Economic, Social and Cultural Rights and other treaty monitoring committees, in decisions of national and international courts, and in other sources.[84] Whether minimum core obligations, taken as a whole, will be implemented depends more than anything else on the willingness of most states to respond to responsible domestic constituencies as well as the concerns raised by international supervisory bodies.

Violations by states of their core minimum obligations relating to labour and work may generate international remedies that are unilateral, regionally multilateral, or globally multilateral. Such responses may be linked to other states' flows of trade, investment and/or economic assistance or kept separate from threats or actions of such kinds. Supervision may be largely dependent on self-reporting and monitoring by each state or also respond to information from NGOs, other states, and diverse intergovernmental organisations. Actions of the international community may result primarily from the dynamics of exchanged information and explanations or from systematic investigations. These actions may be expressed through criticisms and reports and may also involve threats to place states on blacklists or affect their entry into or expulsion from particular IGOs.

International remedies relating to aspects of the right to work may also depend on actions of transnational enterprises, international trade union confederations, or consumer or human rights NGOs. These may involve corporate codes of conduct regarding labour rights and mechanisms for "social labelling" that can alert consumers to the countries and companies that do meet core labour standards.[85] It is striking how diverse these international

---

84 These sources include in General Comment No 9: *The domestic application of the Covenant* (1998) CESCR UN Doc E/C.12/1998/24 and General Comment No 10: *The Role of National Human Rights Institutions in the Protection of Economic, Social and Cultural Rights* (1998) CESCR UN Doc E/C.12/1998/25. See also Scheinin "Economic and social rights as legal rights" and Rosas and Scheinin "Implementation mechanisms and remedies" in Eide et al (eds) Economic, *social and cultural rights: A textbook* (1995) Martinus Nijhoff 21 and 355 respectively.

85 Spar and Yoffie "Multinational enterprises and prospects for justice" (1999) 52 *Journal of International Affairs*: 557-81; De Wet "Labor standards in the globalized economy: The inclusion of a social clause in the General Agreement on Tariff and Trade/World Trade Organization" (1995) 17 *Hum Rts Q* 443.

mechanisms are and how little consensus exists concerning their application.

In contrast to the positions of most labour and human rights organisations many states and employers' organisations take the position that economic globalisation will, without outside interference, assure gradual compliance with international standards. This is projected to occur as freer trade and investment raise standards of living and multinational enterprises bring superior labour practices into additional countries. Such a position was stated by leaders of numerous developing and transitional states at the 1996 Singapore Ministerial Conference of the World Trade Organization (WTO).[86] This viewpoint is not necessarily intended to blunt ongoing efforts to supervise the implementation of international labour standards and human rights through the ILO and UN, but many states are clearly trying to block the WTO or any other international actor from using findings concerning violated labour standards to invoke trade sanctions. Such an explicit linkage, utilising a social clause or social charter, has been supported by international trade union confederations and some industrialised states during the initial years of the WTO.[87] However, it appears that the majority of WTO member states will not allow such linkages and sanctions to be established through that organisation.

This does not necessarily preclude such linkages through bilateral agreements or unilateral actions by a trading partner, a donor state, multinational enterprises, or a collective entity such as the European Union. Nor does it preclude strong criticism of the most obvious violators of work-related rights through ILO or UN processes. The major organisations with authority concerning the right to work are increasingly focussing on the most serious kinds of violations, and there is growing consensus that these need to be addressed effectively. Since the most appalling violations of the right to work are crimes that constitute grave violations of human rights, they may ultimately be judged by an international criminal court or other judicial authority. The ICC Statute, adopted in 1998, included as enumerated acts constituting crimes against humanity enslavement, "sexual slavery", "enforced prostitution", and apartheid.[88]

---

86   See ILO document GB. 268/WP/SOL/1/3, Corr and Add 1, Appendix II.
87   De Wet "Labor standards in the globalized economy: The inclusion of a social clause in the General Agreement on Tariff and Trade/World Trade Organization" (1995) 17 *Hum Rts Q* 443 at 456-58; Charnowitz "Promoting high labor standards" (1995) 18 *The Washington Quarterly* 403
88   Bassiouni "Policy perspectives favoring the establishment of the International Criminal Court" (1999) 52 *Journal of International Affairs* 795 at 801; Human Rights Watch *Summary of the key provisions of the ICC Statute* (1998).

The international community looks to South Africa for leadership in efforts to prevent and redress abuses of the right to work at home and abroad. The pertinent duties to respect, protect and fulfil are defined by international human rights instruments and labour standards as well as by those charged with their interpretation and implementation. South Africa's implementation of these duties will occur in the wake of apartheid's legacy and South Africa's impressive recent experiments in defining an exceptionally broad approach to constitutional rights.

THE RIGHT TO WORK: A RESPONSE TO RICHARD SIEGEL

Kenneth Creamer

1 INTRODUCTION

Richard Lewis Siegel's excellent paper maps out international developments with regard to the right to work in a way that is highly informative to a South African readership.

The most important contribution of the paper is its clear division – disaggregation – of the right to work into separate critical aspects, as this helps to give greater clarity of meaning to a right which has been described as "a complex normative aggregate, and not a single legal concept".[1]

Indeed, I hope that Professor Siegel's paper will serve as a catalyst to greater discussion in South Africa as to how we should understand this complex right. Despite having some resonance in the constitutional right of South Africans to choose their "trade, occupation or profession freely",[2] the right to work is of course not included "in name" in our Bill of Rights.[3] Nevertheless the right, being part of international law, must be considered in the interpretation of rights in the Bill of Rights.[4]

---

1   Drzewicki "The right to work and rights in work" in Eide, Krause and Rosas (eds) *Economic, social and cultural rights: A text book* (1995).
2   Section 22.
3   Chapter 2 of the Constitution of the Republic of South Africa, 1996.
4   Section 39(1)(b) of the Constitution obliges courts, when interpreting the Bill of Rights, to consider international law.

2 METHOD

This responses analyses each of the three critical aspects of the right to work with respect to their applications to the South African context, highlighting the ideological and interest based conflicts at play concerning each of these aspects.

The response concludes with a brief note of caution and a comment on globalisation and human rights.

As I read it Professor Siegel's paper contends that the development of an understanding of the "core minimum content" of the right to work should pivot around three aspects:
- full employment;
- non-discrimination; and
- free choice of work

It is useful to deal with each of these in turn.

2.1 Full employment

The right to work has been interpreted as placing an obligation on the state to put in place *active employment policies* to promote increased employment with the aim of achieving full employment.

It is instructive to analyse the effect of the adoption of such an obligation in the current South African context.

Such an obligation could be interpreted to place a positive obligation on the state to develop active employment policies for those who lose their jobs through privatisation or state asset restructuring. For example, it may entail that restructuring is necessarily required to include social planning aspects aimed at retraining workers who lose their jobs through restructuring with the aim of easing their re-entry into the formal labour market or into other economic activity. Moreover, execution of the entire restructuring exercise would be subject to the requirement that in the short-term job losses are kept to a minimum and that in the long run new employment opportunities are generated.

The right to work could even be interpreted to place obligations on the state with regard to the extension of appropriate regulation and obligation on the private sector with regard to the development of social and development plans and industry specific plans aimed at boosting employment levels. A nascent move in this direction is occurring in various economic sectors in decline, such as the mining industry and in clothing and textiles. The obligation should not necessarily be limited to such sectors.

A key issue in South Africa currently is whether the country's macro-economic policies are suitable to meet South Africa's employment creation challenge. For example, there is dissonance regarding current government target investment levels, with the 2000 budget listing a target for gross domestic fixed investment at around 19% of GDP, whereas a 1998 report of the Reserve Bank of South Africa suggested that investment should reach 25% of GDP in order to effectively begin reducing unemployment levels.

In interpreting the obligation on the state to put in place an active employment policy the ILO has held that the accurate reporting of employment data and adequate consultation with employers and employees are "essential" to the development of such policies.

Against these criteria, it is worth noting the following:
- There has been some controversy about the change in the measurement of unemployment adopted by government. A more restrictive but internationally accepted standard for measurement of unemployment has seen disillusioned work seekers excluded from unemployment figures and "official" unemployment levels falling from over 35% to around 24%. In the context of unemployment levels which are amongst the highest in the world, where the rate of disillusioned work seekers may be extraordinarily high, we need to question whether the shift is in line with the right to work's requirement that there be "accurate reporting of employment data".
- The declaration of the country's macro-economic policies as "non-negotiable" appears to conflict with the stipulation that there be adequate consultation with employers and employees about employment policies. The failure of the 1998 Presidential Job Summit to deal adequately with disputes related to the macro-economic policies and to develop a new employment-creating macro-economic consensus also flies in the face of any claim that consultation on employment creation policies has been adequate. There is conflict over how higher levels of formal employment will be achieved as different economic theories, ideological positions and class interests inform various strategic approaches. On the one hand are those who argue that the free market left alone will lead to full employment, on the other there are those calling for higher levels of state intervention and guidance to lift the economy onto a new path of development and employment creation.

Inevitably these policy disputes will have to be resolved at a political level, but the ILO's interpretation that the right to work stipulates the need for "consultation" on these matters may assist in their resolution.

2.2 Non-discrimination

The paper outlines the argument in terms of which unfair discrimination is viewed as violating the right to work, arguing that the core minimum obligations of the right to work require *inter alia*:
- an avoidance of the intensification of practices of unfair discrimination;
- an obligation to establish remedying procedures; and
- effective monitoring of such developments.

In post-apartheid South Africa, labour legislation seeks to put in place mechanisms for widespread corrective action with the aim of fundamentally altering the legacy of racial, gender and other forms of unfair discrimination which have led to a highly fragmented and stratified labour market. This is strongly re-enforced through the Constitution's overarching concern with equality.

One aspect that is likely to continue to be problematic is the fact that the right to choose a "trade, occupation or profession freely" is explicitly limited to South African citizens.[5] In the context of a politically and economically volatile Southern African region and increasing concerns about rising levels of xenophobia, particularly against South Africa's nearest neighbours, this limitation may be construed as discrimination running contrary to the internationally recognised right to work. This problem is likely to intensify as South Africa and its neighbours advance along the timetable toward greater economic integration in the SADC region, with the creation of a free trade area planned for later this year.

---

5   Section 22 expressly determines that "every citizen", and therefore only citizens, has the right to choose their trade, occupation or profession freely.

2.3 Work chosen freely

The paper reminds us that in ILO documents "apartheid was considered an indirect form of forced labour" i.e. a form of slavery. Given the historical effort through war and taxes to force black labour from the land and bring slaves from Malaysia and indentured labour from India, and the use of influx control to leave mothers and children in rural ghetto bantustans while channeling cheapened male labour to restricted manual labour, this is an accurate and telling description.

The correction of this legacy will require a wide range of structural solutions, in particular increased access to basic and higher education. Following the German example of the early 1970s, Davis has argued that positive obligations could be placed on the state to provide access to all to education and training (even at the higher education and professional education level) based on the right of SA individuals to choose their trade and their rights to equality and education.[6]

South Africa's new democratic political and labour law dispensation is putting in place corrective measures, but as Professor Siegel's paper argues, a "core minimum" of this aspect of the right to work is "an adequate standard of enforcement" of this new dispensation. Those most vulnerable to forced labour in the present day – and to other violations of accepted international customary law, such as slavery and forced association – are those working on the farms, those working in homes as domestic workers, and children and adults – particularly illegal immigrants – working in the informal economy where they have no protection afforded by trade unions. An "adequate standard of enforcement" must be seen to be sufficiently resourced and managed in particular by the Department of Labour to offer protection to these most vulnerable groups: through effective systems of inspection, leading to the detection and prosecution of offenders.

3 NOTE OF CAUTION

An issue not explored in Professor Siegel's paper is the fact that a negative, libertarian interpretation can be given to the right to work. In terms of this *laissez-faire* approach the right to work can

---

6   Davis "Economic Activity" in Chaskalson *et al Constitutional Law of South Africa* (1996 3 rev 1999) Juta 29 at 29 – 16.

be used as a bulwark against regulation and social protection. For example, arguments have been made that it gives individual workers a right to choose to work at a standard below legislated conditions – based on each such worker's supposed freedom to contract.

For example, in the 1905 case of *Lochner v New York*[7] legislatively prescribed maximum working hours were struck down by the US Supreme Court. Fortunately, this anti-regulation trend was later reversed by the US courts in a series of decisions in the 1940's[8] which looked more kindly on the regulation of working relationships and contracts that sought to advance the public interest.

In the South African context there can be no doubt that there are forces that would try to use such an interpretation of the "right to work" to, for example, weaken trade union rights, challenge closed and agency shops and challenge minimum employment standards.

4 RIGHT TO WORK AND GLOBALISATION

Professor Siegel's paper raises the issue of the impact of globalisation on international compliance with human rights laws and standards. Although some would argue that globalisation leads to a "race to the bottom" where all standards are eroded and others would argue that globalisation is leading to greater advances and compliance, I would submit that the answer lies in the nature and type of globalisation that is allowed to occur.

The extent to which the rule of law and regulation is able to transcend global economic and political relations and the extent to which consensus emerges – and effective enforcement mechanisms are constructed – around rules of trade and investment, the environment and labour and human rights norms, will determine the content of an increased global economic integration.

Therefore the paper's suggestions of strategies such as social labeling, which will enable consumers to know more about the social content of the goods that they wish to purchase, is a positive contribution.

In searching for a better global enforcement mechanism, the paper also raises the question of linking labour standards to the

---

7   198 US 45 (1905).
8   Eg *Nebbia v New York* 291 US 502 (1934); *West Coast Hotel Co v Parrish* 300 US 379 (1937).

operation of the WTO – an issue that stalled talks in Seattle in 1999. The issue is complex because, in the context of massive inequality between the rich and poor nations, the poor want greater access to First World markets and the rich are accused of using social issues as a new form of barrier or protectionism.

These are issues which will have to be resolved if the right to work and the related labour rights are to gain any effective enforcement mechanism at a global level.

5 CONCLUSION

Professor Siegel's is a useful, highly informative paper, which will assist South Africans in developing a deeper understanding of the international jurisprudence on the right to work, as well as assist in developing an understanding of the evolving core content of this right in the global context. The issue of the right to work raises serious challenges to the nature of the global and domestic economic system, but for these challenges to be advanced effectively much work lies ahead, both in developing the conceptual definition of the right and with regard to discovering the force of its practical applications.

THE MINIMUM CORE CONTENT OF TRADE UNION RIGHTS IN THE SOUTH AFRICAN CONTEXT

Colin Fenwick

1 INTRODUCTION

The South African Constitution (1996 Constitution) contains many significant provisions with respect to the promotion and protection of fundamental human rights. Some of these are of particular interest to an international observer charged with responsibility to offer comments that might be relevant and helpful in the South African context. A good example is the requirement that all courts, when interpreting the Bill of Rights, must have regard to international law,[1] and that they must promote the fundamental purpose of the Bill of Rights.[2] Further, in the interpretation of any legislation, South African courts must prefer, where possible, an interpretation that is consistent with international law over any that is inconsistent with international law.[3]

In the particular area of trade union rights, there are several other important factors that must be borne in mind in shaping comments about the relationship between the South African and

---

1 Constitution of the Republic of South Africa, 1996 (1996 Constitution) section 39(1)(b).
2 1996 Constitution section 39(1)(a).
3 1996 Constitution section 233.

international contexts. First, South Africa has ratified ILO Conventions No. 87 on Freedom of Association and Protection of the Right to Organise (Convention 87)[4] and No. 98 on the Right to Organise and Collective Bargaining (Convention 98),[5] which are the most important ILO instruments on freedom of association.[6] Secondly, South African law gives practical effect to the trade union rights protected in section 23 of the 1996 Constitution.[7] Trade union rights are protected in detail in the Labour Relations Act 66 of 1995, as amended by the Labour Relations Amendment Act 42 of 1996 and the Labour Relations Amendment Act 127 of 1998.[8] The Labour Relations Act 1995 also creates institutions for resolving labour disputes, including the Commission for Conciliation, Mediation and Arbitration, labour courts and a labour appeals court.[9] These features of the Labour Relations Act 1995 are perhaps not surprising, in light of the involvement of the ILO in South Africa's labour relations, and in the drafting of the present laws. An ILO Fact Finding and Conciliation Commission examined South Africa's labour laws in detail in 1992,[10] and ILO

---

4 Freedom of Association and Protection of the Right to Organize Convention 1948 (No 87) (Convention 87).
5 Right to Organize and Collective Bargaining Convention 1949 (No 98) (Convention 98).
6 Other ILO instruments relating to freedom of association include the Convention concerning organisations of rural workers and their role in economic and social development 1975 (No 141) (and its accompanying Recommendation No 149), the Convention concerning protection of the right to organise and procedures for determining conditions of employment in the public service 1978 (No 151) (and its accompanying Recommendation No 159), and the Convention concerning protection and facilities to be afforded to workers' representatives in the undertaking 1971 (No 135) (and its accompanying Recommendation No 143). On freedom of association and its importance to the ILO see: ILO *Freedom of Association and Collective Bargaining, General Survey of the Committee of Experts* (1994) (ILO General Survey); ILO *Digest of decisions and principles of the Freedom of Association Committee of the Governing Body of the ILO* (4 ed 1996) (ILO Digest); Swepston "Human Rights Law and Freedom of Association: Development through ILO Supervision" (1998) 137 *International Labour Review* 169-94; and Pankert "Freedom of Association" in Blanpain (ed) *Comparative labour law and industrial relations in industrialized market economies*, (3 ed 1987). On international labour standards generally see De la Cruz et al *The International Labour Organization – the international standards system and basic human rights* (1996).
7 Subsections 23(1) (the right to fair labour practices), 23(2) (the rights of workers to form and to join trade unions and to exercise associated rights); 23(3) (the rights of employers to form and join employers' organisations and to exercise associated rights); 23(4) (the rights of workers' and employers' organisations to autonomy, and in particular to engage in collective bargaining); and 23(6) (legislation recognising union security arrangements in collective agreements is preserved from challenge under the Bill of Rights).
8 Labour Relations Act 1995 ss 4 (right to form and to join trade unions), 5 (protection from discrimination in exercising the rights conferred by section 4) and 8; and chs VI (rights of workers' and employers' organisations, and provisions for registration and regulation of organisations) and IV (regulation of the exercise of the right to strike).
9 Labour Relations Act 1995 ch VII.
10 ILO *Prelude to change: Industrial relations reform in South Africa: Report of the Fact-Finding and Conciliation Committee on Freedom of Association concerning the Republic of South Africa* (1992).

officials had a hand in helping to draft the Labour Relations Act 1995.[11] The third preliminary point to make is that there is already much literature in South Africa that examines the constitutional provisions relating to trade union rights, and the Labour Relations Act 1995. That literature draws on ILO standards, European human rights instruments and comparative jurisprudence, particularly of other countries with a bill of rights, including Canada and India.[12]

It is also important to be aware that the system appears to be working in practice, and to be working in conformity with international standards. The labour courts interpret the Labour Relations Act 1995 in terms of its compliance with the 1996 Constitution, as they are bound by the Labour Relations Act 1995 to do.[13] Furthermore, the Constitutional Court has already used ILO standards to reach an important decision defining the ability of government to limit the rights of workers engaged in the defence forces to exercise their rights under section 23 of the 1996 Constitution.[14] Some indication that the system is (apparently) working well can be found in the views of the ILO,[15] and of the United States government, whose Country Reports on Human Rights Practices remark positively on South Africa's protection of "worker rights."[16]

It is also true, however, that labour relations laws must be applied effectively in practice. It must therefore be noted that the International Confederation of Free Trade Unions has reported

---

11 See *Explanatory Memorandum to the Labour Relations Bill 1995* reproduced in part in (1995) 16 *ILJ* 278, 280.
12 See for example Brassey & Cooper "Labour Relations" in Chaskalson *et al Constitutional law of South Africa* (1996 3 rev 1999); Juta and Hepple "Can Collective Labour Law Transplants Work? The South African Example" (1999) 20 *ILJ* 1. See also Du Toit *et al Labour Relations Law – A Comprehensive Guide* (3 ed 2000) Butterworths in which international and comparative perspectives on South African labour relations laws are frequently covered.
13 Labour Relations Act 1995 section 3. For a decision of the Labour Appeal Court putting these principles into practice, see for example *Concorde Plastics (Pty) Limited v NUMSA (Labour Appeal Court, JBG)* 1997 (11) BCLR 1624; 1997 SACLR 28.
14 *South African National Defence Union v Minister of Defence* 1999 (4) SA 469 (CC).
15 See for example ILO *Report of the Committee of Experts* (1999) 280 (Individual Observation concerning Convention 87, in which the Committee noted "with satisfaction" that the Labour Relations Act 1995 "constitutes a considerable improvement over the previous legislation") and 344 (the Committee made a similar Individual Observation concerning Convention 98).
16 See for example the report for the year 2000, available at http://www.state.gov/g/drl/rls/hrrpt/2000/. The expression "worker rights" appears in several US trade laws that link trade preferences to compliance with internationally recognised worker rights, as defined. For an overview and criticism of these legislative regimes see Alston "Labor Rights Provisions in US Trade Law: 'Aggressive Unilateralism'?" (1993) 15 *Hum Rts Q* 1.

that some farm labourers experience difficulty in exercising their trade union rights, and that police have fired rubber bullets at striking workers.[17]

Against this background, I would like to offer a few observations about three areas of particular interest in the South African context. The first is the relationship of trade union rights to other human rights. The second is the use that can be made of international law, and particularly ILO standards and their interpretation, in understanding how section 23 of the 1996 Constitution protects trade union rights. The third is how the framework of government obligations to respect, to protect, to promote and to fulfil fundamental rights could be used to understand government obligations in the specific context of trade union rights. Before doing so, however, it is important to provide a working definition of "trade union rights", and to identify their sources in international law.

2 TRADE UNION RIGHTS IN INTERNATIONAL LAW

Trade union rights include the following rights:
- The right of workers, without discrimination or prior authorisation, to form and to join trade unions of their own choosing;
- The right of trade unions to function autonomously. They must be able to draw up their own rules and constitutions, to devise and to pursue their own programmes of action and activities, and to form national and international relationships with other trade unions; and
- The rights of workers to organise, to engage in collective bargaining, and to take direct action in support of workers' economic interests, particularly by exercising the right to strike.

The international instruments that are most important for understanding these rights are the ILO's Conventions and Recommendations. The crucial instruments are Convention 87 and Convention 98. Another, new ILO instrument that is likely to become increasingly significant is its 1998 Declaration of Fundamental Principles and Rights at Work.[18] The Declaration effectively binds all ILO members to promote these trade union rights (and other

---

17   International Confederation of Free Trade Unions *Annual Survey of Violations of Trade Union Rights* (2000) 37.
18   (1998) 37 *ILM* 1237.

fundamental labour rights) whether or not the states are parties to the conventions in question.[19]

Other international and regional instruments also protect trade union rights. At the international level, these include the Universal Declaration of Human Rights,[20] the International Covenant on Civil and Political Rights,[21] and the International Covenant on Economic, Social and Cultural Rights[22] (the Covenant). Regional human rights instruments for Africa, the Americas and Europe also protect trade union rights. Although the issue is beyond the scope of this present work, it is important to note that there are differences between international instruments in the way these rights are enunciated and protected. There are also, of course, differences among international and regional instruments, and among national constitutions and laws.

3 THE RELATIONSHIP OF TRADE UNION RIGHTS TO OTHER HUMAN RIGHTS

Trade union rights are economic and social rights: the business of trade unions is the protection of the economic and social interests of their members. Hence, trade union rights are protected in Article 8 of the Covenant, which specifically refers to the right to form unions "for the protection and promotion of economic and social interests."[23] That trade union rights are economic and social

---

19 Fundamental Declaration Article 2: ILO members must, by virtue of their membership, "promote and realize . . . the principles concerning" freedom of association and the right to collective bargaining (Article 2(a)); the right not to be subjected to forced or compulsory labour (Article 2(b)); freedom from harmful and hazardous child labour (Article 2(c)); and freedom from discrimination in employment and in remuneration (Article 2(d)). For a brief analysis and overview of the Fundamental Declaration see Kellerson "The ILO Declaration of 1998 on fundamental principles and rights: A challenge for the future" (1998) 137 *International Labour Review* 223.
20 Universal Declaration of Human Rights, UN GA resolution 217 A (III) of 10 December 1948 (hereinafter UDHR), Articles 20 (freedom of peaceful assembly and association), and 23(4) (the right to join trade unions).
21 International Covenant on Civil and Political Rights, *opened for signature* 16 December 1966, *entered into force* 23 March 1976, 999 UNTS 171 (hereinafter ICCPR). Although it permits certain limitations, Article 22 of the International Covenant on Civil and Political Rights protects the right to form and to join trade unions in terms that are very similar to those used in the Universal Declaration of Human Rights.
22 Article 8.
23 Covenant Article 8(1)(a). Interestingly, there may be some ambiguity about the characterisation of trade union rights as economic and social rights in the South African context. Some of the important literature on economic and social rights in the 1996 Constitution says nothing about trade union rights as protected in section 23 of the 1996 Constitution. See for example de Vos "Pious Wishes or Directly Enforceable Human Rights?: Social and Economic Rights in South Africa's Constitution" (1997) 13 *SAJHR* 67, and Liebenberg

rights is further demonstrated by the significant role of the ILO in the drafting of Articles 6 to 9 of the Covenant.[24] These provisions have been described as a summary of ILO instruments on the topics that they cover.[25]

There are of course differences in states parties' obligations with respect to trade union rights under Article 8, compared with rights under other articles of the Covenant. The most significant of these is that the rights protected in Article 8 are to be implemented immediately, rather than progressively. States "undertake to ensure" the rights protected by Article 8 of the Covenant, which suggests that they must be implemented immediately.[26] The time frame for implementation, however, does not affect the characterisation of the right as economic and social.

Trade union rights do, however, have a close relationship to the more general right of freedom of association. ILO instruments refer to freedom of association, and a number of the early authors who are associated with the exposition of trade union rights refer to "freedom of association for trade union purposes".[27] The relationship between the two is clear: without the general freedom of association, the specific example of its exercise in the collective functions of trade unions would not be possible.

Nevertheless, merely protecting freedom of association has not always been sufficient to support the exercise of specific trade union rights and activities. It has been difficult for trade unionists to persuade courts that trade union interests and activities, such as closed shops, strikes, and collective bargaining, are necessarily protected by the simple protection of freedom of association. In most cases in which trade unions and their members have sought to rely on the general freedom of association, courts have preferred its protection of individual interests over the collective interests that

---

"Socio-economic Rights" in Chaskalson *et al Constitutional law of South Africa* (1996 3 rev 1999) Juta. Both De Vos and Liebenberg begin their analysis with section 24 of the 1996 Constitution.

24   See for example Alston "The Committee on Economic, Social and Cultural Rights" in Alston (ed) *The UN and Human Rights – A Critical Appraisal* (1992) Clarendon Press 473, 498. Article 6 of the Covenant protects the right to work, Article 7 protects the right to fair working conditions, and Article 9 protects the right to social security.

25   De la Cruz *et al The International Labour Organization – the international standards system and basic human rights* (1996) 128.

26   Alston and Quinn "The nature and scope of states parties' obligations under the International Covenant on Economic, Social and Cultural Rights" (1987) 9 *Hum Rts Q* 156, 185-86.

27   Valticos "The International Labour Organization: its contribution to the rule of law and the international protection of human rights" (1968) 9 *Journal of the International Commission of Jurists* 3, 13 and Jenks "International protection of freedom of association for trade union purposes" 1955 *Recueil des Cours* 31.

are so important for trade union activities.[28] Freedom of association is, after all, usually expressed as a right of individuals: as a right to associate with other like-minded individuals, or to form an association of such people.[29] Yet the right necessarily also has a collective character, encompassing "the collective right of an existing association to perform activities in pursuit of the common interests of its members."[30] Arguably, decisions that have limited the ability of trade unions to pursue essential goals of the association, such as collective bargaining, have relied too heavily on the individual character of the right, to the detriment of its essential collective aspect.

Difficulties for trade unions and for trade union activities that might arise from relying on the general right of freedom of association are unlikely to arise in South Africa. The 1996 Constitution distinguishes specifically between the freedom of association in general, which is protected in section 18, and freedom of association for trade union purposes, which is protected in detail in section 23.

4 THE USE OF ILO STANDARDS IN UNDERSTANDING THE SCOPE OF FREEDOM OF ASSOCIATION FOR TRADE UNION PURPOSES

The 1996 Constitution requires courts to refer to international law, and the South African Constitutional Court has already decided one case on trade union rights with reference to ILO standards.[31] Therefore, my observations on this point will be brief. I hope nevertheless that they may offer some further strength to arguments that might be put concerning the constitutionality of efforts to implement section 23 of the 1996 Constitution.

In my view, the *minimum* level of protection of trade union rights that must be provided is protection that complies with ILO standards, as a *matter of law*. The argument is based first on the relationships between the ILO and the Covenant, and between the ILO and the United Nations Committee on Economic, Social

---

28 See for example the discussion in Davis "Constitutionalization of Labour Rights" in van Wyk *et al Rights and Constitutionalism – The New South African Legal Order* (1994) 439, 441-44, and Lawyers Committee for Human Rights *The Neglected Right: Freedom of Association in International Human Rights Law* (1997) 12.
29 Nowak *UN Covenant on Civil and Political Rights: CCPR Commentary* (1993) 387.
30 Nowak *UN Covenant on Civil and Political Rights: CCPR Commentary* (1993) 387.
31 *South African National Defence Union v Minister of Defence* 1999 (4) SA 469 (CC).

and Cultural Rights (CESCR or the Committee). Second, it is based on the way that ILO standards are drafted, negotiated and implemented.

4.1 The relationship of the ILO to economic and social rights

Article 8 of the Covenant prohibits states parties that are also party to Convention 87 from relying on Article 8 to derogate from their obligations under Convention 87.[32] So in this sense, Convention 87 provides a minimum standard for states that are parties to both instruments. The ILO was closely involved in drafting Article 8 and other provisions of the Covenant. The Covenant envisages that specialised UN agencies with responsibility for areas covered by the rights in the Covenant might report to the Committee on Economic, Social and Cultural Rights.[33] This approach is further supported by the Limburg Principles, which suggest that the experience of specialised agencies of the UN, including of course the ILO, "should be taken into account in the implementation of the Covenant and in monitoring states parties' achievements."[34]

To this end, the ILO reports annually to the Covenant Committee on matters relating to implementation of obligations with respect to trade union rights.[35] In practice, the ILO's reports are provided by its Committee of Experts on the Application of Conventions and Recommendations (the ILO Committee of Experts) to the Covenant Committee, pursuant to a decision of the ILO Governing Body.[36] The reports draw broadly on the observations and findings of the ILO's supervisory system concerning the application of those ILO Conventions by the States concerned, insofar as the points at issue appear to have a bearing on the provisions of the Covenant.[37]

---

32 Article 8(3).
33 Article 18.
34 The "Limburg Principles on the Implementation of the International Covenant on Economic, Social and Cultural Rights" in International Commission of Jurists *Economic, Social and Cultural Rights – A Compilation of Essential Documents* (1997) 63, 66 (para 5).
35 ILO General Survey para 14. The 24th, 26th and 27th ILO reports (UN Docs E/1998/17, E/C.12/1999/SA/1 and E/C.12/2000/SA/1) are available from the website of the UN Office of the High Commissioner for Human Rights: www.unhchr.ch.
36 These decisions were taken by the ILO Governing Body at its 201st Session (Nov 1976) and at its 236th Sesssion (May 1987): ILO *Twenty-Sixth Report of the International Labour Organisation on Progress in Achieving Observance of the Provisions of the International Covenant on Economic, Social and Cultural Rights* UN Doc E/C.12/1999/SA/1 para 1.
37 For a detailed explanation of the ILO's sophisticated and complex systems for supervising Member States' compliance with ratified Conventions see De la Cruz *et al The International Labour Organization – the international standards system and basic human rights* (1996) ch 6.

Moreover, an official from the International Labour Office attends the sessions of the Covenant Committee as a representative of, and liaison with, the ILO.

4.2 ILO standard-setting

The ILO's experience in setting and supervising standards on economic, social and cultural policies is of particular significance in identifying the minimum obligations of States parties to the Covenant. Universality of standards is a fundamental part of the ILO's basic approach. Together with the methods of setting ILO standards, this enables the ILO to avoid many of the problems of immediate or progressive implementation that arise in the more general context of economic, social and cultural rights, as for example under the Covenant. Variations in economic and social conditions are central to these differences. The ILO approach is to take them into account during the process of formulating the normative content and text of ILO instruments. Indeed, the ILO Constitution obliges the ILO Conference to take into account local conditions when considering the adoption of standards.[38] To facilitate this, a lengthy process of examination and comparative analysis of national law and practice precedes the consideration by the ILO Conference of any proposed international instrument.[39]

In this way, unequal economic development of countries informs, as appropriate, the normative content of ILO standards at the time they are being adopted. Application in different circumstances is further facilitated by flexibility clauses and mechanisms in the text, so that standards are universal.[40] Nevertheless, the ILO does not envisage that this principle will lead to immediate or simultaneous adoption in all countries of all the ILO's standards. Rather, the ILO's policy is "to insist that social development of countries should keep pace with their economic development, considering that the two sides of the equation are inseparable."[41]

A significant consequence of the ILO's approach to standard-setting is that ratification of ILO instruments cannot be made subject to modifications, reservations or understandings. Precisely

---

38 Constitution of the International Labour Organisation Article 19(3).
39 See for example De la Cruz et al *The International Labour Organization – the international standards system and basic human rights* (1996) ch 3.
40 De la Cruz et al *The International Labour Organization – the international standards system and basic human rights* (1996) 27.
41 De la Cruz et al *The International Labour Organization – the international standards system and basic human rights* (1996) 28.

because the ILO Constitution obliges and empowers the organisation to consider differing economic and social conditions in setting the content of its normative instruments, "it is not possible to introduce flexibility which is not provided for in the text."[42] The acceptance of reservations would also be inconsistent with the adoption of standards by the ILO's (tripartite) conference, as reservations would be solely within the preserve of governments. Furthermore, permitting reservations "would interfere with the uniform development of labour legislation".[43]

Relating this understanding of ILO standard-setting to the analysis and interpretation of Article 8 of the Covenant leads to a number of conclusions. The role of the ILO in formulating the text of Article 8, and the express preservation of Convention 87 in Article 8(3) suggest that Convention 87 can be used as a source to amplify the meaning of the obligations in Article 8 itself. It follows that interpretation of Convention 87 by the ILO's supervisory bodies may also be employed to help understand Article 8 of the Covenant. More fundamentally, the ILO's basic approach to the universality and application of its standards is of considerable importance in arriving at a framework for minimum obligations under Article 8.

ILO standards on freedom of association, which are more detailed than those in the Covenant, may therefore be relied on *in their entirety* to elucidate the minimum content of the obligations in Article 8. Although they are more detailed, and therefore not "minimal," they are nevertheless applied by the ILO as *universal minimum standards*. This is an approach which the ILO can pursue because it adopts its standards *after* taking into account all the factors that might otherwise be used as arguments concerning the scope of the obligation to implement them. In short, ILO principles on freedom of association can and should be referred to as the touchstone by which to interpret and apply Article 8 of the Covenant.

How then does this argument apply in the South African context? It might add something to the ways that international law can (and must) be relied upon pursuant to sections 39 and 233 of the 1996 Constitution. Instead of mounting arguments merely concerning consistency of national law and practice with international law, as required by these constitutional provisions, it could

---

42　De la Cruz *et al The International Labour Organization – the international standards system and basic human rights* (1996) 42.

43　De la Cruz *et al The International Labour Organization – the international standards system and basic human rights* (1996) 50.

be argued that the content and meaning of trade union rights must be determined by reference to ILO standards, as minima. In other words, ILO Conventions and their interpretation are not simply points of comparison, but standards that must be met and applied.

5 OBLIGATIONS TO RESPECT, TO PROTECT, TO PROMOTE AND TO FULFIL TRADE UNION RIGHTS

As a general principle, I define the basic obligation of governments in the area of trade union rights as being to provide a positive legal framework for their exercise, and to ensure an administrative and social environment that is conducive to their exercise in practice. Before looking at specific obligations concerning particular aspects of trade union rights, it is useful to outline some broad principles concerning the different types of obligations in this area.

5.1 The obligation to respect trade union rights

The obligation to respect trade union rights requires that the legal framework, administrative actions and government policies not interfere with the ability to exercise the rights. At the core of states parties' obligation to respect the rights contained in the Covenant is the concept that they must "refrain from interfering with the enjoyment" of those rights.[44] This obligation is expressed in Convention 87, Article 3(2), which provides that "[t]he public authorities shall refrain from any interference which would restrict this right or impede the lawful exercise thereof."[45] Moreover, Article 8(2) of Convention 87 provides that "[t]he law of the land shall not be such as to impair, nor shall it be so applied as to impair, the guarantees provided for in this Convention."[46] The obligation to respect freedom of association for trade union purposes has been neatly expressed by the Committee of Independent Experts on the European Social Charter, which has found that Article 5 of the

---

44 "Maastricht Guidelines on Violations of Economic, Social and Cultural Rights" in International Commission of Jurists *Economic, Social and Cultural Rights – A Compilation of Essential Documents* (1997) 79, 83 (para 6).
45 Convention 87 Article 3(2).
46 Convention 87, Article 8(2).

European Social Charter imposes both negative and positive obligations.[47] The negative obligation is a requirement for "absence, in ... municipal law ... of any legislation or regulation or any administrative practice such as to impair the freedom."[48]

Between them these provisions encapsulate the essential conditions which state action must meet in order to respect the right of freedom of association for trade union purposes. They show also that the obligation to respect the rights must be observed on at least two levels of state action: administrative and legislative. More than that, however, states must respect trade union rights in practice: the state and its agencies must refrain from violating these rights, as might happen, for example, where the police break up a lawful strike.

5.2 The obligation to protect trade union rights

The obligation to protect trade union rights requires specific legal and administrative measures to ensure that workers and unions may exercise their rights without third party interference. In its consideration of states parties' reports the Covenant Committee has repeatedly stressed the importance of providing a positive legal framework for the exercise of the rights protected by Article 8 of the Covenant.[49] The Covenant Committee has not, however, made any statement of general principle as to how states parties must implement the obligations in Article 8. Nor has it yet issued a general comment on Article 8.

In the context of the broader freedom of association, one commentator has suggested the following general statement of States' obligations:

> States have a positive duty to provide a legal and regulatory framework enabling individuals who wish to work together

---

47 Article 5 obliges States parties to the European Social Charter to ensure or promote freedom of association for trade union purposes, among other things by ensuring that their laws do not, and are not applied so that, they impair the exercise of the freedom.
48 Council of Europe *The right to organise and bargain collectively – protection within the European Social Charter* (1996) para 9.
49 See for example: Report of the Covenant Committee's 1st Session UN Doc E/1987/28 para 33 (Netherlands (Antilles) – the Covenant Committee asked for more information as to the "positive legal protection" provided for certain rights under Article 8), and para 160 (Czechoslovakia – the Covenant Committee addressed the issue of whether there was a positive legal basis for establishment of unions), and Report of the Covenant Committee's 6th Session UN Doc E/1992/23 para 75 (Afghanistan – the Covenant Committee inquired about the legal framework for freedom of association for trade union purposes).

in a legally recognized form to do so. More broadly, this means a framework designed to facilitate freedom of association rather than to inhibit it.[50]

This general statement of obligation is based in part on a 1991 general comment of the UN Human Rights Committee, on the obligation in Article 2(1) of the International Covenant on Civil and Political Rights, "to ensure to all individuals within its territory" the rights it contains. Therein, the Human Rights Committee reminded states parties that this requires them to undertake "specific activities."

Drawing these sources together, one can then assert as a general principle that governments must provide a legal framework, and an administrative and social environment, which facilitate the exercise of freedom of association for trade union purposes. The Committee of Independent Experts on the European Social Charter has expressed the positive obligation of states parties under Article 5 of the European Social Charter as requiring them "to take adequate legislative or other measures to guarantee the exercise of the right to organise, and in particular to protect, workers' organisations from any interference on the part of the employer."[51]

More broadly, however, the obligation to protect requires that governments maintain a climate of civil and political liberties in which workers are able to exercise their trade union rights. Finally, the obligation to fulfil means more than merely providing a positive legal framework: there must also be measures for coordinated administration and enforcement of the law. This implicates what the ILO refers to as "labour administration," and in particular the requirements of the Labour Administration Convention (No. 150) and its accompanying Recommendation (No. 158).[52]

5.3 The obligation to fulfil trade union rights

At the core of States parties' obligation to fulfil the rights contained in the Covenant is the concept that they must "take appropriate legislative, administrative, budgetary, judicial and other

---

50 Lawyers Committee for Human Rights *The Neglected Right: Freedom of Association in International Human Rights Law* (1997) 30.
51 Council of Europe *The right to organise and bargain collectively – protection within the European Social Charter* (1996) 11.
52 Convention concerning Labour Administration: Role, Functions and Organisation 1978 (No 150) (1995) (and its accompanying Recommendation No 158).

measures towards the full realisation" of the rights.[53] In this area minimum obligations require governments to take positive steps to ensure that the rights are protected, rather than merely to refrain from interference, or to take steps to ensure that others are restrained from interfering.

5.4 Obligations with respect to the specific elements of trade union rights

In the following sections I apply these general principles to the different elements of trade union rights. Where possible, I refer to those parts of the Labour Relations Act 1995 that implement the rights protected by section 23 of the 1996 Constitution. I do not, however, engage in a detailed comparative analysis of the provisions concerning, in particular, whether or not they comply with pertinent international standards.[54]

5.5 The right to form and to join trade unions[55]

The obligation to respect requires that the positive legal framework should be simple and facilitative, and that it should be administered according to law.[56] Necessary formalities should be prescribed clearly in law,[57] as simple as possible,[58] and administered promptly.[59] Moreover, it is essential that the legal framework not make the exercise of the right to form unions subject to the exercise of administrative discretion.[60] Thus, administrative agencies should not be given power to decide whether or not an applicant for registration as a union should succeed on grounds of necessity, or desirability.

Governments must refrain from discouraging those workers within their jurisdiction, and entitled to exercise the right, from

---

53 "Maastricht Guidelines on Violations of Economic, Social and Cultural Rights" in International Commission of Jurists *Economic, Social and Cultural Rights – A Compilation of Essential Documents* (1997) 79 at para 6.
54 For analysis to this effect see for example Brassey & Cooper "Labour Relations" in Chaskalson *et al Constitutional law of South Africa* (1996 3 rev 1999) Juta.
55 Labour Relations Act 1995 section 4 (right to form and join trade unions).
56 Labour Relations Act 1995 ch V (registration and regulation of workers' and employers' organisations).
57 ILO Digest para 266.
58 ILO Digest para 260.
59 ILO Digest para 251.
60 ILO General Survey paras 77-78.

exercising it in practice. In my view the obligation to respect also prohibits governments from adopting policies, particularly macro-economic policies, which would interfere with workers' ability to exercise this right.

The *obligation to protect* the right to form and to join trade unions requires that the right to participate in a union be adequately supported by procedures for enforcement, including appropriate sanctions for interference with the exercise of the rights.[61] This means therefore that governments must enforce the laws designed to protect the exercise of trade union rights, and that they must maintain a climate of civil liberties in which citizens are able to exercise all their basic rights. Workers should be protected against acts making employment conditional on being, or on not being, a union member.[62] Workers should also be protected against dismissal from employment, or other acts prejudicial to their employment, by reason of union membership, or participation in union activities out of working hours, or during working hours with their employer's consent.[63] The use of penal sanctions as part of the laws providing this protection, both as a punishment and as a deterrent, is "likely to strengthen protection against anti-union discrimination."[64]

Legal provisions for protection are by themselves, however, inadequate to protect workers' rights to form and join unions. The provisions in force must be "coupled with effective and expeditious procedures and with sufficiently dissuasive sanctions to ensure their application."[65] Thus, governments must ensure that such laws are enforced, including by investigation and, where appropriate, prosecution of alleged offenders. Of course, a fundamental prerequisite is the maintenance of a social, legal and political climate in which the lawful exercise of the right is possible without fear of personal harm or attack.

The *obligation to fulfil* the right to form and to join trade unions specifically requires that there be legal means enabling the collective groups we call trade unions to exist in law.[66] Thus, governments must not only ensure that individuals may exercise their

---

61 Labour Relations Act 1995 ss 5, 187, 191 and 193.
62 Convention 98 Article 1(2)(a). This may of course give rise to some inconsistency in those cases where union security arrangements are lawful in a country. According to the ILO Committee of Experts, to the extent that there is conflict between these principles, they are matters to be resolved at the national level: ILO General Survey para 205.
63 Convention 98 Article 1(2)(b).
64 ILO General Survey para 222.
65 ILO General Survey para 224.
66 Labour Relations Act 1995 section 8 and ch VI.

personal right to associate with one another, in the formation of unions, but also that the unions which they form are able to exist and to function so as to enable them to carry out the wishes and purposes of their members.

This is a different matter from ensuring that unions may function freely, as is required by Article 8(1)(c) of the Covenant and is indeed preliminary to it. It requires that there be a possibility for the association, the collectivity itself, to exist in some recognisable form that might be used as a means to carry out the lawful activities which its members wish to pursue.

5.6 The right of trade unions to join with other trade unions

Here the *obligation to respect* requires a simple, positive legal framework that does not interfere with the exercise of the right.[67] It is significant to note that the ILO's general principles concerning permissible limitations on the structure and composition of primary-level trade union organisations apply, with any necessary limitations, to higher level trade union bodies such as federations and confederations.[68]

The *obligations to protect* and *to fulfil* both fundamentally require that these laws should work in practice. Within a domestic legal order which facilitates the formation of and membership in trade unions, governments must ensure that trade unions have a positive legal right to form federations or confederations,[69] and for those organisations to be able to affiliate with international trade union organisations.

5.7 The right of trade unions to function autonomously[70]

The *obligation to respect* requires that the legal framework should not restrain the ability of trade unions to control their own structures and to devise their own programmes of action.[71] In general,

---

67 Labour Relations Act 1995 section 8 and ch VI.
68 ILO General Survey para 195.
69 Labour Relations Act 1995 section 8(c).
70 Labour Relations Act 1995 section 8 and ch VI.
71 Labour Relations Act 1995 ss 8(a) and (b).

legislative provisions should not limit the particular rights of trade union organisations enunciated in Article 3(1) of Convention 87. It should not impose particular constitutions and rules on workers' organisations, although it may require that they have constitutions and rules. The Covenant Committee has remarked on the importance of economic policies in the global economy being consistent with observance of economic, social and cultural rights, particularly freedom of association for trade union purposes.[72]

States must respect the right to engage in collective bargaining, including the right of the bargaining parties to determine the level at which bargaining should occur. The right of the parties to make this determination flows from the fact that collective bargaining should be *voluntary*.[73] As noted below, government may be required to reconsider some of its macroeconomic policies in light of this aspect of trade union rights.

The *obligation to protect* the right of unions to function freely requires that unions be kept free of political domination, that they not be subject to administrative suspension or dissolution, and that relevant laws be adequately enforced. States must enforce legal provisions that protect trade unions against third party interference. They must also take measures, including legal and administrative measures, to ensure that the independence of trade unions and their members remains protected from political interference. Perhaps more fundamentally, trade unions should be protected and secure in their continued existence: they should not be vulnerable to administrative dissolution or suspension. Federations and confederations of workers' organisations should be similarly protected. These rights appear specifically in Articles 4 and 6 of Convention 87;[74] in the context of Article 8 of the Covenant they can be inferred from the right of unions to function freely.

The *obligation to fulfil* the right of trade unions to function freely requires that there be adequate protection from acts of interference with trade unions, and that collective bargaining be actively promoted.

---

72 Statement by the CESCR on "Globalisation and its impact on the enjoyment of economic and social rights" – Report of the Committee's 18th and 19th Sessions UN Doc E/1999/22 para 515, para 3 of the statement on globalisation.
73 ILO General Survey para 249.
74 ILO General Survey paras 180-188.

5.8 The right to strike

The *obligation to respect* this right requires that limitations on its exercise be drawn as narrowly as possible, and that where there are such limitations, they should be offset with appropriate compensation, such as access to speedy conciliation. While the right to strike might be limited for those workers employed in essential services,[75] for example, care must be taken to ensure that "essential services" are appropriately and narrowly defined.[76] Moreover, such limitations must be offset with appropriate compensatory guarantees, or perhaps replaced with agreement on provision of minimum services in some cases.[77] Care must be taken to ensure that any conditions precedent to the right to strike are not so onerous that they vitiate its exercise. Particular attention must be paid in the case of laws requiring workers and unions to hold secret ballots before taking strike action,[78] and on restrictions on the objectives that may be pursued by strike action, particularly attempts to limit the ability of workers to engage in so-called "political strikes".[79]

The *obligation to protect* the right to strike requires that workers and unions be able to exercise the right in practice.[80] This may require legal protection, particularly the right to sue those who obstruct the exercise of the right. It may require that obstruction of the exercise of the right be a criminal offence. The *obligation to fulfil* the right to strike requires that it be incorporated into the domestic legal order, and that government take adequate measures to ensure that workers and unions are able to exercise the right in practice. In common law countries, specific legislative action may be necessary. In the case of the United Kingdom, for example, there is no *right* to strike protected by the domestic legal order. While there is no prohibition on strikes, it can only be said that workers have a *freedom* to strike, subject to the risk that the general law will in other ways impose adverse consequences upon them.[81] Both the ILO and the

---

75 Labour Relations Act 1995 ch IV and particularly ss 70 and 71 (essential services).
76 The ILO defines essential services as those "in which interruption may endanger the life, personal safety or health of the whole or part of the population": ILO General Survey para 159.
77 ILO General Survey para 164 and ILO Digest paras 547, 551 (compensatory guarantees) and paras 556, and 563-568 (negotiated minimum services). See also Labour Relations Act 1995 section 72 (negotiated minimum services).
78 ILO General Survey paras 170-172 and ILO Digest paras 504 to 512.
79 ILO General Survey para 165.
80 Labour Relations Act 1995 ss 4 and 8 and chs IV and VI.
81 In the United Kingdom for example the consequence of striking is that the employer may treat the strike as a repudiatory breach of the contract of employment's fundamental obligation to work. See ILO General Survey para 139.

Covenant Committee have expressed their concern that such a position does not amount to protection of a right to strike.[82]

6 CONCLUSION

Having set out these views on minimum obligations with respect to trade union rights, I want to venture some concluding thoughts about how this approach could perhaps be useful in the South African context. The main reason for this is that good constitutional and national legal protection is not the end of the matter. As I have tried to emphasise, and as the ILO Committee of Experts, for example, constantly reiterates, the important question is usually whether trade union rights may be exercised *in practice,* and not merely whether they are protected in law.

The first issue that arises is the relationship of the obligation to promote and fulfil trade union rights to unemployment, and to work in the informal sector. Generally speaking, people without jobs, or without jobs in the formal sector of the economy, have neither unions, nor an employer with whom to bargain collectively. Looked at from another point of view, it is difficult (although not impossible) for informal sector workers to organise trade unions.[83] It seems to me then that it might be arguable that the obligation to promote trade union rights could be relied upon as a *constitutional* reason why employment promotion, and efforts to increase participation in the formal labour market might be required. In other words, if a regular job in the formal labour market is for all practical purposes a prerequisite to being able to exercise meaningfully the right to form and/or to join a trade union under section 23 of the 1996 Constitution, ought not the government to take effective steps to fulfil that right by ensuring greater possibilities for such labour market participation?

The second point concerns how government coordinates its efforts to promote the exercise of trade union rights. Here again I suggest that the terms of the ILO instruments relating to labour administration could be of particular interest. If, for example, inadequate effort is being made to provide labour inspection and

---

82 ILO General Survey para 139. See also Report of the Covenant Committee's 16th and 17th Sessions UN Doc E/1998/22 para 294 (United Kingdom).
83 While a large majority of new jobs created during the 1990s were in the informal sector, in both Latin America and Africa, "traditional trade unions presence is very weak" – see *ILO Your Voice At Work* (2000) at 10.

education about basic trade union rights, this may arguably be a constitutional failing. I should emphasise here the importance of education and information about trade union rights and their exercise. While trade unions might be expected to offer education to their members, this still leaves to government some responsibility to educate unorganised workers, and perhaps more importantly, to educate employers and employers' organisations.

The third point concerns the impact of globalisation, as manifested in certain economic policies such as privatisation, and flexibilisation of the labour market. There are frequently conflicts between these policies and the ability to exercise trade union rights. As noted, the Covenant Committee has remarked on the need for economic policies in the global economy to be consistent with the observance of economic and social rights.[84] In the area of trade union rights, governments are typically under pressure to limit the ability of workers to bargain collectively at the sectoral level, and to ensure that all collective bargaining only takes place at the plant, or workplace level. As noted above, however, in the view of the ILO it follows from the proposition that collective bargaining must be voluntary that it is for the bargaining parties themselves to determine the level at which bargaining should take place. At present, the Labour Relations Act 1995 provides certain incentives for bargaining at the sectoral level, and also allows the parties to bargain at the workplace or plant level.[85] It may be that section 23 of the 1996 Constitution, and the obligation of government to promote and fulfil its rights, could be used as a means of opposing any proposals to alter that regime, in pursuance of economic policies, in ways that might *compel* the parties to bargain at the workplace, or enterprise level.

The fourth point is simply to note that the arguments I have made about the basic obligations of government could be particularly relevant in instances of "horizontal application" of section 23 of the 1996 Constitution: under section 8(2) of the 1996 Constitution, the Bill of Rights binds non-government actors, to the extent that it is appropriate. This seems to me a very important area to examine, given that on a day-to-day to basis, trade union rights are more usually impaired or denied by private actors, rather than by government directly. It is in this area that there might prove to be considerable scope for requiring government to take greater steps

---

84 Statement by the CESCR on "Globalisation and its impact on the enjoyment of economic and social rights" – Report of the Committee's 18th and 19th Sessions UN Doc E/1999/22.
85 See for example the concise discussion in Du Toit *et al Labour Relations Law – A Comprehensive Guide* (3 ed 2000) 185-186.

to educate employers and employers' organisations about workers' constitutional rights. Furthermore, the extent to which government properly enforces those provisions that protect workers in the exercise of their rights under the Labour Relations Act 1995 and section 23 of the 1996 Constitution could be the subject of scrutiny in the courts on the basis of the minimum core obligations analysis. So too arguably could the extent to which government provides adequate infrastructure and resources for the necessary functions of education and oversight through labour inspection.

Finally, as I have been suggesting, the arguments I have made about how to understand government obligations with respect to trade union rights may potentially be of use in considering, and where necessary resisting, changes to the legal regime, proposed now or in the future.

INDEX

AAAS/HURIDOCS Economic, Social and Cultural Rights Violations Project, 3, 45
Child labour see Children
Children
    affirmative action for, 173–174
    best interest of, 155
    birth registration of, 178, 187–188
    contextual interpretation of rights of, 195–196
    definition of, 177
    discrimination against see Equality
    economic exploitation of see labour
    fair remuneration for, 184–185
    harmful work, employment of children in, 183–184
    labour, child, 180–182, 190, 194–195, 199, 200, 216–217, 219, 221
    minimum core content as applied to section 28, rights of, 193
    minimum working ages for, 184–185, 190
    participation rights of, 176
    prevention rights of, 176
    protection rights of, 176
    provision rights of, 176
    recovery and reintegration services for, 185–186
    resources to realise the rights of, 175
    right to education of, 155
    sanctions and, 188–189
    sexual exploitation of, 182–183, 187, 190, 219–220
    social exploitation of, 182–183
    South African constitutional provisions pertaining to, 192–193
    street children, 180, 183
    trafficking in, 182, 189, 190, 219–220, 221
    young persons as, 177
Civil and political rights
    relationship with economic, social and cultural rights, 1, 3, 15, 166, 169, 186–187, 222
Core content see Minimum core content
Dignity
    basis for socio-economic rights, as, 157
    right to food, link to, 71
    right to housing, link to, 15–16
    right to social security, link to, 140
Disadvantaged groups see Vulnerable groups
Discrimination see Equality
Economic, social and cultural rights
    incorporation into domestic legal systems, 3
    interpreting, 4, 52–53
    justiciability of, 3, 4, 15–17
    non-discrimination in respect of, 3, 15
    South African Constitution, in the, 3–4
Education, the right to
    basic education see primary education
    child labour and, 167
    core content of, 157–164
    empowerment right, as an, 150–151
    free primary education, 161–162
    freedom dimension of, 152, 163–164, 171
    fundamental education see primary education
    higher education, 153, 165
    interdependence with other rights of, 151
    international instruments guaranteeing, 149
    language of choice and, 164–165
    minimum core obligations of, 168–169
    obligation to fulfil the, 167–168
    obligation to protect the, 167
    obligation to respect the, 167
    primary education, 153, 158–162
    privatisation of implementation of, 162
    quality of education, 163
    refugees, of, 165
    school attendance as aspect of, 161
    secondary education, 153, 160, 165
    social aspect of, 152
    vocational training, 165
    vulnerable groups, of, see Vulnerable groups
    women, of, see Women
Equality
    access to food, in, 77–78
    access to health care, in, 32, 35–36, 39, 42, 44, 45–46, 53, 54, 55, 59
    access to housing, in, 15, 18–20
    children, for, 178–180, 189–190
    contextual conception of, 17–18
    education, in, 157–158
    employment, in, 200, 208–214, 230
    liberal conception of, 17
    social security, in 108–109, 118, 125, 129–134, 138, 142, 146
    socio-economic rights, link to, 3
    substantive conception of, 17–18
Eviction, 15
Food, the right to
    access to food as opposed to availability of food, 68
    accessibility of food, 69–71

INDEX

adequacy of food, 71
adequate food, as a right to 69
cultural aspects of, 71
framework legislation for the implementation of, 78
freedom from hunger, as a right to 69
historical development of, 62–63, 66–67
international instruments guaranteeing, 64–67
international obligations with regard to, 79–81
margin of discretion in implementation of, 78
minimum core content of, 72–73
monitoring implementation of, 79
obligation to fulfil, 74–75, 76–77
obligation to protect, 74–75
obligation to respect, 74–75
policy prioritisation in respect of, 72
property in relation to, 78
remedies for the violation of, 79
resource constraints on the implementation of, 82–84
violations of minimum core obligations of, 84–88
violations of minimum core obligations to fulfil, 85–88
violations of minimum core obligations to respect and protect, 84–85
vulnerable groups, of, see Vulnerable groups
women, of see Women
Health, the right to
access to information regarding, 36, 37, 53
health care, as a right to, 26
health protection, as a right to, 32, 42–43
historical development of, 28–30
impact of HIV/Aids on, 48–50, 58
international instruments guaranteeing, 30–32
judicial decisions in respect of, 46–48
measurement of implementation of, 35
minimum core obligations of, 39–40, 44, 55
monitoring the implementation of, 33–34
obligation to fulfil, 37, 54, 57
obligation to protect, 36, 54, 57
obligation to respect, 36, 54, 57
other national constitutions guaranteeing, 32
privacy and confidentiality in relation to, 58
public health, as a right to, 25–26
racism in access to, 45–46
regional instruments guaranteeing, 31–32
resources required to implement, 38–39
South African constitutional provisions guaranteeing, 26, 41–42
vulnerable groups, of, see Vulnerable groups
women, of, see Women
Housing, the right to
discrimination in respect of, 15
minimum core content of, 21–23
obligation to respect, 14–15
vulnerable groups, of, see Vulnerable groups
International Labour Organisation
Convention 102 of the, 102–109
history of the, 101
right to social security and the, 101–109
standards for trade union rights of the, 241–245
tripartite structure of the, 101, 244
International Monetary Fund, 81, 162
Limburg Principles on the Implementation of Economic, Social and Cultural Rights
status and nature of, 2
Maastricht Guidelines on Violations of Economic, Social and Cultural Rights
food, the right to, and the, 76
social security, the right to, and the, 117, 122
status and nature of, 2
work, the right to, and the, 201–202, 211
Minimum core content
abstract nature of concept of, 90–92
applicability of concept to non-qualified South African constitutional socio-economic rights, 193
ceiling, as a, 97–98
concept of, 4–6, 156–157, 170, 174–175, 199–200, 203, 206
floor, as a, 162, 199–200
resource implications of, 6–7
shifting nature of, 92–96
terminology related to, 4, 169
Minimum state obligations see Minimum core content
Organisation for Economic Cooperation and Development, 200, 201
Social security, the right to
administrative justice and, 147
administrative problems and, 143
Care dependency grant, 139
Child support grant, 139, 141
Compensation for Occupational Injuries and Diseases, 140, 142

Foster child grant, 139
Grant for the aged, 139, 141
Grant for the disabled, 139, 141
Grant-in-aid, 139
HIV/Aids and, 144
historical development of, 100
level of benefits with regard to, 106–107
minimum core content of, 119–122, 148
Occupational retirement insurance, 140, 142
privatisation of, 114, 118, 121, 123–126
progressive realisation of, 147–148
protected classes of persons with regard to, 103–105
scope of, 145
social protection, as a right to, 111
South African system of social security, 139–140
unemployment insurance, 140, 142
War veterans' grant, 139
women, of, see Women
Socio-economic rights see Economic, social and cultural rights
State obligations
conduct, of, 10, 160
fulfil, to, 9, 166
protect, to, 9, 166
respect, to, 8–9, 165–166
result, of, 10, 160
Street children see Children
Sub-commission on the Promotion and Protection of Human Rights, 2, 80
Trade union rights
horizontal application of, 255
informal sector work and, 253–254
international instruments guaranteeing, 238–239
obligation to fulfil, 248, 250, 252, 254
obligation to protect, 246–247, 249, 250, 251, 252
obligation to respect, 245, 248–249, 250, 251, 252
right to form and join trade unions, as a, 238, 248–250
right to strike, as a, 252–253
right of trade unions to function autonomously, as a, 238, 251–252
right of trade unions to join with other trade unions, as a, 250
right of workers to organise, as a, 238
right to freedom of association, as a, 240–241
South African constitutional provisions guaranteeing, 236
South African legislation detailing, 236
United Nations Commission on Human Rights, 2
United Nations Committee on Economic, Social and Cultural Rights, 1–2
General Comment No 3 of the, 3, 5–6, 119, 168, 169, 187, 188, 202–203
General Comment No 12 of the, 67–68, 165
General Comment No 13 of the, 151–152, 153–154, 165, 168
General Comment No 14 of the, 34–37, 39–40, 51–52, 53–57
Vulnerable groups
access to education for, 162–163
access to food of, 70, 87
access to health care, 54
employment for, 231
equal access to resources for, 16
special measures to meet the needs of, 25–26, 28
Women
right to education of, 164–165
right to food of, 97, 98
right to health of, 45–46, 64, 67, 69
right to social security of, 115, 135, 152
Work, the right to
aliens, of, 240
child labour and, see Children
collective bargaining and, 210
discrimination with regard to, see Equality
forced labour and, 209, 210, 224–231, 232
freedom of association and, 210, 225
freedom to choose work and, 209, 225, 229, 241
full employment and, 211, 214–218, 238–240
globalisation and, 242–243
obligation to fulfil, 216, 221
obligation to protect, 216, 221
obligation to respect, 215, 232
safety and health standards and, 211
slavery and, 209, 210, 224–225, 229–230
termination of employment and, 211
unemployment and, 209
World Bank, 91, 121, 133
World Health Organisation, 39, 43, 48